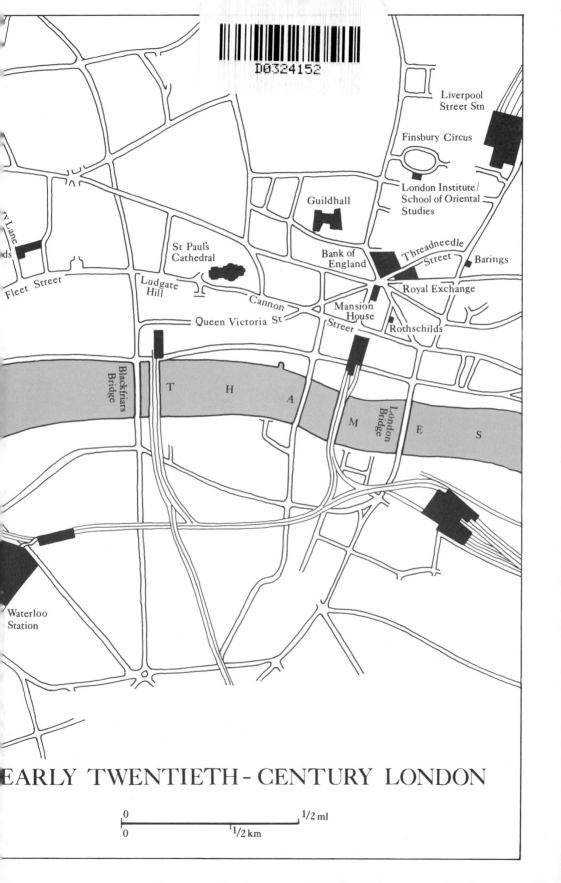

EARLY TWENTIETH - CENTURY LONDON

LONDON AND THE INVENTION
OF THE MIDDLE EAST

London and the Invention of the Middle East

Money, Power, and War, 1902–1922

Roger Adelson

YALE UNIVERSITY PRESS
NEW HAVEN AND LONDON   1995

To Jean Marshall
for her hospitality in London
and
Sharon and Al Viscito
for their support in Arizona

Set in Bembo
Printed and bound in Great Britain by St Edmundsbury Press

Library of Congress Cataloging-in-Publication Data

Adelson, Roger.
    London and the Invention of the Middle East, 1902–1922/ Roger Adelson
        p.   cm.
    Includes bibliographical references and index.
    ISBN 0–300–06094–7
    1. Middle East—Foreign relations—Great Britain. 2. Great Britain—Foreign relations—Middle East. I. Title.
ds63.2.g7a34   1994
327.41056'09'041—dc20   94–36262
                                                              CIP

A catalogue record for this book is available from the British Library

CONTENTS

LIST OF ILLUSTRATIONS

ACKNOWLEDGEMENTS

Besides the many scholars and historians whose published works appear in the endnotes to this book, I wish to acknowledge the teachers, colleagues, students, institutions, and editors that have been indispensable to its publication.

In alphabetical order, I thank the following teachers: Roderic Davison introduced me to the modern history of the Near and Middle East; Jack Gallagher urged me not to become imprisoned by the official record; Dietrich Gerhard alerted me to the significance for the Middle East of Anglo-Russian pre-World War I diplomacy; Albert Hourani helped me understand the Middle East on its own terms and carefully criticized two-thirds of this manuscript before his death; Elizabeth Monroe tutored me in how to write about the Middle East for a wide audience; John Pocock refined my analysis of the British policy-making process; and Theodore VonLaue stimulated my thinking about the comparative history of the non-European world.

Among colleagues, I must thank the following: Walter Arnstein insisted on historical precision in the manuscript; Richard Barlow encouraged me not to rush my doctoral thesis to publication and read the manuscript; Peter Calvocoressi deepened my understanding of the British and the Middle East and has stimulated much of my work; Roy Foster made suggestions as to the way Ireland affected British policies toward the Middle East; Rose Greaves offered insights into the history of British Petroleum and Persia; Cameron Hazlehurst shared his knowledge of British political and publishing circles; Peter Iverson was a good listener and provided good advice; Elie Kedourie indicated to me the significance of British attitudes toward the Middle East before World War I; Roger Louis encouraged the highest standards of scholarship in reviewing my work; Richard Martin deepened my understanding of Islam; Peter Mellini encouraged me to examine Lord Cromer's post-Egyptian career; Roger Owen made clearer the complex economic history of the Middle East and read the entire manuscript; Elliot Palais provided expert reference and library assistance; Joshua Sherman shared his insights into the British and Zionism, as well as the Palestine mandate; and Retha Warnicke provided much support in the preparation of this book.

Several graduate students deserve my thanks: Susanna Dyer copy-edited the last chapters of the manuscript; Jennifer Hardy copy-edited the first chapters of the manuscript; Marsha Havens took great editorial pains with the first draft of the full script; John Radzilowski helped me meet a couple of deadlines; Pam Rector assisted me in many ways during the preparation of the book; Michael Steiner researched the connection between Britain's quality press and the Middle East and helped with the early drafts of the manuscript; and William Hull examined British parliamentary debates on the Middle East and the issue of British casualties in World War I.

There are many institutions which I should like to acknowledge: Arizona State University provided me with three faculty awards for research in the British Isles and granted me a year and a half of sabbatical leave to research and write this book; the Bank of England Library assisted with the research; Birmingham University Library permitted me to study its manuscripts; the Bodleian Library, Oxford, gave me access to several important manuscript collections; the British Library permitted me to use its books, periodicals, and manuscripts; Churchill College, Cambridge, cooperated with my archival requests; the City of London Library assisted with background research; Colindale Newspaper Library provided me with scores of volumes of British periodicals; Durham University permitted me to work in its Arab archive; the Guildhall Library facilitated my research in its archival and photographic collections, Hulton Deutsch allowed me unusually wide access to its vast photographic and illustrative resources and gave permission to reproduce some in this book; *The Illustrated London News* Library cooperated fully with my photographic requests; the Imperial War Museum permitted me to study its manuscripts and photographic collections and to reproduce some of the latter; the India Record Office and Library let me use archives and reproduce photographs; the Institute of Historical Research, London, afforded me a research base in London; the Middle East Centre, St Antony's College, Oxford, allowed me to see collections of private papers and photographs, and to reproduce some of the latter; the National Portrait Gallery Library gave me access to its collection; the Public Record Office assisted me at its Chancery Lane, Portugal Street and Kew offices.

My main editorial debt is to Robert Baldock, my editor at Yale University Press, London, and his able staff. He encouraged me to write a more ambitious book than I had originally intended, insisted that I trim the manuscript and reconfigure some early and late sections of the book, supported my enthusiasm for illustrations, invented the book's main title, and made the text leaner and clearer. Finally, I thank Beth Luey, director of the scholarly editing and publishing program at Arizona State University and consulting editor of *The Historian*, who read the entire manuscript, made many suggestions of substance, and taught me the art of editing. I regard Beth and Robert as the editorial godparents of the book.

Introduction

The World's Greatest Metropolis

AT THE BEGINNING of the twentieth century, London was the largest and richest, as well as the most influential and powerful, city in the world. Its population of 4.5 million was followed by New York's 3.4 million and Paris's 2.5 million. Each of the following seven largest cities – Berlin, Chicago, Vienna, Canton, Tokyo, Philadelphia and St Petersburg – had populations less than a third the size of London in 1900.

London was the centre of the capitalist market system, of international finance and overseas trade. All the world kept time by London's observatory at Greenwich. Britain's capital dominated the communication networks of the early twentieth century. Its extensive telegraphic wire services, numerous journalists, varied periodicals and large publishing houses extended the power and influence of the city throughout the English-speaking world and beyond, while entrepreneurial opportunities and cosmopolitan values prevailed even over the narrow religious and partisan attitudes of the British Isles.

At that time London was the capital of the British Empire, which ruled a quarter of the globe and its peoples. Queen Victoria was related to most of the royal houses of Europe and reigned over millions more Asians and African than Christians and English-speaking peoples. Britain had far greater seapower than France, Germany, Russia or the United States. Any ambassador to the Court of St James held his country's most prominent posting abroad. London was indeed the world's greatest metropolis.

From early in the new century, some individuals and institutions in London began to fear that Britain was losing its imperial ascendancy in the area between Europe and India. In 1902, the term 'Middle East' was constructed to describe the area north and west of India, and to distinguish it from the Near East and the Far East.

London's general indifference towards the inhabitants of the Middle East at the beginning of the twentieth century probably had as much effect upon the region as any aspect of British policy. A few groups in London maintained humanitarian concern for religious and ethnic minorities in the Middle East, but these were completely eclipsed by the priorities of policy. Those in London who made, conducted and influenced British strategy in the Middle East were far more interested in political considerations than in the Middle East itself, although it was here that Britain had cemented its influence since the middle of the nineteenth century. The first priority of London's policymakers was to defend the Empire and India, a priority they saw as justifying British protection of the Suez Canal and domination of the Persian Gulf. The second major concern was to maintain the balance of power in Europe, and the third to exploit the area's copious resources of oil, discovered near the Persian Gulf, to meet the needs of the British navy.

In the 1850s, British troops had been sent to the Crimea to fight alongside the French and Turks against Russia, while in the 1860s the City of London advanced huge loans to Constantinople to help defray the costs of that war. In the 1870s, the British government bought 49 per cent of the shares in the Suez Canal Company. The French-built canal was vital to the British, and they were its primary users. A permanent British presence at Suez was reinforced in the 1880s by the British occupation of Egypt, and in the 1890s by the Anglo-Egyptian occupation of Sudan. These initiatives in northeast Africa complemented Britain's economic, naval and diplomatic predominance over the Turkish Empire and Persia. Given diminished confidence in the regimes of the sultan of Turkey and the shah of Persia, both deeply in debt and offering low returns to their bondholders, increased attention was paid to the Arab lands on either side of the Suez canal. In addition to occupying Aden, Egypt and Sudan, the British indirectly ruled the Arabs along the coasts of the Persian Gulf, the Arabian peninsula and the Red Sea. Ensuring that Arab leaders maintained a pro-British stance was, of course, far less costly than occupying the area with British troops. The indirect approach also acknowledged the fact that the British in India did not want to upset the Muslims. Before the discovery of oil in the region, the Middle East was plainly not perceived to be particularly significant.

Following Japan's defeat of Russia in 1905, the old geopolitical bogey of Russian armies rolling over the Indian subcontinent gave way to new fears of German railways bringing troops to challenge British ascendancy. To counter German influence, Britain instigated a defensive diplomacy with France and Russia. It traded recognition of France's predominance in Morocco in return for French acknowledgment of British dominance in Egypt. Meanwhile, Persia was divided into a British southern sphere, a Russian northern sphere, with a neutral area in between.

Seeing Britain becoming more closely allied to Russia in Persia, the Young Turks, who overthrew the regime of the Ottoman Sultan in 1908, rebelled against the traditional Turkish alliance with Britain. Suspecting the Young Turks were puppets of the German kaiser, the Foreign Office backed Italian, Greek, Bulgarian, Serbian and Macedonian initiatives against Turkey. While Berlin actively sought the support of the Turks and the Bulgarians, London policymakers alienated both. When war broke out in Europe in the summer of 1914, British relations with the Turks deteriorated and the conflict was extended to the Near and Middle East. During the war, the campaigns in Gallipoli, Sinai, the Arabian peninsula, Palestine,

Syria, Iraq and Persia were largely British operations, with more than a million British and Indian troops in the area between 1915 and 1919. Many undertakings were made to the Arab, Armenian, Egyptian, Greek, Kurdish, Persian and Zionist nationalities which, after the war, were found to be difficult and sometimes impossible to honour.

Postwar allied diplomacy alienated most of the nationalists of the Near and Middle East, although Britain did succeed in establishing collaborative regimes in Egypt, Palestine, Transjordan and Iraq. At the same time, Britain managed to preserve its pre-war hegemony over Suez, Sudan, the coasts of the Arabian peninsula and the Persian Gulf. Anglo-Afghan, Anglo-Persian and Anglo-Turkish relations, however, were not as smooth as London policymakers had expected. Even war was feared when Turkey threatened British troops in 1922. Deprived of the support of the British press, the Conservatives and the dominions, the prime minister was compelled to resign. War, however, was avoided.

London policymaking in the Middle East in the early twentieth century reflected historically significant changes in the waging of war and making of peace. Like the other Great Powers, Britain was increasingly affected by scientific and technological change. While the role of the state in developing and deploying atomic power since World War II is well known, the significance of the military-industrial complex, and its expectations of official support at a much earlier period is interestingly revealed in Maurice Pearton's *The Knowledgeable State: Diplomacy, War, and Technology since 1830*. The object of weapon and other manufacturers was to 'convince government that the interests of the nation and finance were identical. To this end, industrialists had to spend more time in their own ministries of foreign affairs and concern themselves with those sections of public opinion which could be induced to support them.'[1] Pearton also contrasts the era of nineteenth-century diplomacy, when conservative aristocrats determined the larger objectives of the state, with the bureaucratic defence planning of the twentieth century, when diplomacy became subordinated to the state.

The change to long-term, detailed planning effectively transferred power from its traditional or titular holder to the bureaucrats, military or civilian, responsible for drawing up the plans. The more comprehensive they were, the fewer options were open to policy in any given situation, and the greater the psychological pressure to carry them out. Moreover, because of its complexity, the 'Plan' needed to be carried out entirely or not at all. Careful gradations of response to threats or challenges, possible during the pre-industrial era, were progressively ruled out.

> The lengthening time scales of manufacturers and the need to spread budgetary costs contributed their degree of inflexibility to policy, and reinforced the tendency to regard a plan as a blueprint or formula which would inevitably produce the desired result.[2]

Although there was no single British plan for the Near and Middle East, a Plan was developed in association with France which, after 1911, would determine British policy in the Near and Middle East in the event of war with Germany. Although British interests were closely bound up with the defence of India and the Suez Canal, the level of comprehension of the Middle East was surprisingly poor. Official reports from the area were heavily prejudiced: the British in India fundamentally believed all Arabs were primitive, though at the same time they feared alienating the Muslims. Reports were dutifully stamped, minuted and filed in Whitehall, through local intelligence had very little effect upon the decisions of politicians in Westminster. Indeed, the most crucial British decisions about the Middle East were taken by politicians who had, at best, only a nodding acquaintance with the Islamic world, or, at worst, found the beliefs and customs of Muslims contemptible. Overall the individuals and institutions involved with British policy in the Middle East displayed what today would be regarded as bigoted and chauvinistic attitudes towards the indigenous peoples of the area. In any event, those who made, conducted or influenced British policy were more affected by what they read in the press, or heard in Parliament, or understood from a selected group of experts, such as the Lords Cromer, Curzon, Kitchener and Milner, or even from Lawrence of Arabia. They also reflected what people in London thought was happening, or might happen, in the region, rather than what actually occurred.

The centralized, bureaucratic style of planning initiated by the Committee of Imperial Defence and its associated interdepartmental institutions in the early 1900s was new to London. These, together with the limited intelligence emanating from the region, were the only resources on which to base strategy in the Middle East. It should be emphasized that, in the early twentieth-century, cabinet ministers lacked diplomatic precedents. It explains both the exaggerated fears of aliens, and the unrealistic expectations of what Britain could achieve.

The literature on British policy in the Middle East during the early twentieth century is substantial.[3] The bureaucracy of Whitehall generated extensive documentation: departmental records are voluminous. Indeed, the era following the introduction of the telegraph and typewriter (but before the introduction of the telephone, recording machines and computers) provides the historian of policymaking with valuable sources. But despite this enormous paper trail, many of the most important conversations were not recorded, even in that golden age of diaries and the daily exchange of letters and telegrams.[4]

Financial interests in the City of London had a substantial stake in the Middle East, and British commerce exceeded that of any European rival. (For historians, access to business records of the City is unfortunately much more restricted than to government archives.[5]) Then, too, the British government, which from 1875 held the largest number of shares in the

Suez Canal Company and after 1914 became the majority shareholder in the Anglo-Persian Oil Company, was deeply enmeshed in the area. In terms of the British press, the quantity of newspapers and the variety of periodicals published in London in that era of expanding literacy and popular readership clearly had an enormous impact upon public opinion. The contempt the cheap papers and cartoons exhibited towards Middle-Eastern leaders, religions and peoples, as well as the patronizing attitude so often exhibited by the 'quality press' towards sultans, shahs, khedives, sheikhs, Muslims, Turks, Persians, Egyptians and Arabs, hardened during the war. After it, the hatred and resentment generated by nationalism at home and abroad was increasingly apparent.[6]

The views of politicians at Westminster were a matter of public record, though cabinet discussions at 10 Downing Street were confidential. Gossip and leaks, however, provoked the introduction of official secrecy laws even before the 1914–18 war brought its own censorship. From Hansard and from the minutes of cabinet meetings, it is possible to trace the details of the evolution of policy and its defence in Parliament, while memoirs and diaries enable historians to read between the lines of official records.[7]

So much has been written about such looming figures as David Lloyd George and Winston Churchill that it almost seems necessary for historians to cut them down to human size.[8] Although we may be awed by the power such men wielded, we need not be overawed by the men themselves. One way for historians to retain a sense of proportion is to imagine themselves as silent observers in a conference room of the period, seated at a large table with these men during political discussions, when mannerisms, voices, charm, wit, flexibility, and stubbornness often affected the direction of policy.[9] For example, Lloyd George disliked having to listen to the high staccato voice of Lord Kitchener, the larger-than-life imperial soldier whose face appeared on recruiting posters in the 1914–18 war, and George V dreaded having to endure Churchill's pushiness. Equally, historians need not be overawed by the figures of cabinet ministers ensconced behind impressive desks in large Whitehall buildings, giving orders to be followed by their subordinates and officers posted overseas. It is when we are alert to personal idiosyncrasies and the complexities of political hierarchies that we can grasp who and what prevailed in 'the corridors of power'.[10]

In the early twentieth century, London policymakers confidently assumed that Britain was able to administer the Middle East as well as it ruled large parts of Asia and Africa. They were, however, confronted by two new developments: nationalism and oil. The British Empire, as a Christian entity, provoked widespread suspicion and fear among Muslims. But while in India the British exaggerated Pan-Islamic movements, in London Islam was virtually dismissed from the official mind: a persistent cultural myopia insulated policymakers from the beliefs and values of most people in the Middle East. For the first fifteen years of the twentieth century, expressions of nationalism within the Turkish empire were largely ignored by the British who, in the main, adhered to the traditional alliance with Turkey. As far as oil was concerned, the British believed that it belonged to those that discovered and exploited it, in accordance with concessionary practices operating since the late nineteenth century.

Powerful as Britain was at the turn of the century, the wishes of British policymakers were not simply obeyed without question by Middle Eastern rulers and their peoples: initiatives often encountered the same geographical, cultural, religious and socio-economic obstacles that Islamic empires had earlier faced in the region. And there were indeed some who, knowing the languages and customs of the area far better than the foreigners, made as much use of the British as the British made of them. In regard to question of religion, in particular, the peoples of the Middle East rarely accepted any interference in the way they handled their affairs and ran their lives.

Chapter 1

British Ascendancy

THERE WERE MANY in London, at the beginning of the twentieth century, who believed Britain should defend its imperial predominance in the area lying between Europe and India more vigorously. Britain had already won economic, naval and diplomatic ascendancy in the region known in 1902 as the 'Middle East'. But before the discovery of oil, what it principally represented was arid land, highly-populated riverbanks and coastlines, and ancient Islamic beliefs that conditioned the region's societies and governments. It seemed, in London, to have little to offer the Empire.

Officials in London supported those Middle Eastern rulers that cooperated with Britain, together with cosmopolitan individuals and groups with westernized values. But the vast majority of the poor and illiterate had nothing in common with the British Empire.

By isolating Russia from the Turkish and Persian empires, by confining the Russian navy to the Black Sea, and by developing communications and extending loans and subsidies throughout the area, Britain had, by the middle of the nineteenth century, achieved a clear paramountcy. In the last decades of the century, as the regimes of the sultan and shah weakened, the British government purchased nearly half the shares of the Suez Canal Company, occupied the island of Cyprus, took over Egypt and Sudan, and transformed the Persian Gulf into a British lake. With that level of political investment, political leaders in London paid careful attention to what happened in the Middle East, or what they feared might happen.

NEW WEALTH AND TECHNOLOGIES

During the early and middle decades of the nineteenth century Britain used its developing industrial economy and technological superiority to export machine-made textiles to western Asia and northern Africa, and elbow out its competitors. British merchants of the old Levant, Muscovy and East India trading companies had operated in the region for centuries, but the volume of trade was small in comparison with that of the shipping firms of the port cities of the Italian peninsula and southern France. Venetian trade was the oldest in Europe, while that of Marseilles dominated until the Revolutionary and Napoleonic Wars disrupted French commerce in the Mediterranean. Despite this, the French label

'Levant', the land of the rising sun, survived. Levantines referred to Europeans generally as 'Franks', and French remained the most important European language in the Middle East until it was subsumed by English in the twentieth century.

Since defeating French forces in India during the mid-1700s, the British had both dominated the foreign trade of the subcontinent and patrolled much of the Indian Ocean, including the Persian Gulf and the Red Sea. By the mid-1800s the British had become the leading exporters of manufactured goods in the world, and the major shippers in the area. Subsequently the British established a growing financial presence in an area which ranged from the Mediterranean to India. In the 1850s and 1860s, when the French invested in Egypt and Algeria, the British gained the financial initiative in the Turkish and Persian empires. Loaning money to the sultan and shah was not, in this instance, simply a matter of finance, but also a question of imperial strategy.[1]

Britain in the nineteenth century had two strategic preoccupations: the defence of India and the so-called 'Eastern Question'. To protect its interests in India, British forces confronted French ambitions in Egypt and the eastern Mediterranean during the early 1800s, first by a naval blockade of Bonaparte's Egypt and then through a diplomatic assault on the growing military power of Muhammad Ali, an officer in the Turkish imperial army whom the British saw as a French puppet. In 1840 Britain insisted that Muhammad Ali's army be dismantled. It opposed, but did not stop, the construction of the Suez Canal, which had been devised by French engineers, built by Egyptian labour, and underwritten in the 1850s and 1860s principally by French investors. Britain also acknowledged French protection of Christians in the Levant during the 1860s. Unlike France, Britain needed to balance its concern for the thousands of Christians in Islamic empires with the interests of the millions of Muslims that Britain ruled elsewhere, particularly in India. Britain thus found it more difficult than the French to champion non-Muslim minorities in the Islamic world. At Constantinople, the capital of the Ottoman Empire, the British enforced the capitulations, privileges dating from the sixteenth century that exempted Europeans from Turkish law and taxes. When Christian and Jewish minorities in the region became successful entrepreneurs, Britain officially protected them, especially the rich merchants and bankers who bought *barats* that entitled them to the same capitulatory privileges enjoyed by European traders.[2]

While displacing the French commercially and linking with Greek merchants and other minorities in the Eastern Mediterranean, Britain opposed Russian expansion in central Asia and secured its position throughout the Indian subcontinent and Indian Ocean. The British defended India's northwest frontier, subsidizing rulers or arming indigenous leaders who cooperated with them against the Russians. Where cooperation failed, they dispatched military expeditions against central Asian foes in what some termed the 'Great Game' in Persia, Afghanistan and beyond. Success in central Asia probably owed less to the British themselves than to central Asia's vast, mountainous aridity, as well as to Russia's fundamental military limitations, despite its expansionist menace.[3]

If the tsar's navy were to pass from the Black Sea through the Turkish Straits and into the Mediterranean, British naval supremacy would be threatened. This factor embroiled Britain in 'the Eastern Question', a term devised to characterize the rivalry over the military vacuum created by the decline of the Ottoman Empire. During the Crimean War (1854–6), the British joined the French and the Turks to defeat the Russians, loaned money to Turkey, and passed reforms guaranteeing favourable treatment for Europeans and minorities in the Ottoman Empire. During the 1860s and 1870s the British developed extensive telegraph links with India, but only a few miles of railways in the Anatolian peninsula, and always on terms satisfactory to British investors. Britain also backed Turkey abroad, protecting the territorial integrity of the Turkish Empire. In 1874, however, when the heavily indebted Ottoman dynasty repudiated half the interest on its debt, the confidence of London's banking houses collapsed, and the government was forced to reassess its position.

Instead of relying on European diplomacy, Britain took immediate action to secure its strategic and economic interests. In 1875 it borrowed sufficient funds from London financial institutions, especially the Rothschild banking house, to buy 49 per cent of the shares of the Suez Canal Company from the debt-ridden khedive of Egypt. This historic purchase protected the British sea route to India and placed the costs of the Suez Canal under British control. Britain and France also established an Anglo-French debt commission to monitor the repayment of loans made to the khedive of Egypt.

In 1876, when the bankrupt Turks faced insurrection in the Balkans and constitutional crisis in Constantinople, Britain was not unduly concerned – until Russia declared war on the Ottoman Empire in 1877.[4] Turkish reprisals against Christian nationalists in Bulgaria had so outraged British public opinion in the 1870s that some opposed the conventional pro-Turkish assumptions. Even so, no matter the concern expressed in British churches for Christian coreligionists living under Ottoman misrule, no matter how outraged journalists became over 'the terrible Turk', and no matter how many anti-Turkish speeches were delivered at public meetings, those that determined policy in Britain still preferred the Turkey they knew to its unknown successor. The government endured public recrimination rather than forfeit influence over the Turks and submit to European rivals eager to fill the power vacuum.

After Turkey's defeat in the Russo-Turkish War, Britain took an active role at the Congress of Berlin, in 1878, where some Balkan nationalities gained a degree of territorial independence. Britain itself acquired Cyprus, which became a staging post for the Royal Navy, and established an important precedent for British actions in Egypt. In 1881, the British secretly accepted the French takeover of Tunisia, another part of the Turkish imperial realm. Content with its diplomacy, Britain felt Turkey could not complain since it still controlled some of Europe, much of northeastern Africa, and all of southwestern Asia.[5]

Following the Congress of Berlin, Britain and France established the Ottoman Public Debt Administration (OPDA) to protect their financial stake and manage the collection of Turkish revenues. The OPDA was based in London, but the administration of the debt was centred in Constantinople. There, a huge number of accountants and tax collectors soon outnumbered the staff of the Turkish financial department: Turkey was forced to spend substantial amounts servicing the Ottoman debt rather than meeting its own needs, a factor which caused it to look increasingly to Berlin.

Britain's naval presence in the eastern Mediterranean increased as a result of its control of the Suez Canal and of Cyprus. Cypriots were taxed to help meet the Ottoman public debt, for Cyprus remained nominally a part of the Turkish Empire and paid suzerainty to the Porte, the name given to the Ottoman court and the seat of imperial government.

In 1882 the British bombarded the Egyptian port of Alexandria in order to secure the Suez Canal. France was asked for support, but hesitated. While Britain expected France to accept its move into Egypt – in return for London's acceptance of the 1881 French takeover in Tunisia – the French were in fact alarmed. For the following two decades, Britain and France became rivals over the partition of Africa. In 1879, the British had replaced the uncooperative Egyptian khedive with a compliant ruler, while maintaining the pretence of suzerainty to the Porte. The costs of British occupation were borne by Egypt's taxpayers, just as those of India had long paid for their own defence. Although Egypt was a poor country, the strategic importance of the Suez Canal persuaded the British to remain despite earlier expecting the occupation to be temporary.[6]

Additional territorial expansion involved the so-called reconquest of the Sudan in 1898. This vast desert, except for the area adjacent to the Upper Nile, had been conquered by Muhammad Ali's Egyptian army in the 1820s, but ceded in the 1880s when Egypt's forces were defeated by partisans of a self-proclaimed mahdi, Muhammad Ahmad. 'Chinese' Gordon, the British general sent to supervise the evacuation of Egyptian forces from the Sudan, died at Khartoum in 1885. His martyrdom was more an imperial humiliation than a real threat to Anglo-Egyptian security, yet Anglo-Egyptian forces returned to the Sudan and obliterated the mahdi and his followers in the late 1890s. London justified the expansion in Egypt and the Sudan as strategically offsetting the French colonial presence throughout northwestern Africa.[7]

A further manifestation of the defence of India came in eastern Africa, where Britain acquired more territory than any rival power. But even this fell short of the ambitions of some British imperialists, who sought control of all ports, railways and coasts from the Cape to Cairo; enterprising London mapmakers duly met the growing demand.

British influence in East Africa seemed as vital to the defence of India as control of the seaways between Europe and the Indian subcontinent. Since the French had sway in northern Africa and the Russians in central Asia, the British needed a presence in southwestern Asia to guard the Suez Canal, Egypt and the Sudan. Britain already dominated the Persian Gulf, while Aden, an important coaling station for steamships, was seen as crucial, as was the patrolling of the Red Sea to guarantee the free passage of Muslim pilgrims to the western Arabian peninsula. Since the cost of the defence of India was borne by Indian taxpayers, London itself avoided the burden.[8]

Britain clearly dominated the waterways and coasts, if not the lands, where the African, Asian and European continents joined. As defined by parliamentary statute of 1889, the British navy was required to be larger than the next two navies combined, be they French, Russian, or – later – German. The Indian Army could be deployed more rapidly than troops stationed in Europe, using bases in India, Aden, the Suez Canal, Egypt and Cyprus. Britain maintained a leading diplomatic profile in Constantinople, and posted more consular and intelligence officers throughout Turkey's Asiatic empire than any European rival. In Constantinople the British shared their financial influence with French investors, and their role as military advisers with German officers, but the British navy alone patrolled the eastern Mediterranean, the Red Sea and the Persian Gulf.

LONDON'S ARCHITECTURE OF POWER

The steady growth of British wealth and power since the seventeenth century is reflected in the architecture of London. Within an area of a few square miles in Westminster, Whitehall and St James's, decisions were taken that profoundly affected the world. Here too, the Middle East was invented.

Ten Downing Street, the residence of the prime minister, was erected at the end of the seventeenth century by George Downing. Its plain, dark brick exterior, with simple Georgian doors and windowframes, was overshadowed by the construction, in the 1860s, of a multi-story office building opposite, blocking most of its light. The house, however, links with adjoining properties and opens onto a high-walled garden on the south side of Horse Guards Parade. Apart from its grand S-shaped staircase, 10 Downing Street has developed a warren of rooms added and altered to suit the requirements of Chatham, Pitt, Palmerston, Disraeli, Gladstone, Salisbury and other incumbents. The Cabinet Room, in the northwest

1   The Cabinet Room at 10 Downing Street in 1922. A map of the Near and Middle East hangs by the prime minister's chair.

corner of the ground floor, offers a fine view of the garden. In this large chamber, with its high, undecorated ceiling framed by superb Corinthian columns, successive premiers administered the Empire.[9]

The headquarters of the navy dominated the northwestern side of Whitehall. The Old Admiralty Building, erected in the 1720s by a naval comptroller, was the official residence of the first lord of the Admiralty until he moved next door into the new Admiralty House, constructed in the 1780s. Winston Churchill resided there from 1911 to 1915, when as first lord he presided over meetings of the Admiralty Board in a large panelled room. Close to Admiralty House is Trafalgar Square, with Nelson's Column standing as a heroic reminder of the central role of the navy in British history.

The need to fund enormous naval expenditure, as a crucial part of British policy relating to the Middle East, enhanced the influence of the financial district of London, known as the City. The City subsidized the Ottoman debt from the 1850s, and loaned funds to the British government to buy into the Suez Canal Company in 1875 and the Anglo-Persian Oil Company in 1914.[10]

Mansion House, the Royal Exchange and the Bank of England were located at the intersection of nine streets that came together in the centre of the crowded square mile of the City of London.[11] Mansion House was erected in the mid-1700s, shortly before the Seven Years War, when the British forced the French out of North America and the subcontinent of India. It is the official residence of the lord mayor, whose position requires him to entertain the leaders of business and government. Elected by liverymen and aldermen who owe their vote to tradition and economic

2 A picture postcard before World War I that depicts the two most important financial institutions in the City of London: the Bank of England, on the left, and the Royal Exchange, on the right.

power, he rides, on the second Saturday of each November, in a gilded four-ton coach, the highlight of a parade that symbolizes the ongoing wealth and independence of the City.

The Royal Exchange, close to the Bank of England, is the City's commercial and trading centre, and was modelled in the 1560s on the Dutch exchange. It was reconstructed after the Great Fire of 1666 and rebuilt in the 1840s by Sir William Tite. Over the central portico is a weather vane and an eleven-foot-long gilded grasshopper. Above the massive row of columns is a typanum, bearing an inscription from the Psalms, 'The Earth is the Lord's and the Fulness thereof', a mark of piety recommended by Albert, consort to Queen Victoria.

The business of the Royal Exchange is conducted in private, as is that of the Bank of England nearby. Founded as a private company in the 1690s by William Paterson, a Scot, to loan money to William III, the Bank of England in due course obtained a monopoly on issuing paper money and holding the nation's gold reserve. As the British government was subsidized by the rich, the Bank not only controlled the national debt – the grease that lubricated an increasingly expensive British defence machine – but also secured influence over other banks in the country. The Bank of England played a substantial role in all matters of public finance throughout the eighteenth and nineteenth centuries, and its role has increased alongside public indebtedness since World War I. Designed by Sir John Soane and completed in 1808, the Bank, when viewed from

3   Mansion House, the opulent official residence of the Lord Mayor of the City of London since the middle of the eighteenth century, shown here in a photograph taken on the eve of World War I.

Threadneedle or Princes streets, appears as a brooding fortress. Behind its two-storied, massive grey walls lies a succession of halls and courts hidden from public view until the Bank of England museum was opened in the 1990s. Today, during the evening rush hour, a detachment of the British army still marches to guard the bank – the only national troops permitted within the City.[12]

Parliament, since the middle of the nineteenth century, has been housed in the rebuilt Palace of Westminster on the River Thames. Boldly redesigned by Charles Barry and framed by Big Ben Tower on one side and Victoria Tower on the other, medieval Westminster Hall remains its centrepiece. The Tudor Gothic decoration, so scrupulously crafted in great detail, gives the palace a rich historical exterior that complements Westminster Abbey, opposite, where the coronation has taken place of almost every British monarch since William the Conqueror.

The monarchy too has played a central role. By the beginning of Queen Victoria's reign (1837–1901), Buckingham Palace had become the principal royal residence in London, following the smaller Palace of St James. Although ambassadors continued to present their credentials to the Court of St James, the ceremony, along with that of ministers kissing the hands of the monarch upon assuming office, actually took place at Buckingham Palace. Edward VII (who reigned from 1901–10) and George V (1910–36) influenced Middle Eastern policy only very marginally during the first two decades of the twentieth century.

Whitehall, the avenue connecting Westminster with Trafalgar Square, is lined with edifices that house the great departments of State, the Treasury, Foreign Office, India Office, Colonial Office and War Office. These, together with the Admiralty, became so routinely involved in the administration of the British Empire in the late nineteenth and early twentieth centuries that they came to represent 'the official mind of imperialism'.[13] Middle Eastern policy was part of this process, and despite the arrival of telegraphic communication, high policy continued to be defined by a small group of powerful ministers with direct access to the prime minister and his cabinet.[14]

The social hub for Downing Street, Westminster and Whitehall was located conveniently nearby in Pall Mall and St James's Street. The gentlemen's clubs to be found in the area originated in such eighteenth-century meeting places as St James's and Boodle's, designed by Robert Adam, Brooks's by the architect Henry Holland, and the Pantheum and White's by James Wyatt in the 1770s. White's became a particular favourite of those involved in Middle Eastern affairs in the early twentieth century. The number and size of the clubs increased during the nineteenth century, when many were associated with specific political parties or professions. Although each developed its own character, all were highly exclusive, membership depending on nomination and recommendation. In the 1820s John Nash created the United Service Club, later reconstructed by

Decimus Burton, the architect of the Athenaeum. During the 1830s Charles Barry was the architect of the Travellers' and Reform clubs. In the 1840s Sydney Smirke created the Carlton, the core of British Conservatism that was to admit Margaret Thatcher only after she had become prime minister. It was at the Carlton that the decision was made to change the Conservative leadership in 1911, and to abandon the coalition in 1922. The ambience of the Carlton and similar men's clubs replicated the public school and university experiences of most of their members.

It was within these governmental, quasi-governmental and non-governmental institutions in Westminster, St James's, and the City – and virtually nowhere else – that the most important issues involving the Middle East were discussed and decided. Unlike any other comparable capital city in Europe, an identifiable and compact geographical area provides the historical context for those who invented the Middle East.[15]

THE POWER OF THE PRESS

The effective operation of the City's money-market, the Bank of England, and London's powerful joint-stock banks depended upon reliable daily access to news. Reuters Telegraph Company, located from the 1870s until after World War I in a Georgian house on Old Jewry street, provided its subscribers with fund quotations from the ten leading world exchanges; cotton, corn and flour reports from twenty-four locations; the rate of exchange for bills and discount reports from seventeen sources; and metal and wool prices from many areas. Providing rapid and accurate information on specie, freight, mails and petroleum as well, Reuters was indispensable to the City and by the end of the nineteenth-century had become the principal news agency for the entire British Empire.[16]

The main thoroughfare from the City of London to Westminster bears the name of the old Fleet River, a sewer before it was covered and entubed in the 1760s. Fleet Street, colloquially designated 'the street of ink', became synonymous with London's press, which grew rapidly in number after the mid-nineteenth century. In 1860 London had fifteen daily morning and evening newspapers; by 1900 there were a total of 150 in London and the provinces. Newspaper readership quadrupled between 1896 and 1914.[17]

Since its first publication in 1785, The Times, known as 'The Thunderer', has exercised such continuous influence that it has sometimes mistakenly been regarded as an official organ of government. The newspaper with the largest range of foreign correspondents, The Times covered the Crimean War in the 1850s, sustained the British defence of India after the mutiny, supported the British occupation of Egypt in the 1880s and hailed the reconquest of the Sudan in the 1890s, endorsed

British paramountcy in the Persian Gulf, and approved British imperial expansion in eastern and southern Africa at the end of the century. *The Times* was read by, and to some extent possibly influenced, almost everyone of importance, even though it had a daily circulation of fewer than 50,000 in 1914.

To the right of *The Times,* on the political spectrum, were the *Morning Post*, first published in the 1770s; the *Daily Telegraph*, launched in the 1850s; and the *Evening News*, which first appeared during the 1880s. Most of the papers saw themselves as having a conservative or independent viewpoint, but some, such as the Liberals' *Daily Chronicle, Daily News* and *Morning Leader*, inclined more to the political left. Identification with the Conservative or Liberal parties often rendered editorials on foreign policy predictable, although Fleet Street, taken as a whole, was relatively bipartisan in its handling of the Middle Eastern issues during the first decades of the twentieth century.

The four most popular London newspapers sold over 2,500,000 copies daily in the years before 1914. The *Daily Mail* had a circulation of 900,000; the *Daily Sketch,* 750,000; the *Daily Mirror,* 650,000; and the *Daily Express,* 400,000. These and similar papers fed the public's appetite for the sensational reporting of murders, suicides, accidents, natural catastrophes, disturbances at home, riots abroad, and especially wars. Patriotically championing the British Empire, these popular newspapers made huge profits for their owner-publishers, the press lords to whom London's political elite needed to pay careful attention.[18]

Most of the weeklies, quarterlies and provincial dailies also had offices near Fleet Street. The most influential quality periodicals at the beginning of the twentieth century were, from right to left on the political spectrum, *Blackwood's Magazine, The Quarterly Review, The Edinburgh Review, The Fortnightly Review* and *The Nineteenth Century.* These five publications gave increased attention to the Middle East in the first decades of the twentieth century. Indeed, the numbers of articles on the Middle East increased, relative to other areas, as follows:

Years	Middle East	Africa	India	Ireland
1902–14	190	291	256	305
1915–23	194	123	131	171[19]

Another journalistic area influential at the beginning of the twentieth century was London's religious press. One historian has recently estimated that there may have been as many as 25,000 distinct titles of religious newspapers, magazines and reviews printed in the nineteenth century. The leading religious papers, with 100,000 subscribers at the beginning of the twentieth century, included the nonconformist *Christian World* (established in 1857), the Roman Catholic *Universe* (1860), the High Anglican *Church Times* (1863), the *Methodist Times* (1885) and the Protestant *British Weekly*

(1886). Because most Christians knew the geography of the Holy Land better than they did that of the political Middle East, the religious press tended to reinforce Christian suspicions of Jews and hostility towards Muslims.[20]

No London institution paid more attention to Fleet Street than Parliament, and this was particularly true of members of the House of Commons. Members of Parliament who held electorally safe seats could choose to ignore the press, but those in marginal seats needed to take Fleet Street very seriously. The celebrated example occurred after 1876, when Gladstone skilfully used press indignation over Turkish atrocities against the Bulgarian Christians to besmirch Disraeli, the Conservative prime minister, for deals with the Turks at the Congress of Berlin, and win the famous Midlothian campaign of 1879–80. The House of Lords was less vulnerable to press comment, and indeed included within it peers whose fortune had been made in Fleet Street rather than in the City.[21]

In the early twentieth-century the Middle East increasingly became a topic of debate in both the House of Commons and the House of Lords. It is revealing to note the average number of occasions each year on which the Middle East was raised, in comparison with other areas:

Years	Middle East	India	Ireland	Russia
1902–14	231	442	446	29
1915–23	265	402	700	171[22]

NINE MINISTERS OF STATE

This book focuses on nine British men whose cabinet careers and backgrounds most affected British policy towards the Middle East during the first two decades of the twentieth century. None was elected through any specific expertise. None believed that he was under any obligation to consult with leaders of the Middle East. None seriously questioned the information he received from Whitehall and from officials on the spot, and scarcely any cared about the region their decisions affected.

The nine leaders are listed alphabetically with their relevant ministerial posts, as follows:

Herbert Henry Asquith: chancellor of the Exchequer, 1905–8; prime minister, 1908–16;[23]

Arthur James Balfour: prime minister, 1902–5; first lord of the Admiralty, 1915–16; foreign secretary, 1916–19;[24]

Winston Churchill: colonial under secretary, 1905–8; first lord of the Admiralty, 1911–15; chancellor of the duchy of Lancaster, 1915–16; minister of munitions, 1917–19; secretary of war and air, 1919–22; colonial secretary, 1921–2;[25]

Lord Curzon: lord privy seal, 1915–16; war cabinet member, 1916–19; foreign secretary, 1919–22;[26]

Edward Grey: foreign secretary, 1905–16;[27]

Lord Kitchener: war secretary, 1914–16;[28]

Lord Lansdowne: foreign secretary, 1900–5; minister without portfolio, 1915–16;[29]

David Lloyd George: chancellor of the Exchequer, 1908–15; minister of munitions, 1915–16; war secretary, 1916; prime minister, 1916–22;[30]

Lord Milner: war cabinet member, 1916–18; war secretary, 1918–19; colonial secretary, 1919–21.[31]

The personalities of each of these men will come under scrutiny in later chapters, but here it may be revealing to compare their socioeconomic backgrounds, their religious outlook and their political views in relation to Britain, its empire and the Middle East. A composite profile suggests more similarities than differences among them, these similarities indeed contributing to the bipartisan consensus conventionally reached on British policy towards the Middle East.

Five of the nine cabinet ministers were aristocrats: Balfour and Lansdowne inherited the most; Curzon twice revitalized his wealth by marrying American heiresses; Grey was content to survive on a more meagre income; Churchill supplemented his income through the prolific publication of articles and books. Milner and Kitchener were middle class in the sense that their fathers had worked for a living, while the backgrounds of Asquith and Lloyd George were modest. All but Grey became members of at least two clubs: Balfour, Curzon, Churchill, Kitchener and Milner were members of the Athenaeum; Asquith, Milner and Lansdowne of Brooks's; and Balfour and Lansdowne of the Travellers' club.

Six were born to Anglican parents, and Asquith eventually joined the established Church. Balfour worshipped as an Anglican when in England and as a Presbyterian when at his family estate in Scotland. Only Lloyd George did not conform to the state religion. He made his political reputation initially as an outspoken nonconformist who advocated the disestablishment of the Anglican Church in Wales. Lloyd George's popularity with nonconformists was enhanced by the *British Weekly*, the biggest Protestant religious newspaper. Indeed, apart from Lloyd George, a Welshman, all were firmly English.

In respect of education, Balfour, Curzon and Lansdowne each went to Eton, Balfour proceeding to Cambridge University, while Curzon and Lansdowne went up to Oxford, as did Asquith, Grey and Milner. Kitchener and Milner briefly attended secondary academies in Europe; Kitchener's schooling in Switzerland made him fluent in French and Milner's residence in Germany enabled him to master German. Knowledge of foreign languages made some suspect that Kitchener and Milner had Continental loyalties, and it was perhaps for this reason that Churchill

4 The nine cabinet ministers who most influenced Middle Eastern policies from 1902 to 1922. Left to right, top row: Asquith, Balfour, Churchill; middle row: Curzon, Lloyd George, Grey; bottom row: Kitchener, Lansdowne and Milner.

deliberately mispronounced the French he knew, as had Palmerston the previous century. Kitchener and Churchill had studied at military academies, and only Lloyd George had no formal higher education.

Most had travelled extensively, though Lloyd George and Asquith were too poor to go abroad in their youth. Two who travelled little were Grey, who rarely left his country estate except when compelled to be in London, and Balfour, who was prone to seasickness. Much of Churchill's travelling involved military postings or journeys to battlegrounds as a military writer. Curzon travelled purposefully in Asia as a young man, and made a reputation for himself as an author; at the age of thirty-nine he was appointed viceroy of India. Lansdowne spent a dozen years as governor of Canada and viceroy of India. Milner worked for three years in Egypt as a young administrator, and eight in South Africa. Kitchener lived the longest abroad, principally as an army officer. For twenty years he spent more time in Asia than in the British Isles, and was the only one of the nine with personal experience of the Arab world through travel or residence. Not one of these men doubted the superiority of British civilization.

In 1902 all nine men were in vigorous middle-age: Lansdowne, the eldest, was fifty-seven, Balfour fifty-four, and Kitchener fifty-two. The rest were in their forties, except for Lloyd George, who was thirty-nine and Churchill a mere twenty-eight. All made their careers in Parliament except for Milner, who stood unsuccessfully for a seat in the Commons, and Kitchener. Most owed their careers to non-parliamentary factors, to their families, their connections, or – as in the case of Milner and Kitchener – their imperial accomplishments. A ministerial career was earned through loyalty to party; the proconsuls, Milner and Kitchener, were appointed only through the exigencies of war.

Balfour, Curzon, Lansdowne, Milner and Kitchener were Conservatives, while Asquith, Grey and Lloyd George were Liberals. Churchill shifted from the Conservative to the Liberal bench in the aftermath of the Boer War. During the conflict in South Africa (1899–1902), the Conservatives, as well as Asquith and Grey, supported the British against the Boers. Lloyd George, however, was outspoken in his criticism of Conservative conduct during the War, but even he eventually accepted the consensus. By 1911, Lloyd George was fraternizing conventionally in London clubs and the great country houses. And he became the first to enjoy the benefits of Chequers, a country home allocated to the prime minister.

In making decisions about the Middle East, all nine acknowledged the principle of collective cabinet responsibility. Yet it did not blur their individuality, their personalities, or their political peculiarities. Matters of defence required ministers to keep their deliberations confidential, but confidentiality was sometimes notably lacking with regard to issues involving the Middle East. Before the 1914–18 War, cabinet secrets were sometimes leaked to the press. During the war differences between 'Easterner' and 'Westerner' strategists were sometimes pivotal, and led to the fall of one prime minister and the rise of another in 1916. After 1918, and the lifting of censorship, the views of individual cabinet members became widely known and discussed. Policymaking became a topic for gossips, loquacious wives, manipulative officers and officials, as well as eager journalists.

LABELLING THE MIDDLE EAST

The term 'Middle East' first appeared in the September 1902 issue of London's *National Review*, an influential conservative monthly. The man who coined the term was Alfred Thayer Mahan (1840–1914), a US naval officer and lecturer who first came to attention in the early 1890s with the publication of two books on the historic influence of British sea power. The books initially attracted less attention in the United States than in London, where they supported the argument for an augmented British navy. During Mahan's highly successful three-week visit to England in 1894, he was received at court, entertained by the prime minister, Lord Rosebery, and the opposition leader, Lord Salisbury, fêted at banquets in his honour, and awarded honorary degrees at both Oxford and Cambridge universities. Mahan, moreover, was the first foreigner allowed to enter London's exclusive Army and Navy Club.

The *Times* indeed compared Mahan to Copernicus: just as he had been the first to teach that the earth and other planets revolved around the sun, so Mahan was the first to show that history was determined by the powers that controlled the seas.[32] Mahan, a devout Episcopalian, cut a fine figure in London, and was immensely well-received by the press.

Mahan's *National Review* article bore the title 'The Persian Gulf and International Relations'. Repeating George Washington's principle that international relations should be determined by justice and interest, Mahan believed that Britain should bear the greatest responsibility for protecting the Persian Gulf in order to fulfil its obligations to India and to secure its sea route to the Far East, which, according to the author, had already become 'an advanced post of international activities, of very great and immediate importance'.[33] Just as Russia's railway across the Siberian vastness had linked its huge Asiatic empire to the North China Sea and the Pacific Ocean, so Mahan believed that Russian advances in central Asia and northern Persia brought the country too close to the Persian Gulf. Praising the British for their control of the Suez Canal and Egypt, Mahan regarded south Persia as 'the logical next step beyond Egypt' for Britain.

> The Middle East, if I may adopt a term which I have not seen, will some day need its Malta, as well as its Gibraltar; it does not follow that either will be in the Gulf. Naval force has the quality of mobility which carries with it the privilege of temporary absences; but it needs to find

5   A. T. Mahan.

on every scene of operation established bases of refit, of supply, and in case of disaster, of security. The British Navy should have the facility to concentrate in force if occasion arise, about Aden, India, and the Gulf.[34]

To secure itself at sea, Britain needed to defend its commerce and communications across the Suez route to India, thereby offsetting Russia's huge land empire.

To Mahan, German proposals to build a railway to Baghdad and beyond called for British attention, even though he saw railways as more expensive and less effective than 'nature's own highway' that connected the Mediterranean Sea to the Indian Ocean. Mahan doubted that the Great Powers of Europe would accept British control of the Baghdad Railway as well as over the Persian Gulf, but he believed that the British should not abandon their 'advantages, except as the result of war, if a rival think that result will repay the cost'. He believed Britain should cooperate with Germany's railway scheme, and together hold Russia in check while they settled the political problems surrounding the status of the Asiatic provinces of the Turkish Empire. He deplored the xenophobic outbursts of both the German and the British press, and believed that the Teutonic states, including the United States, could make a 'balanced and conciliatory adjustment on all sides'. Mahan's tone was conspicuously more restrained than the normally anti-German tone of the *National Review*.[35]

Not only did *The Times* reprint excerpts from Mahan's article, but its leading anti-German journalist penned a powerful series of twenty articles, beginning in mid-October 1902, under the heading 'The Middle Eastern Question'. The author, whom the newspaper designated 'a special correspondent from Teheran', was the influential head of *The Times'* foreign department, Valentine Ignatius Chirol.[36]

Chirol (1852–1929), one of Britain's most influential journalists, was the son of an Anglican and a prominent Englishwoman who had converted to Roman Catholicism. Raised a Catholic and educated in Germany, Chirol graduated from the Sorbonne in Paris. Outspoken in his criticism of Germany, Chirol was banned from the country in 1892. In 1897 he became head of the foreign department of *The Times*. Humourless and self-important, Chirol took his journalistic mission very seriously, maintaining extensive contacts inside as well as on the fringes of British policymaking.[37]

Chirol's articles were reprinted in 1903 as a book called *The Middle East Question or Some Problems of Indian Defence*. He acknowledged Mahan's original use of the term Middle East, but applied it more broadly. To Chirol, the Middle East included not just the Persian Gulf and its coasts, but all land as well as sea approaches to India: Persia, the Persian Gulf, Iraq, the east coast of Arabia, Afghanistan and Tibet, or 'those regions of Asia which extend to the borders of India or command the approaches to India, and which are consequently bound up with the problems of Indian political as well as military defence'. Chirol thus tied the Middle East to the defence of India and related it to British interests throughout southern Asia, but not yet to the Suez Canal.

In 1896 Chirol had published *The Far Eastern Question* to alert London to the danger that Japan's military success over China might enhance Russia's position in eastern and central Asia, where it posed a yet greater threat to British defences. Chirol now urged the strengthening of British defences on India's northwest frontier, although few needed to be reminded of tsarist expansion in Asia. Chirol also noted two new factors: first, Russia's oil wealth, centred around Baku, which then produced half the world's petroleum. Baku had grown from a population of only 60,000 in the 1880s to over 250,000 in the 1900s, making it, after St Petersburg, the next most modern city in Russia. To Chirol, increased Russian influence in northern Persia had to be offset by greater British power in southern Persia. Reviving earlier British anxieties over Russia's Siberian Railway, Chirol noted a second new factor in 'the German railway invasion of Asiatic Turkey'.[38] Chirol linked the Middle East to Germany's interests in Anatolia and the Balkans, which he termed the Near East.

Chirol's views looked back to British and European involvement in Asia during the nineteenth century and forward to the geopolitical linkages of the twentieth century, reflecting the speed of modern transportation and

6   Valentine Chirol.

communication. Technological progress had the effect of bringing more of the East to the attention of more of the West.

Before the last half of the nineteenth century, Asia had simply been known as 'the East', the exotic and alluring Orient of wealth and spices evoked by Shakespeare, Milton and others. In the late 1700s, the French had coined the phrase 'Near East' to refer to the Ottoman Empire. Bonaparte's expedition to Egypt and French interests in the Levant had provoked the British into an aggressive defence of India in the eastern Mediterranean. The expansion of British economic and military activity in China during the early 1800s encouraged the British to distinguish between the Far East and the Near East. Such distinctions were necessary since the advent of steam-powered ships and locomotives meant the West was no longer confined to Asian coasts, and since laying of telegraph wires brought superior communication with the East.[39]

Chirol's concept of the Middle East gave further definition to the existing geopolitical distinctions in Asia. To him, the central issue was

Russian expansion in Asia. Japan had begun to intervene powerfully in the Far East, while Germany was attempting to exert pressure in the Near East. Chirol wanted the British to take more interest in the Middle East.

When *The Times* concluded its publication of Chirol's series of articles in 1903, it ceased to place the phrase the 'Middle East' in quotation marks. In 1904, the British geographer Halford J. Mackinder challenged Mahan's emphasis on sea power by reasserting the greater strategic significance of land power. In an article for London's *Geographical Journal*, Mackinder argued that the inner area of Eurasia remained the most pivotal region in world politics, and that it was beyond the reach of maritime powers.[40]

It is clear that, whatever the view of other strategists, Chirol's readers expected their government to defend British interests between Europe and India. How best to do that preoccupied Whitehall, Westminster, Fleet Street and the City during the early years of the twentieth century. Even before the 1914–18 war, Downing Street, the Foreign Office and the Admiralty had adopted policies that palpably altered the balance of power in the Middle East. During the war, when British military forces occupied so much of Western Asia, the Middle East label would gain momentum in Whitehall. After it, when Churchill became colonial secretary and head of the newly-created Middle East Department, Mahan's identification of the Middle East with the Persian Gulf and Chirol's preoccupation with India's defence expanded to encompass Iraq, Palestine, the Sinai and the Arabian peninsulas, as well as the Suez canal.

Chapter 2

The Status Quo: 1902–1905

WHEN THE SOUTH African war ended in the summer of 1902, Arthur Balfour became Britain's new prime minister. He presided over a Conservative administration that faced a sizeable national deficit, and, concerned with paying for the war and the enormous costs incurred in building up the navy, he opposed new initiatives in the Middle East. At the same time Downing Street ceded none of Britain's economic, naval and diplomatic advantages in a region Balfour fully recognized as of major strategic importance.

The government maintained British control over the Suez Canal and British dominance throughout the Indian Ocean and the Persian Gulf. Whitehall officials were not as anxious as the Anglo-Indians about Russian expansion into central Asia, particularly northern Persia, provided Russia built no railways and maintained no bases in the Persian Gulf. This frustrated the viceroy of India, whose hand was further weakened by Japan's victory over Russia several years later. Russia's defeat also made France more amenable to settling some of its imperial differences with Britain. The 1904 Entente Cordiale recognized the British occupation of Egypt in exchange for French claims in Morocco.

In 1906, London's Germanophobic press was satisfied to learn that Britain stood with France on Morocco. Two years previously, the Tory press had been emboldened when it successfully blocked German efforts to secure financial backing and government support in London for building a railway through Asiatic Turkey to Baghdad.

Despite a variety of religious and humanitarian protests against the Turks, the Conservative cabinet maintained existing Anglo-Ottoman relations so as to secure the Turkish Straits, the waterway connecting the Black Sea with the Mediterranean. The foreign secretary, Lord Lansdowne, along with his European counterparts, had difficulty pressing the sultan to control the armed bands operating in Macedonia. The plight of Christians and Jews in the Turkish Empire found more verbal than real support from the British government.

LONDON'S MOOD AFTER THE SOUTH AFRICAN WAR

The dawn of a new century is time to take stock, and the columns of

British newspapers, journals and magazines were occupied in 1899 and 1900 with comment on what the British had done in the past century and what they should do in the next. The reflection was intensified by the war in South Africa, where the British army, which had been fighting since 1899, gained the offensive only in the spring of 1900 and failed to defeat Boer guerrillas until the spring of 1902. Media retrospective was stimulated too by the death of Queen Victoria in January 1901, her sixty-four-year reign having lasted longer than any European monarch except Louis XIV. Journalists asked how the Edwardian era would compare with the greatness of the past.

Amid this public soul-searching was a view that the Boer War had underlined Britain's strengths and weaknesses. Fleet Street approved the determination of political leaders, the patriotism of the people, and the high costs of the war. Reports in the latter part of 1901 that revealed the brutal methods of British troops against Boer guerrillas, such as raids on villages and the internment of Boer women and children, tarnished the lustre of victory just as the public began to weary of the war. British isolation from the other Great Powers seemed less splendid now than it had in the late Victorian era. Although expecting no support from the French and their Russian rivals during the South African war, London had been shocked that the kaiser and the German press had gloated over British reverses. While the Foreign Office appreciated US neutrality, the British public seemed baffled. Though volunteers from Australia, Canada and New Zealand had enlisted with the British army in South Africa, some in London regarded the colonies as lukewarm in their support.

The high cost of the war was met by increased taxes and government borrowing that increased inflation and provoked anxiety. With the economic recession of 1903–5, some Conservatives advocated abandoning free trade for tariff reform, which would have involved an imperial tariff to protect trade within the British Empire against US and European competition. However, many Conservatives opposed the idea, which they thought would lead to unpopular increases in food prices. Tariff reform revived memories of the early nineteenth-century Tory identification with the high price of bread resulting from the Corn Laws, the repeal of which in the 1840s had torn the Tories apart and left them as a minority party for two decades.

Facing such political and economic constraints, Conservative policy-makers perceived the Middle East primarily in terms of controlling its waterways. The Suez Canal, the Persian Gulf and the eastern Mediterranean were all dominated by the British navy as the Suez route to India grew in importance in relation to the longer oceanic route around the African continent. For the British, strategic defence remained of paramount significance until oil became the dominant feature during the middle decades of the twentieth century.

BALFOUR AT DOWNING STREET

Balfour became prime minister in July 1902. He succeeded his uncle, Lord Salisbury, then seventy-one years old, who had remained as prime minister despite declining energy and failing health until the conclusion of the war in South Africa. During the war, however, Balfour had assumed increasing direction of affairs, and his appointment came as no surprise.

Arthur James Balfour (1848–1930) was one of Britain's most wealthy and powerful individuals. At the age of eight, when his father died, Balfour inherited the Scottish estate and fortune his grandfather had made as a contractor in India. Balfour's mother, a sister of the third marquess of Salisbury, inculcated religious devotion and bookish pursuits in her frail, shortsighted, son. His mother, sister, two brothers and their spouses, who stimulated his interest in philosophy and science, had rather more impact upon him than did his years at Eton and Cambridge. Orthodox in his religious and political views, Balfour had a low opinion of history and no expectation that humanity could do better in the future. In a book published in 1895, he wrote:

> We survey the past and see that its history is of blood and tears, of helpless blundering, of wild revolt, of stupid acquiescence, of empty aspirations. We sound the future, and learn that after a period, long compared with the individual life, but short indeed compared with the divisions of time open to our investigation, the energies of our system will decay, the glory of the sun will be dimmed and the earth, tideless and inert, will no longer tolerate the race which has for a moment disturbed its solitude. Man will go down into the pit, and all his thoughts will perish.[1]

Balfour led an active social and intellectual life that centred on his large London town house at 4 Carlton Gardens and his Scottish estate, Whittinghame. Although at ease with his family and closest friends, the impeccably dressed bachelor appeared aloof and cold to others. Tall and lean, languid in posture, Balfour viewed the world cautiously through his pince-nez, paying as little attention to public opinion as he could.

It was, however, politics that was the centre of Balfour's life. Elected to the House of Commons in 1876 he had served his apprenticeship under Salisbury, who had appointed him first his parliamentary private secretary and then his minister for local government, Scotland and Ireland. In the latter position, amid passions stirred by Home Rule, Balfour used more sticks than carrots, gaining praise from Conservatives and Unionists while being designated 'Bloody Balfour' by the Irish and their Liberal supporters. He subsequently led the House of Commons and headed the Treasury during the later 1890s. Though no orator, Balfour was effective on paper

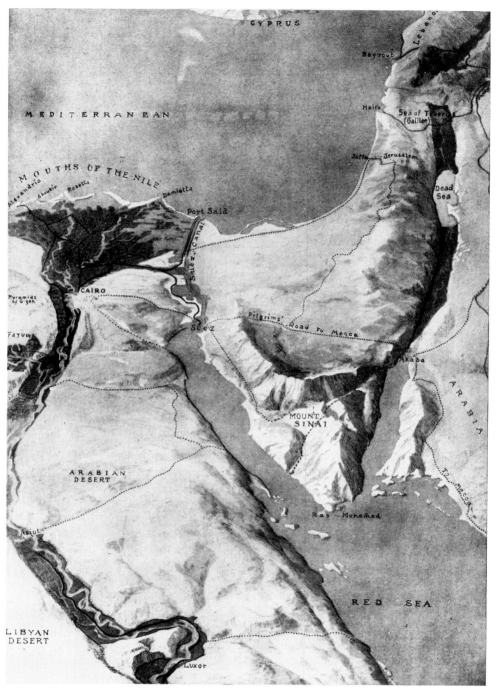

7 The topography around the Suez Canal, of which the British government owned 49 per cent of the company stock. The canal was defended by the British occupation of Egypt. Given the millions of Muslims in the British Empire, access to Mecca also needed to be secured.

and in the conference room, where his intellect overcame the nonchalance he affected in public.

Balfour inherited his political credo and his view of imperial and international affairs from his uncle. Like Salisbury, Balfour believed in maintaining the Church, Crown and Empire through aristocratic and financial leadership: wealth, a powerful navy and enlightened rule overseas had facilitated peace and fostered the growth of world trade. The empire was a great asset, but the British needed to protect their naval supremacy and economic investment to maintain their worldly preeminence.

In December 1902, six months after he became prime minister, Balfour established the Committee of Imperial Defence (CID). An outgrowth of a cabinet defence committee formed in 1895, the CID added to its membership the officers in charge of the army and navy. The new committee set out to coordinate the various defence agencies and determine strategic priorities. In 1903 Balfour became the CID's chairman; the following year he raised it from an advisory to a policy-making body and dominated it as prime minister. He was the only permanent member; he decided which ministers and opposition members would attend it and which civilian and military officials would be asked to appear before it; he established the CID Secretariat, which monitored all memos and minutes; he convened the meetings and established the agenda. In this he had the approval of Viscount Esher (1852–1930), who, at the same time, played a pivotal role in reorganizing the War Office. In 1903 Esher wrote to Balfour: 'I look to the Defence Ctte. as the crowning stone of the edifice. We begin constructing from the top, an inversion of the usual method, necessary in this case, for many and vital reasons.'[2] Balfour's reorganization of British imperial defences indeed proceeded from the top down. The CID held eighty meetings between December 1902 and December 1905, with Balfour contributing twenty memos on Indian, colonial and home defence. Balfour determined strategic priorities and decided which matters were 'vital', 'important' or merely of 'local' significance.[3]

Balfour's approach to British defence was more geopolitical than economic or ideological. He believed that a powerful British navy was the key to the defence of the British Isles and Empire; he rarely concerned himself with promoting British trade and commercial interests; and did not favour one foreign power or group over another. Paying close attention to maps, ships and armies, he understood how central Asia's high mountains and arid plateaux formed a more powerful barrier to Russian expansion towards India than any buffer the British might establish in Afghanistan. Balfour disliked Russia's ascendancy in northern Persia but allowed it so long as Russia built no railways in eastern or southern Persia and no bases on the Persian coast of the gulf. The British should dominate the coasts of the Persian Gulf through their treaties with local leaders, and British communications with Bombay and Karachi, seaports vital to trade with India, should remain secure.

To Balfour, a large Indian army, led by British officers, was vital to the British Empire. In a 1904 memorandum for the CID, he estimated British armed forces and their distribution as follows:

100,000 Indian infantry available for use outside India
 52,000 Indian infantry for India's internal security
 33,000 British infantry for colonial garrisons
 27,000 British infantry for the British Isles[4]

Indians not only constituted 72 per cent of British imperial troops but bore all the costs of the army, including the purchase of arms from British manufacturers. British naval domination of the Persian Gulf was also essential for India's defence and indeed something of a bargain for the British at the same time.

For Balfour, as for his Conservative predecessors, the Suez Canal was vital. Although the British government had owned 49 per cent of the Suez Canal Company stock since 1875, the canal was operated from the company's headquarters in Paris. Balfour was content so long as user fees were kept low, since over 80 per cent of the shipping that passed through the waterway was British. With the security of the canal guaranteed by British ships based in the Mediterranean Sea, Red Sea and Indian Ocean, he regarded the Suez Canal as virtually British.

Provided the British navy was more powerful than the French and Russian fleets combined, Balfour believed that it would prevail from the British Isles to India. From 1889 to 1897 Balfour and the Conservatives supported its expansion and development, the costs of which increased from over £15 million to almost £24 million per year, an increase of 65 per cent. The increase was met by increasing taxes, reducing colonial military activities and avoiding confrontation with Europe's Great Powers. Between 1897 and 1905 annual naval expenditure increased by another 78 per cent.[5] The growth in size and in operating costs of the British navy, combined with a huge increase in cost-per-unit production of battleships and cruisers and the costs of the war in South Africa, worsened the deficit when the economic recession of 1903–5 itself diminished government revenue. 'I am in despair about the financial outlook', the head of the Admiralty wrote to Balfour in October 1903.[6] But the prime minister neither slowed the pace of naval expansion nor reduced the overwhelming British naval superiority in the Mediterranean.

Compared with the Suez Canal and the Persian Gulf, Balfour believed the Turkish Straits connecting the Black Sea with the Mediterranean Sea were less important. If Russia were to gain access to the straits, the British would still have their naval bases and soldiers garrisoned on Cyprus, at Alexandria, on Malta and at Gibraltar; Russian access to the straits would not alter the strategic advantages the British enjoyed in the Mediterranean unless the Russian navy were joined by the French; and if Russia were to capture Constantinople, other European powers would doubtless support Britain, so it would not have to act alone.

Although Balfour recognized the importance of the Suez Canal as a lifeline to India, he wrote in 1904 that 'Egypt has for us no strategic importance'. Several thousand Anglo-Egyptian forces led by British officers and paid for by Egyptian taxpayers were sufficient: 'The final fate of Egypt, however, in case of war, is quite independent of the success or failure of the local military operations, and would depend upon the general issues of the great struggle.'[7] Sending more men to Egypt would 'lock up troops much required elsewhere', so the defence of Egypt was not part of his overall design.

Balfour's strategic position on the Middle East was enunciated and refined at meetings of the CID between 1902 and 1905, in his handwritten letters to the sovereign following each cabinet meeting, and in his correspondence with the foreign secretary. In 1904 Balfour used the term Middle East with greater frequency. Provided the British maintained their own naval supremacy throughout the area, Balfour believed British India would be secure. Any difficulties that arose in the Balkans, the Anatolian peninsula and the Levant could be handled diplomatically with the other Great Powers. Localised difficulties in the Arabian peninsula or in northeastern Africa would involve only small expeditionary forces paid for by India or Egypt.

Balfour only once departed from these strategic priorities, but soon regretted his decision to fight Somali rebels in eastern Africa led by 'the mad Mullah'. In 1902 he observed that offensive operations were difficult because the enemy retreated and made it 'almost impossible to strike or at least to be *sure* of striking an effective blow', while defensive operations were 'never conclusive' and the garrison had nothing to do while waiting for the enemy to strike.[8] Nevertheless, Balfour accepted the recommendations of Egypt and Whitehall, and authorized the Treasury to pay for an Indian expeditionary force to join Italian troops in attacking the mullah's forces. By the spring of 1904, however, Balfour was upset by the Indian command 'pouring money into the Somali sands', where neither British nor Indian interests were involved, though he did not know how to end the ineffective operations there.[9]

Balfour's strategic priorities appear to have been based not simply on his assessment of immediate situations but also upon the lessons he had learned from Lord Salisbury. Since the mid-1870s, Russia and France had been Britain's main competitors in Suez, Cyprus, Egypt, Sudan, Aden, the Persian Gulf and beyond. Balfour's long ministerial experience had taught him how to handle British officers. He knew of 'prancing proconsuls' who made demands that overextended British imperial resources in Asia and Africa. And his caution stood him in good stead with the viceroy of India, the ambassador to the Turkish Porte, the consul general in Egypt and the minister in Persia, as well as with other British officers in or on the edges of the Middle East.

The prime minister also resented the influence on British imperial strategy of the press which, in his view, had too much access to governmental secrets. In the spring of 1904, when appointing the secretary of the CID, Balfour was so concerned about the man's 'well known connections with the Press' that he made it 'perfectly clear' to him 'that all conversations to the Press – direct or indirect – must henceforth cease'.[10]

Balfour also tried to distance himself from London groups concerned with the plight of Jews in Russia and Europe or of Christian minorities in the Turkish Empire. He did not even oblige his friend and confidant, Baron Rothschild (1840–1915), head of the banking house, the most prominent Jew in the United Kingdom and a powerful figure in the innermost circle of the Conservative party. Responding to 'Natty' Rothschild when he set up a London committee to help Rumanian Jews, Balfour expressed his 'deepest sympathy' for the committee's goals but then observed:

> In the course of our long experience we have seen minorities monstrously ill-used in more than one country – Bulgarians, Armenians, Christians, Jews, to say nothing of aborigines in various parts of the world. Their wrongs have deeply moved public opinion in many countries, and not least in America and Britain. Societies have been formed for their protection, speeches denouncing their oppressors have been made without number, pressure has been put upon various Governments to intervene on their behalf; but I am doubtful whether any of these proceedings have done good to those they were intending to benefit, while they have undoubtedly produced much international bitterness.[11]

Politically important though Rothschild was, the strategic priorities of empire and the financial imperatives of the City of London took precedence over humanitarian concerns.[12]

LORD LANSDOWNE'S DIPLOMACY

After Balfour, the senior individual determining British policy in the Middle East was Lord Lansdowne. As head of the Foreign Office from 1900 to 1905, Lansdowne was routinely involved in the complexities of diplomatic relations with Austria-Hungary, France, Germany, Japan, Russia and the United States, as well as in the strategic or merely local matters that arose in Persia, the Turkish Empire, Egypt and surrounding areas, in India, northeastern Africa and the Balkans. Much of Lansdowne's diplomacy was conducted through foreign ambassadors in London.

In November 1900, after Salisbury had appointed him foreign secretary, Lansdowne wrote to Balfour acknowledging 'the weight of your opinion with the Prime Minister, I am grateful to you for whatever share you may have had in my appointment'.[13] Lansdowne and Balfour had known each other since their schooldays at Eton in the 1860s: Balfour continued to call Lansdowne 'Clan', an abbreviation for Viscount Clanmaurice, Lansdowne's title as a boy. Colleagues in Salisbury's cabinet since the mid-1890s, they had established a close working rapport, relying on each other's candour, political loyalty and forthright opinion.

Henry Charles Keith Petty-Fitzmaurice, the fifth marquess of Lansdowne (1845–1927) was born at Lansdowne House, the most imposing structure in Berkeley Square and one which survives unaltered after becoming part of the Lansdowne Club in the 1930s. It was his ancestor Lord Shelburne, the first marquess, who, as prime minister, signed the peace treaty with the United States in the Round Room at Lansdowne House. One of Henry's great grandfathers was Talleyrand, the great French diplomat. His mother was the daughter of a French count and a Scottish baroness, from whom he learned French and, on her death in 1895, inherited large Scottish estates. Lansdowne was a sportsman rather than a student at Eton and needed special coaching for university. At Oxford he came under the influence of Benjamin Jowett, the master of Balliol College, who encouraged his privileged student to serve the British Empire. Lansdowne was twenty-one when he inherited his title, seat in the House of Lords, and vast estates in England and Ireland from his father. At the age of twenty-four he married the youngest of a duke's six daughters, who bore him four children.

Initially Lansdowne's favourite home was in Ireland. He had ancient Irish ancestors, but the estates his family had purchased a century before were largely undeveloped. In the 1870s Lansdowne enlarged his cottage at Derreen, planted trees and laid gardens to create an ideal estate. Happiness, however, was denied Lansdowne when he came under criticism for mismanaging his vast estates, when the Irish Land League urged tenants to withhold rents from English landlords, and when Gladstone's Home Rule Bill drove him from the Liberal party and into the Unionist ranks in 1886.

Lansdowne had previously served as governor-general of Canada for five years, Gladstone having temporarily removed him from the Irish controversy. In 1888 Salisbury appointed him viceroy of India, where he passed six years without major incident, sufficiently proving his loyalty to be promoted to the War Office in 1895. As secretary of state for war, Lansdowne implemented administrative changes recommended by a commission in 1890 and worked closely with Balfour's new defence committee. He stoically endured an angry press blaming him for British military reverses in the first months of the South African war, but somewhat retrieved his reputation once tougher and abler commanders such as Roberts and Kitchener were appointed in the field.

8   The Shah of Persia on board the royal yacht in 1902. Front row: the Prince of Wales, the Shah, Queen Alexandra, Edward VII and the Princess of Wales; back row: the Shah's entourage.

Lansdowne's standing and experience equipped him well for the extravagant displays that diplomacy required. As foreign secretary, he lavishly entertained prominent foreigners at Lansdowne House and at Bowood, his estate in Wiltshire. In India he was host to Archduke Franz Ferdinand, heir to the Austro-Hungarian Empire, and to the tsarevitch, later Nicholas II of Russia.

In August 1902, during a ten-day state visit to London by the shah of Persia, Lansdowne was required to smooth over difficulties arising out of the actions of the uncooperative new king, Edward VII. The shah's planned visit in 1901 had been delayed because the court was in mourning for the death of Queen Victoria. The shah had expected to receive the Order of the Garter, just as Victoria had bestowed it on his father. but Edward refused on the grounds that a Christian decoration given to the Muslim leader of Persia would prompt similar requests from the Turkish sultan and the Chinese and Japanese emperors. Lansdowne saw to it that the shah's preferences were honoured, to have time free from the usual schedule of public appearances, to see ballet rather than opera and, above all, to attend a military rather than a naval review. But the shah, instead of being welcomed at Buckingham Palace, was compelled to travel with Lansdowne by rail to Portsmouth, where he was received by the king aboard the *Victoria & Albert*. While on board, Lansdowne read a memorandum amending the Order of the Garter to make non-Christians eligible; the shah was expected to be among its first recipients. Lansdowne wired the news to Tehran but the king continued to deny the honour to the shah, suggesting instead a jewelled portrait of himself. Having already promised the Garter and telegraphed his commitment to Tehran, Lansdowne enlisted the support of Balfour to explain to Edward the consequences that could ensue if the promise were not kept. The king eventually yielded, and a Garter Mission was sent to Tehran.[14]

The shah's visit had not enhanced the British position in Tehran, even though Anglo-Persian relations had traditionally been difficult. The shah's excessive spending had worsened Persia's debt, a factor since the 1870s when Russia and Britain had competed for influence by making loans in return for concessions. There was, for example, the sixty-year concession concluded in 1901 by British oil entrepreneurs in exchange for £20,000 cash, £20,000 in shares, and an annual royalty of 16 per cent of net profits. Lansdowne himself was not concerned with oil, which was discovered in southern Persia only in 1908, but he did favour good relations with the shah in order to counterbalance Russian influence.

Besides his diplomatic manner, Lansdowne's fluency in French enabled him to converse readily with ambassadors in London in what was still Europe's language of diplomacy. He met regularly with Paul Cambon, French ambassador to the Court of St James from 1898 until after the 1914–18 war, as well as with other European ambassadors, realizing that neglected ambassadors might embarrass His Majesty's Government through leaks to the press or complaints to their home capitals.

One of Lansdowne's most intractable diplomatic problems arose from the decline of Turkish power in southeast Europe. The Foreign Office continued to seek good relations with the sultan, as well as with the shah, to counterbalance Russian influence. Lansdowne agreed that European diplomacy should aim for peace in the Near East, despite intense religious hatred and political suspicion among newly independent countries in the Balkans and competition among their Great Power protectors. Like Salisbury, Lansdowne regarded amicable relations with both the Austro-Hungarian and Russian empires as more important for Britain than any nationality or minority in the Balkans.

In 1902, an insurrection broke out in Macedonia, which the sultan failed to pacify. Throughout 1903 Lansdowne backed an Austro-Hungarian and Russian scheme for a Christian gendarmerie in the areas of Christian dominance and a Muslim gendarmerie in the predominantly Islamic areas of Macedonia. The gendarmerie would be led by European officers and paid for by customs duties that European creditors allowed the Turks to increase.[15]

But Lansdowne's diplomacy did too little, according to several London religious and relief organizations. Christian papers were as furious in 1903 about his apparent indifference towards their coreligionists as they had been in the late nineteenth century about Turkish attacks on Bulgarians and Armenians. The *Church Times* reported a large gathering at St James's Hall, at which the bishop of Hereford stated: 'If there was any one cause in the world in which Lord Lansdowne might be provided with a big revolver, this is the one.'[16] The protestant *British Weekly*, angry over the 'Sultan's savage and ferocious troops' being 'allowed to pillage Christian provinces, to burn the villages, and to massacre the innocent inhabitants' while 'England is silent, and her influence dead or disregarded' asked, 'Who can wonder at that when her Foreign Secretary is Lord Lansdowne?'[17] The ultramontane Roman Catholic *Universe* called for nothing less than 'the crushing out of Mohammedanism in Europe' and 'the freeing of the Holy Land, of Calvary, and Nazareth, from the filthy pagan government' of the Turks.[18]

Although such indignation was expressed in the religious weeklies, most of Fleet Street recognized that the complicated issues of Macedonia could not be settled by the Foreign Office alone and that the Great Powers had to exert concerted pressure on the Porte. Frustrated as he was with Constantinople, the foreign secretary could use his leverage over the sultan to bring order to Macedonia only by acting in conjunction with Austria-Hungary and Russia.

What happened in the Balkans was a repeat of what had occurred during the 1890s on the island of Crete, when insurrection fomented by Greek annexationists provoked a Turco-Greek war that led to European intervention. Backed by its powerful navy, Britain compelled the sultan to appoint a Christian governor to Crete and to reorganize the island's gendarmerie, courts and finances, a step that eased both tensions in the Aegean and anxieties in European capitals.

Lansdowne thus assumed Lord Salisbury's traditional role as intermediary between Balkan Christians and the Porte. But, as with the earlier settlement on Crete, local passions ran so high among guerrillas and nationalists that it was incumbent upon the Foreign Office, in league with the other Great Powers, to prevent the Balkan conflict from developing into a European conflagration. Lansdowne confided to Balfour that he anticipated 'the best Greeks' would moderate nationalist ambitions for the annexation of Crete and the extension of Greek influence in Ottoman Macedonia.[19] No Hellenophile, however, Balfour viewed the Bulgarians as 'the only Nationality in the Balkans with the making of a nation in them' who 'would be much more efficient guardians of the Straits than Turkey seems ever likely to be'.[20] The more frustrated Lansdowne became with the Turks, the better the Greeks and Bulgarians seemed to him. In the latter part of 1905, when the sultan refused to comply with Great Power demands for Macedonian reforms, Lansdowne co-ordinated a naval demonstration and occupation of the island of Lemnos, an effective piece of gunboat diplomacy which forced the sultan to yield.

Lansdowne and Balfour were in agreement over the maintenance of the diplomatic status quo in the Near East and the strategic status quo in the Middle East. But when Lansdowne took steps to limit British commitments in America and the Pacific, he often needed to be more persuasive.

Lansdowne's first major initiative as foreign secretary during the winter of 1900–1, when the South African war was proceeding more satisfactorily, was a rapprochement with the United States. In addition to acknowledging the economic, linguistic, cultural and other ties between Great Britain and America, Lansdowne was willing to recognize US paramountcy in the western hemisphere in exchange for greater US appreciation of British imperial interests in Africa and Asia. Although Russian and French battleships outnumbered those in Britain's Pacific fleet, the Admiralty could not afford to send more ships. Even as the British began to retreat from the Americas, however, the Foreign Office did not automatically defer to the United States and instead at the end of 1902 joined Germany and Italy in blockading Venezuela after it refused to meet its debt obligations. The US president so resented this action that the matter was turned over to the Hague Tribunal and the blockade was lifted, reducing Anglo-American friction. Despite Canadian protests, Britain also deferred to the US over the long drawn-out Alaskan boundary dispute. The Anglo-American rapprochement subsequently took years to manifest itself, unlike the more surprising ties the British rapidly forged with Japan.[21]

Lansdowne's second major diplomatic initiative was the Anglo-Japanese alliance, whereby Britain recognized the growth of Japan's power in the Far East following its victory over China in the 1890s. Anglo-Japanese diplomacy emerged out of Britain's longstanding enmity towards Russian expansion in Asia, but also related immediately to Lansdowne's wish, particularly during the South African war, to break out of diplomatic isolation and reduce British naval responsibilities in the Pacific. In the autumn of 1901, the first lord of the Admiralty reported that Britain's Pacific fleet had four battleships to France and Russia's nine. He argued that an Anglo-Japanese combination could secure British naval superiority in the Pacific and release more ships to strengthen the home fleet.[22]

At the end of 1901, when Lansdowne began negotiations with Japan, Balfour expressed interesting reservations in a twenty-page letter written after a lengthy talk between the two men. Although the prime minister agreed that the Far East was important, if not vital, Balfour was concerned about the negative impact an Anglo-Japanese alliance might have on Germany. The British could ill afford to alienate Germany in case Russia and France declared war on Britain, particularly in India, which he believed was 'the weakest spot in the Empire' and the defence of which would scarcely be helped by a Japanese alliance. Instead, Balfour believed, Britain should seek closer relations with Berlin since Germany's alliance with Austria-Hungary and Italy – the Triple Alliance – could continue to restrain French and Russian ambitions:

It appears to me therefore that the only arguments left us for rejecting Germany's advances are that the sentiments of the German and English peoples are at present so hostile as to make negotiations undesirable (an argument of transitory value); or else that we cannot trust the leaders of the Triple Alliance (an argument which, even if it were true, is one which can hardly be used in public). As a matter of fact, I suppose none of us think that the Japanese are more to be relied upon than European governments.[23]

Balfour's concern over France and Russia made him more conciliatory towards Germany, even as he acknowledged how powerful anti-German public opinion was in Britain. Lansdowne also recognized these views in the letter he sent immediately to Balfour:

While I feel the force of your argument, there is, I think, this to be said on the other side: that the chances of the *casus foederis* arising are much fewer in the case of the Anglo-Japanese agreement than they would be in that of an Anglo-German agreement. The area of entanglement seems to me much more restricted under the former and, if this be true, the fact diminishes the difficulty of explaining to the Germans why we are prepared to face the one but not the other liability.[24]

Lansdowne was correct about his diplomacy not backfiring in Berlin. Apart from its significance for the Anglo-Japanese alliance, Lansdowne and Balfour's exchange also indicates the importance both leaders attached to anti-German opinion in Britain as the diplomatic isolation of Lord Salisbury's era was brought to an end.

BRITISH OPPOSITION TO THE BAGHDAD RAILWAY

By the late 1890s, the Germans proposed extending their Southern Anatolian Railway to Baghdad and the Persian Gulf. This attracted much attention in London during the autumn of 1902 and spring of 1903. But the British media were not essentially interested in the visits that the kaiser had paid to Constantinople in 1889 and 1898, nor in the German construction of the Anatolian railway. After the Boer war, however, Conservative newspapers strongly opposed the government's backing of German railway projects. Balfour, Lansdowne and the leading supporters of the Conservative administration, financial circles in the City of London, as well as diplomatic, naval and military officials in Whitehall, argued that as the railway would be built in any event, Britain should be part of the project to protect its own interests and maintain predominance in the Persian Gulf. But Balfour's administration surrendered to Conservative anger in Fleet Street and Westminster, and Lansdowne tried to keep the lines of

THE TEUTONISING OF TURKEY.

GERMAN KAISER. "GOOD BIRD!"

9   A cartoon of the 1900s

communication open with disappointed financiers in the City and with diplomats in Berlin. He was reassured by Balfour that the British would once again support the railway when Conservative tempers had cooled.[25]

Before examining the public controversy and the strategic issues of the Baghdad Railway, it is necessary to understand how European finance and railways operated in the Ottoman Empire. What Berlin did in the early 1900s followed precedents London and Paris had established in the late 1800s.

Britain's economic interests in the Ottoman Empire centred on the Public Debt Administration (PDA). In 1881 the huge indebtedness of the Ottoman regime had been restructured by two major foreign-controlled banks, the (French) Imperial Ottoman Bank and the (German) Deutsche Bank, which, despite political differences, had cooperated with London in protecting shareholders from the Ottoman public debt. The PDA derived most of its revenue from a tobacco tax and from the state's monopoly on salt, as well as from duties on stamps, alcoholic beverages, fish, silk, from the annual tribute paid by certain provinces, and from a variety of taxes on loans and financial guarantees given to foreign railway promoters. The regular payment to bondholders steadily increased the value of shares in the Ottoman public debt, making it a safe investment for British and other investors.

The PDA obtained thirteen further loans for the Turkish regime on terms that were probably better than it might otherwise have obtained, but the conditions usually included provisions that helped European investors and promoters far more than the Ottoman empire. Between 1886 and 1906 the sultan's government borrowed 120 million Turkish pounds ($£T$), of which it actually received $£T108$ million. In addition, the administrative costs of the PDA escalated during these years as a result of its huge staff spread over 800 separate salt duty and tax-collecting offices throughout the Turkish Empire. There were almost 5,000 officials, the majority of them European, excluding those employed by the Regie, a French agency created in 1881 to collect the tax on tobacco, with extra profits for itself in addition to the large sums remitted annually to the PDA. In 1903 the PDA forced Turkish authorities to accept additional unprofitable administrative costs to pay for Macedonian reforms. In 1905 it also blocked the Ottoman attempt to introduce a new agricultural tax. In short, while British and European bondholders made a handsome profit, the sultan's regime fell so deeply into debt that it seemed unlikely to be able ever again to order its finances.[26]

The payment of interest on the PDA was the second most substantial charge the Turks faced at the beginning of the twentieth century. Their largest expenditure went on defence, with an army of more than one million, modern weaponry, and a fleet of large ships, torpedo boats and two submarines. And, in acquiring arms from the main British and German weapon manufacturers, the Turks 'were regularly coerced or seduced into buying the latest weapon from the factories of Vickers or Krupp'.[27]

Besides having a stake in the PDA and Turkish defence, the British also had an interest in the operation of existing railways and construction of new networks in the Ottoman Empire. After the Crimean War, the British led the way in securing favourable concessions from Constantinople for building and operating railways in southwestern Anatolia, with the French following in Lebanon and Syria. The Germans did the same in southern Anatolia after Russia opposed the laying of railways in the northern part of the peninsula because it would bring Turkish troops too close to the tsar's forces. By the late 1890s the Germans proposed extending their southern Anatolian Railway to Baghdad and the Persian Gulf. Most of the British could see some value in such a construction blocking Russian expansion in Persia and linking with a British railway stretching from Egypt to the Persian Gulf.

Independent of European support, Sultan Abdul-Hamid launched the Hejaz Railway. This was begun in 1900 and completed in 1906, and aimed to convey Muslim pilgrims from Syria to Mecca, a pan-Islamic gesture paid for by Muslims. The Hejaz Railway was the only railway in the Turkish Empire not under European control.

British and European railway developers demanded – and for various reasons received – concessions far more beneficial to them than to the Ottoman Empire. First, the concessions were usually long-lasting – often ninety-nine years – and renewable. Second, the Porte provided land on either side of the line, as well as supplying developers with capital raised by the sale of Ottoman bonds. Third, Europeans secured what was called 'the kilometric guarantee', which ensured developers a profit for every kilometre of railway they operated. Fourth, the railway paid no taxes on either revenue or property. Finally, there were additional 'minor' concessions granted to European developers, such as freedom from customs duties on all imported material and machinery; the acquisition of lucrative mining and forest rights on either side of the rails; the operation of their own support facilities, such as warehouses, elevators and dockyards; the right to manufacture their own bricks and tiles; and access to water and water power free of charge. These concessions facilitated complete European economic control over the territory through which the railways passed.[28]

Even these advantages were deemed insufficient by the City of London in 1902, when Germany sought financial backing for its proposed Anatolian Railway to Baghdad and the Persian Gulf. A representative of Baring Brothers, the largest banking firm in the City, reported that British investors expected no economic support from the Treasury, but would not respond to the German enterprise unless it did.

When the Baghdad Railway proceeded in 1899, Berlin was careful to inform London. Lansdowne prepared a memorandum for Edward VII, in preparation for his 1901 visit to Germany. It indicated that Britain did not oppose the German plan provided it did not disturb Britain's position in the Persian Gulf. The memo, which was mistakenly shown to the kaiser, also referred to the maintenance of the status quo in Kuwait. German railway developers were encouraged, although the precise status of Kuwait remained unclear since Berlin saw it as part of the Ottoman Empire. Lansdowne equivocated rather than press the view of the viceroy of India, who regarded Kuwait's ruler as a British client whose harbour was essential to British shipping and to trade in the Persian Gulf.

While it would take another decade to determine the status of Kuwait and the terminus of the Baghdad Railway, the Germans proceeded to complete their surveys of the area. In the spring of 1902 Constantinople formally granted Berlin the Baghdad concession. The track was to be built in sections from Konia in southwestern Anatolia through the highlands and mountains, which would involve costly blasting and tunnelling, then south to Aleppo and east across the desert to Mosul and the River Tigris. The railway would proceed to Baghdad, follow the Tigris, and end at the Persian Gulf, adding 2,000 miles to the existing 600 miles of Anatolian railway. All was public knowledge: *Die Bagdadbahn*, (1902) and *Le chemin de fer de Baghdad*, (1903)were published at the same time as Chirol's articles for *The Times* and his subsequent book, *The Middle East Question*.[29]

In the spring of 1901 Lord Lansdowne had been approached first by Lord Revelstoke on behalf of Baring Brothers and then by other representatives of leading financial institutions, as well as by less reputable City figures, to enquire if the government would approve preliminary financial negotiations with Germany for investment in the Baghdad Railway enterprise. Lansdowne went methodically through the options: the government would demonstrate its goodwill by granting a postal subsidy for the proposed railway to carry mail to India, by agreeing to increase the Ottoman customs tariff, and by securing a terminus in Kuwait for the railway, provided the allocation of stock shares was divided equally among investors within the international consortium. German, French and British financiers would each be offered 25 per cent of the shares; 10 per cent would go to the Anatolian Railway Company; and the remaining 15 per cent would be offered to the stock markets. This arrangement, similar to others agreed in earlier decades, seemed viable to Lansdowne and to the City. A British syndicate, led by Revelstoke, continued negotiations with their German counterparts.[30]

By early April 1903 the Baghdad Railway had turned into a heated issue in both Fleet Street and Westminster. Lansdowne alerted Revelstoke to a campaign led by the *National Review*, the *Spectator* and *The Times* that strongly opposed British support of the Baghdad Railway. Balfour responded to a question in the House of Commons, acknowledging that the government could slow the project but believing Britain should be involved since the railway would be built with or without London's public support. The Conservative press's response was hostile.[31]

Lansdowne observed that Whitehall's representatives had agreed it would be a mistake to oppose the project, provided the British acquired an equal share in administering the railway and its terminus on the Persian Gulf. Lord Revelstoke confirmed that the project was financially sound and compatible with British interests. Meanwhile, angry letters appeared in *The Times* from Lynch Brothers Steamer, with interests on the River Tigris, and from the Peninsular and Oriental Steam Navigation Company, which carried mail to India.[32] Editorials and letters also appeared in other newspapers expressing concern that international management of the railway, particularly the equal number of directors for Britain, France and Germany, which would give the Germans 10 per cent control of the Anatolian Railway.

Conservative opposition to the Baghdad Railway intensified when the chancellor of the Exchequer introduced his strictly free-trade budget on 23 April. This infuriated the protectionists, led by the colonial secretary, Joseph Chamberlain, a champion of tariff reform. Facing a deep division in party ranks, Balfour backed down.[33] *The Economist* welcomed the announcement: 'This nation does not want the German partnership at the present time on any terms and wants it as little as anywhere, in the region between Constantinople and the Persian Gulf.'[34] Balfour had survived a storm by opposing any City backing for the German railway, which temporarily relieved the pressure from Chamberlain's tariff reformers. As the prime minister's hold on his party weakened, Conservatives proved unwilling to share any of the Middle East with Germany.

Given such Germanophobia in Fleet Street and divisions in Westminster, the City dropped the matter. The issue nevertheless survived. In the spring of 1905 the German railway syndicate, still in need of London money, initiated a proposal that met Whitehall's main concern – the effective neutralization of the terminus at the head of the Persian Gulf. Lansdowne brought the British ambassador in Constantinople up to date on the matter, anticipating that the new proposal 'would be much more popular with the public'. The foreign secretary believed the cabinet would 'probably agree', but that the Treasury was 'unlikely' to provide any more money, and he expected the French ambassador 'confidentially' to agree. Even so, British Germanophobia remained an obstacle, as Lansdowne wrote to his ambassador in Constantinople:

> But pray remember that any proposal involving cooperation with Germany will be regarded with utmost suspicion in many quarters here. If therefore an arrangement is to be come to, I should like to be able to show that it really has the effect of placing an obstacle in the way of the German Government to obtain an exclusive hold on Asia Minor .... Our position would, I think, be considerably strengthened if we could obtain our concession direct from the Sultan, instead of by the grace and favour of the German groups or the German government.[35]

When Balfour reported to Edward VII on the cabinet's endorsement of the 1905 German proposal for the Baghdad Railway, he noted that 'any such cooperation would be exceedingly unpopular in the present state of public opinion'. Yet, Balfour thought it 'inadvisable to shut the door absolutely against any arrangement, keeping in mind that our interest was mainly, though not wholly in the Persian Gulf and in the proposed railway'.[36]

RESTRAINING THE VICEROY IN THE PERSIAN GULF

British involvement in the Middle East continued to be justified on the grounds of defending India, and British policy towards Persia and the Persian Gulf between 1902 and 1905 was determined by the administration in London. London's role had been defined by the Government of India Act in 1858, by which the viceroy of India was made responsible to the India Office. This was led by the secretary of state for India and advised by the Council of India. London's influence was facilitated by telegraphic communication: the British in the subcontinent ceased to enjoy the independence that had characterized the rule of the old East India Company. From the second half of the nineteenth century, India had usually to cede to imperial interests as perceived by London.

The Indian army, comprising Indian soldiers and British officers, formed the largest infantry in the British Empire. Its soldiers were available for service outside India and formed a rapid deployment force of sorts, dispatched to Abyssinia in the 1860s, to Malta in the 1870s, to Egypt in the 1880s, and to the Sudan in the 1890s. Deploying Indian troops outside India required parliamentary authorization, but the cabinet circumvented this with a clause allowing the use of troops 'in urgent necessity or to repel invasion', as in China during the Boxer Rebellion and in South Africa during the Boer War.[37] The costs of the Indian army were met by India's taxpayers; the British government neither funded the army nor compensated the government of India for the overseas services of its soldiers.

Important though the Indian army was, the secretary of state for India was a much less prominent figure in the cabinet than the foreign secretary. The India Office and the Foreign Office shared the same building, the India Office occupying only three floors along one side. Its staff was small when compared with the number of British officials in India. In addition to officials posted to the winter capital in Calcutta and the summer retreat in Simla, hundreds of Anglo-Indians worked for the Bombay and Madras presidencies. Others were distributed in urban districts and rural postings throughout the subcontinent. Since the cost of the India Office was met by Indian taxpayers, the secretary of state for India did not have to report to Parliament. Yet, because the viceroy of India and the secretary of state for India were both appointed by the prime minister, Downing Street retained ultimate authority.[38]

George Nathaniel Curzon (1859–1925) assumed the viceroyalty in 1899, the first of three posts to which he aspired. The ambitious Etonian and Oxonian, designated 'a superior person' by 'The Souls', saw his position of viceroy as the first step to becoming foreign secretary, and then prime minister. Curzon was only thirty-nine and already well known for his five extensive Asian trips and the resulting numerous articles and three books – *Russia in Central Asia* (1889), *Persia and the Persian Question* (1892) and *Problems of the Far East* (1894). He emphasized the importance of defending the subcontinent from Russian expansion on India's northeastern and northwestern frontiers, preserving British paramountcy in the Persian Gulf, blocking Russian inroads into southern and eastern Persia or Afghanistan, and countering Russian influence over the shah and his ministers in Tehran. British telegraph wires buzzed between India, London and Persia in 1900, when a Russian gunboat stopped at several Persian Gulf ports, and in 1901, when a Russian merchant ship unloaded cases of kerosene and bales of cotton. London agreed that the Persian Gulf must remain under British control but suspected Curzon of being unduly aggressive.[39] Although his internal administrative reforms remain controversial, historians agree that Curzon's policies won only limited support from the India Office, the Foreign Office and from Downing Street at a time when London was preoccupied by the Boer War and by the need to limit imperial commitments.

The priority in London was a strong stance in the Persian Gulf. Before Curzon left for India, he recommended a British protectorate over Kuwait to reduce the possibility of a Turkish deal with other powers giving them access to the port at the head of the gulf. Lord Salisbury reminded Curzon that increased costs in Kuwait would have to be borne by the government of India. In 1899 one of Curzon's officers pressured the sultan of Muscat to cancel a French lease for a coaling station, pressure which contravened a treaty of 1862 but had the effect of ending French influence in Muscat. The same year, Curzon persuaded the sheikh of Kuwait not to surrender territory to any other power, land to which Turkey had lain claim since the 1870s. When pro-Turkish Arabs and Turkish officers put British ties with Kuwait to the test, Curzon ignored them. Lansdowne, as foreign secretary, did not pursue the matter for fear it would anger Constantinople and upset Great Power relations. Curzon took risks and, according to the British ambassador in Constantinople who particularly resented the hard line in Kuwait, endangered Anglo-Ottoman relations. To the Foreign Office, Curzon's preoccupation with defending India had blinded him to the risks involved in Britain's departing from its traditional defence of the Ottoman Empire, in which the City of London still had substantial financial investments and with which the British had more trade than other European country.

Curzon's expansion policy was not confined to the Persian Gulf. In 1901 he invited to India the new amir of Afghanistan, who refused to come. The same year, Curzon's plan to send a small British military mission to Tibet against the uncooperative Dalai Lama was blocked by the prime minister. Curzon persisted, and in 1904 a British mission went to Tibet and extracted a treaty in India's interests. Pressure on the nizam of Hyderabad reflected similar goals, as did Curzon's recommendations regarding Persia and the Persian Gulf.

Curzon's worst fears about the British losing to Russian influence in Tehran were confirmed after he became viceroy. He had blamed Russia for most of Persia's ills and conveniently ignored Britain's role, particularly in terms of economic and oil concessions. Whitehall took the Russian threat less seriously than Curzon: old nineteenth-century rumours of Russian agents operating in central Asia, Persia and Afghanistan seemed remote to London in the early twentieth century.

Curzon's views of Persia were shared by Sir Arthur Hardinge (1859–1933), who became the British minister to Tehran early in 1901. Neither could agree to Russia's controlling fertile northern Persia, nor could they easily contemplate the prospect of Russia and Britain dividing Persia into spheres of interest, with Britain taking only the desolate south

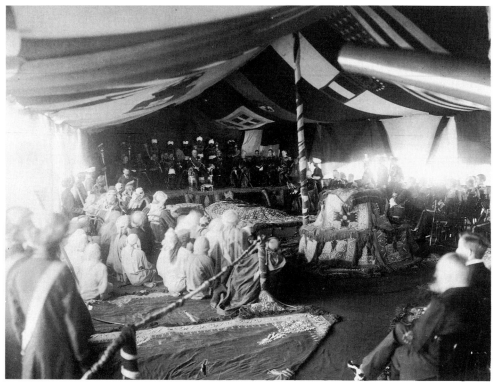

10   The viceroy of India's tour of the Persian Gulf, during which he met with local sheikhs on a British cruiser at Sharja in 1903. Curzon believed such durbars impressed the Middle East and India.

11   The viceroy being carried to shore at Kuwait in 1903. Curzon regarded Kuwait's leader as 'by far the most masculine and vigorous personality whom I encountered in the Gulf'.

to protect its paramountcy in the Persian Gulf. Hardinge recommended offsetting Russian loans to the shah with British loans, which Curzon offered to supply from the government of India or by means of the British Treasury taking over the Imperial Bank of Persia, set up in the 1880s. But Hardinge's proposals to support various political, religious and provincial leaders against the shah and his pro-Russian ministers in Tehran received a cool reception at Lansdowne's Foreign Office.[40]

Curzon's call for bolder strategic initiatives in Persia and the gulf were blocked by the CID. Like his uncle, Balfour knew the obstacles that blocked Russia's route to India unless it built and operated railways in Persia. Balfour, doubting that Afghanistan could be an effective buffer for India's defence, was troubled by reports of Russian interest in the eastern Persian province of Seistan, which bordered Afghanistan, but did not worry as long as no Russian railways were built there. He wished to avoid actions that might make Russia launch a military expedition against India and he wanted the world to view Britain as responding to Russian aggression, not initiating it. Balfour's defensive strategy prevailed over Curzon.[41]

The viceroy had first proposed the idea of a tour of the Persian Gulf in 1901 as a way of demonstrating British paramountcy, but received little support from London. Encouraged by Balfour and Lansdowne's opposition to the Baghdad Railway in the spring of 1903, Curzon revived the idea. Lansdowne informed Curzon that the cabinet would let him proceed provided he neither signed any new agreements nor assumed any new obligations without London's approval.

The tour was made at the end of 1903 in the *Argonaut*, a first-class cruiser of gleaming white and the largest ship to enter the gulf before the 1914–18 war. It was accompanied by a steamship and a flotilla of six British men-of-war. Curzon first dropped anchor at Muscat, where he met a compliant sultan. Then he went to Sharja, where he held a durbar on board and met several local leaders whom the Anglo-Indians called 'trucial chiefs', after the truces they had signed with Britain.

Curzon next proceeded to Kuwait, where he was carried to shore and rode with the chief in a carriage that had been brought from Bombay for the occasion. He reported to London that he regarded the leader of Kuwait as 'by far the most masculine and vigorous personality whom I encountered in the Gulf, with acute intelligence and a character justifying his reputation for cunning and explaining the method by which he had attained his position (wholesale murder of competitors)'.[42]

The next stop was to have been the Persian side of the gulf in Bushire. The Persian governor of Fars had been unwilling to come on board but agreed to come to the landing with his large ceremonial staff and military guard. Curzon declined to stay as a guest of the Persian government or call on the governor before the latter had been received at the government of India's building at Bushire. A further difficulty arose over the issue of the gun salute. Curzon received a thirty-one-gun salute and, although the Persian governor asked for the same, he was awarded only nineteen. Refusing to leave his ship, Curzon departed the next day, blaming the fiasco on the British minister in Tehran. The discordant end to the viceroy's tour presaged more Anglo-Persian difficulties.

The cabinet balked at some of Curzon's plans for the durbar ceremony in Delhi, and a compromise was reached only after he threatened to resign. Historians have seen the 1903 durbar as the high point of Curzon's viceroyalty since his fortunes declined thereafter when he offended influential figures in India's army and his partition of the Bengali province provoked a religious backlash. The reforms Kitchener recommended after he became commander-in-chief of India would have given him greater autonomy from the viceroy. Incensed, Curzon resigned in 1905, the prime minister accepting his resignation. Curzon blamed Balfour and the India Office for treating him shabbily, but in fact they were merely exercising their authority over an ambitious viceroy.[43]

Russia's defeat and the entente with France

Japan's victories over Russia underlined the benefits of the 1902 Anglo-Japanese alliance. The British press celebrated Russia's defeat, particularly the bottling up of the Russian navy after the successful attack on Port Arthur and the forcing of the tsar's army to retreat to Mukden to await reinforcements through the Baltic Sea. (Britain denied the Russian Black Sea fleet access through the Turkish Straits or to British coaling stations.)

Fleet Street and Westminster applauded Balfour for the tough stand against Russia, particularly regarding the Dogger Bank incident of October 1904, when the Russian fleet in the North Sea, en route from the Baltic to the Pacific, mistakenly sank a British trawler and drowned several British on board. Supported by his party, Balfour authorised the British fleet to use whatever force necessary to stop the Russian fleet off Gibraltar. Lansdowne's deft diplomacy eased subsequent tensions, and the French were eventually successful in referring the question to an international commission, which ordered Russia to compensate the British early in 1905.

The single event with the greatest impact on British policy was Japan's annihilation of thirty-two Russian vessels at the decisive naval battle at Tsushima Straits in May 1905. It greatly reduced the Admiralty's Pacific responsibilities and had wider diplomatic consequences. In London as in other European capitals, Japanese diplomatic representation was raised to the level of ambassador. And in August 1905 a revised Anglo-Japanese treaty strengthened the mutual obligations. By the terms of the 1902 alliance, Britain and Japan had undertaken, for a period of five years, to remain neutral unless the other faced *two enemies*. In 1905 the alliance was extended to ten years, if either faced a *single enemy*.[44]

12 The *mahmal*, the black covering for the ka'aba in Mecca, has been made for centuries by Egypt's Muslims. This 1904 photo shows the vast cloth being escorted through the streets of Cairo.

Japan's confirmation of Russia's vulnerability strengthened Britain's position around the Suez Canal and in Egypt. The final two decades of the nineteenth century had seen Anglo-French competition in Africa. In 1898–9, Anglo-Egyptian forces moved south from the Sudan and Anglo-Indian forces north from east Africa to counterbalance a French military mission which had established itself on the Nile at Fashoda. After fifteen tense months, Foreign Office pressure forced the French to evacuate the mission. French interference in Egypt's finances however continued.

The Suez Canal had been completed in 1869, France having the largest stake in the Paris company that operated it. Egypt had raised £11.5 of the £16 million total cost of the canal, yet a Law of Liquidation in 1880 restricted it to fifteen per cent of the profit. In addition to the Suez project, French finance had been active in other spheres of Egypt's economy: during the 1860s and 1870s it organised eight loans totalling over £68 million at high rates of interest. Measures were subsequently taken to regulate Egypt's finances to ensure repayment to European bondholders. The Law of Liquidation also allocated half Egypt's revenue to the debt, and half to state expenses, with any surplus above £8.5 million routed to the servicing of the debt. An economic straightjacket primarily in the interests of France rather than Egypt, the arrangements threatened the security of the British occupation and the defence of the Suez Canal.[45]

The real ruler of Egypt between 1883 and 1907 was the consul general, Lord Cromer (1841–1917). A Baring, and member of one of London's leading banking families, Cromer had served his imperial apprenticeship in

SIR WALTER RALEIGH
THE MARQUIS OF LANSDOWNE.

13   Cartoon, 1904.

India and imbibed the fiscal conservatism that favoured the least burden on the British taxpayer. After two decades in Egypt, Cromer urged the Foreign Office to buy off French interference in the British administration of the country by compensating France elsewhere, perhaps in Morocco. British recognition of French claims in Morocco, Cromer anticipated, could strengthen his hand in Egypt.

Anglo-French relations began to improve during the spring and summer of 1903, when Edward VII's official visit to France was followed by a state visit by the French president to London. Wishing to capitalize on the goodwill, the French Foreign Ministry proposed negotiations to resolve their imperial differences, negotiations which Balfour reported to the king were 'at all events a step in the right direction'.[46]

The negotiations between Lansdowne and the French ambassador, Cambon, which began at the end of the summer of 1903, were critical for European diplomacy. Lansdowne not only kept the prime minister and cabinet fully apprised of the progress of the negotiations, but was in frequent communication with Cromer, and with Cromer's assistant, John Eldon Gorst, then assisting Lansdowne in the Foreign Office.[47]

Besides resolving Anglo-French differences over Egypt and Morocco, Lansdowne and Cambon addressed other issues in North America, eastern and western Africa, southeastern Asia and the south Pacific. Lansdowne yielded little to French demands, and negotiations made little headway until the Russo-Japanese War broke out in February 1904. The possibility of France's most important ally being defeated by London's Pacific ally put Paris in a much more accommodating mood. The main trade-off involved Egypt and Morocco. France recognized the British occupation of Egypt but still obtained guarantees regarding the Egyptian debt and reassurances over free navigation of the Suez Canal. Britain, in turn, supported French predominance in Morocco. The Lansdowne-Cambon talks led to the signing in April 1904 of an understanding, rather than a treaty, known as the Entente Cordiale, the strength of which Germany soon tested.[48]

In March 1905, the German emperor visited Tangier, declaring his support for Moroccan independence and an 'open door' trade policy which he believed the French had ignored. The visit brought panic to Paris, the foreign minister being accused of risking war with Germany. The calling of an international conference by the sultan of Morocco – supported by Germany but opposed by France – forced the hand of the British. Balfour and Lansdowne, eager to allay French anxieties and concerned about trade with Morocco, proposed 'full and confidential discussion . . . in anticipation of any complications'. The precise meaning of this British gesture was debated then in Paris, as it has been by diplomatic historians ever since. Interpreting the Entente Cordiale as the first step towards an Anglo-French alliance against Germany, the French foreign minister urged acceptance of the British offer and the calling of Germany's bluff. The French cabinet, acutely conscious of a national fear of war with Germany, turned against their foreign minister. He resigned when Paris agreed to an international conference on Morocco.

Russia's defeat by Japan had a significant impact not only on European diplomacy, but also in relation to the Middle East and North Africa. The Anglo-French Entente confirmed the British occupation of Egypt and secured the Suez Canal. Balfour had preserved the strategic status quo in the Middle East as Lansdowne had maintained the diplomatic status quo in the Near East.

Chapter 3

Holding the Ramparts: 1905–1911

WHEN THE CONSERVATIVE cabinet relinquished power at the end of 1905, the Liberals formed a government, called for new elections and, early in 1906, won a huge majority of parliamentary seats. Voters appeared ready for a significant change, and yet within three years a government which had pledged to cut expenditure on armaments found itself compelled to build large numbers of new battleships to meet the perceived German naval threat. The unwillingness of the House of Lords to approve the so-called People's Budget of 1909 led to two general elections in 1910. Thereafter the government depended for political survival on the support of minor parties. Tax policies, social reform measures, and Irish Home Rule proved deeply divisive, but greater bipartisanship prevailed in foreign and imperial affairs.

A new foreign secretary built on the strategic pillars erected by the Conservatives. To Anglo-American, Anglo-Japanese and Anglo-French diplomacy, the Liberals added the Anglo-Russian Convention of 1907. Diplomats in London perceived Russia as counteracting Germany's growing military strength and threat to the balance of power in Europe. When, in 1908, Turkish army officers rebelled against the sultan, encouraging Vienna to annex Bosnia-Herzegovina and Sofia to declare Bulgaria independent of the Turks, Britain approved. And the British press, amid mounting hysteria over German militarization, attacked Turkish and German initiatives on behalf of the Baghdad Railway.

After a quarter-century running Egypt, Lord Cromer retired as the empire's greatest expert on a region he regarded as Oriental. The assassination of the pro-British prime minister of Egypt in 1910 led to receptive London audiences for the former US president, Theodore Roosevelt, when he spoke of the necessity for Britain maintaining supremacy along the Nile and the Suez Canal.

THE LIBERALS IN POWER

Balfour resigned in 1905 without dissolving Parliament, which would have required new elections: he believed the Liberals were too divided to form and sustain a government. A Liberal cabinet was put together by Sir Henry Campbell-Bannerman (1836–1908), a rotund Scottish millionaire who had inherited money from his father, a Glasgow businessman, and land

14 London meeting in 1907 with leaders from the overseas dominions, whose defence role had increased. Asquith and Lloyd George sit at opposite ends, Churchill stands behind Asquith.

from his mother's brother. Campbell-Bannerman had led Liberal Radicals in opposition to the Boer War and championed Irish Home Rule, but still persuaded prominent Liberal Imperialists into his cabinet. In January 1906 he called an election and won a large victory.

After Campbell-Bannerman's resignation through illness in 1908, Herbert Henry Asquith (1852–1928) became prime minister. Asquith was a self-made Yorkshireman who, after Oxford, struggled as a London barrister before entering the House of Commons. At twenty-six he had married the daughter of a Manchester physician. After thirteen years of marriage which produced four sons and a daughter, his wife died, leaving him a widower at the age of thirty-nine. Three years later he married Margot Tennant, a brilliant London socialite. The marriage produced five more children, only two of whom survived infancy. A skilful parliamentarian, Asquith maintained party unity, despite radical and imperialist divisions in his cabinet.

For the Liberal party, domestic concerns overshadowed all others save for the expansion of the German navy. Sir John 'Jacky' Fisher (1841–1920), the short and feisty first sea lord between 1904 and 1910, modernized the British navy, concentrated ships closer to home to meet any German threat, and pressed for the building of four new dreadnoughts each year, the Fleet Street refrain being, 'We want eight and we won't wait!' The resultant cost involved increased taxation, and the House of Lords vetoed the 1909 budget. The Liberal majority survived only with the support of Labour and Irish MPs. The price was a constitutional crisis over the Parlia-ment Act of 1911 and over Home Rule for Ireland, and a worsening economy.[1]

With the pressure of domestic issues, Asquith involved himself little with defence matters. The CID met infrequently: Balfour had called over eighty meetings and submitted nearly twenty memoranda between 1902 and 1905, while Asquith called fewer than thirty meetings and submitted no memos between 1908 and 1914.[2] And in defiance of the advice of armed service organizations, he steadfastly opposed conscription.

GREY AT THE FOREIGN OFFICE

Asquith himself paid little attention to the Near and Middle East, leaving it to his foreign secretary, Sir Edward Grey (1862–1933). Grey came from a major political dynasty. He was great-grandnephew of Earl Grey, the Whig prime minister, and his own grandfather had represented northeastern voters for four decades. After his father's death when Edward Grey was only twelve, the boy's life centred upon Fallodon, the family's 2,000-acre estate near the coast of Northumberland. Educated at Oxford, the future foreign secretary knew no foreign languages, had little interest in history, and disliked going abroad. In 1884 Grey married an independent-minded woman from an ancient Northumberland family who preferred country pursuits to city frivolity. In 1906 Lady Grey died, her skull fractured when she was thrown from a carriage. Grey's mother had died a few months before. Grief-stricken, he became married to the Foreign Office.[3]

Grey lacked the confidence and panache of his predecessors, Lansdowne and Salisbury. But it was precisely this dour reserve that enabled him to steer controversial foreign issues through a cabinet split between Radicals and Liberal Imperialists over foreign and imperial issues. The Liberal Radicals who had opposed the British war in South Africa were disparagingly labelled 'Little Englanders' by Liberal Imperialists. To avoid such intraparty fighting, Grey kept controversial foreign matters to himself rather than face the hostile reactions of Radicals in the cabinet. Grey's straightforward use of language, his polite manner when delivering speeches in the House of Commons, and his apparent diffidence towards others suggested sincerity and facilitated the secrecy and discretion he considered essential. British diplomacy needed to be kept from Fleet Street reporters, where proprietors and journalists fed on gossip and contrived leaks to embarrass the Foreign Office. Grey saw few advantages and many risks in press attention; by retaining the confidence of Westminster and Fleet Street, he could minimise public anxiety and popular interference.

The complexities of the administration of foreign policy that faced Grey in the early years of the new century are revealed by the volume of reports received by telegraph from all over the world. In 1905 the Foreign Office employed 150 officials and clerks who handled 110,000 dispatches, while only 40 people had processed 30,000 dispatches in the middle of the nineteenth century. Though a modern bureaucracy, the Foreign Office retained an aristocratic ethos, where 'everything was done to preserve its class character and clannish structure'.[4] Grey never claimed to have mastered world affairs, unlike such Foreign Office mandarins as Lord Hardinge (1858–1944) and Louis Mallet (1864–1936), or such famous British ambassadors as Lord Bertie (1847–1919) in Paris and Arthur Nicolson (1849–1928) in St Petersburg. These diplomats believed they knew how best to juggle the balance of power in Europe: some favoured France, while others saw Russia as the main counterweight to Germany. Their assumptions and conceits defined the way they interpreted the detailed information that reached them. With clear goals in mind, Foreign Office leaders differed only over the best contacts and the most effective verbal formulae for gaining short-term advantage. Diplomatic victories were won, for them, like games or wars, one battle or round of negotiations at a time.

In assessing Grey's career at the Foreign Office, historians have portrayed him as conscientious but too easily dominated by others. It is evident in what he did or did not do in the Middle East between 1906 and 1911. The Foreign Office paid more attention to Europe than to Africa or Asia, but Grey sought to keep the Middle East within the British sphere of interest by backing France from Morocco to Tunisia and by joining Russia in opposing Persian and Turkish nationalism. To avoid war with Germany, Grey conducted what might be generally characterized as defensive diplomacy. Increasingly sharing the views of his colleagues, he feared Germany's new naval power, but was no mere Germanophobe. Neither was he an appeaser, although less strongly identified with the British Empire than were his Conservative and Unionist opponents in Parliament. To Grey, the old rivalry with Russia over Asia had been upstaged by the new European competition with Germany. A powerful British navy not only defended the British Isles and the British Empire but also preserved the peace of Europe. Following the precedent of the European partition of Africa, Grey saw the Near and Middle East mainly in terms of British, French and Russian spheres of interest. His diplomacy therefore alienated not only Germany and Austria-Hungary, but also the Turks, Egyptians and Persians.

The Foreign Office had its own system for dealing with the Middle East, the countries of which were assigned to either the Western Europe or the Eastern Europe Department. Morocco and Tunis alone were part of the former, since Algeria was considered to be as French as Ireland was British. On the other hand, Bulgaria, Greece, Montenegro, Rumania, Serbia, Russia, Turkey, Persia, central Asia, Egypt, Abyssinia and Somaliland were all part of the Eastern Europe Department. To all these countries, the Foreign Office posted British ambassadors, ministers or consuls-general, whose status, salary and size of staffs differed. Table 1 illustrates the relative importance attached by the Foreign Office to the countries of the Near and Middle East, as well as of North Africa.

Table 1
Foreign Office Establishment, Overseas, 1906

Country	Head	Salary p.a.	Staff in capital	Staff in field
Algeria	con.	1,000	2	4
Austria-Hungary	amb.	8,000	11	10
Bulgaria	con.	1,500	3	4
Egypt	con.	6,500	8	15
France	amb.	9,000	17	74
Germany	amb.	8,000	13	59
Greece	min.	3,500	6	17
Italy	amb.	7,000	10	43
Morocco	min.	2,000	12	10
Persia	min.	4,500	10	17
Russia	amb.	7,800	11	38
Serbia	min.	1,800	2	0
Spain	amb.	5,500	9	56
Tripoli	con.	800	3	4
Tunis	con.	900	3	7
Turkey	amb.	8,000	31	65
US	amb.	6,500	8	66

Although the status of the diplomatic posts, salaries and staff were affected by diplomatic customs and local peculiarities, the figures do reveal the extent to which Ottoman Turkey loomed large in the Foreign Office mind. (The figures for 1906 were comparable with those for 1902, 1910 and 1914.)[5] Most consular officials were situated in or near Constantinople and the rest distributed in descending numbers at Smyrna, Salonica, Beirut, Aleppo, Trebizond, Baghdad, Jeddah, Jerusalem, Damascus and Erzeroum. The number of consuls reflects British commercial, intelligence and other activities, with the number of British consuls at Salonica, Smyrna, Beirut, Baghdad, Jerusalem and Jeddah rising between 1902 and 1914.[6]

The figures for Egypt remained virtually the same from 1902 to 1914, but are misleadingly low since they excluded several thousand British military personnel attached to and paid for by the Egyptian government and the Anglo-Egyptian Sudan. In the case of Persia, the number of Foreign Office personnel remained unchanged in Tehran, but British consular officials increased outside the capital from nine in 1902 to twenty-six in 1914, indicating increased British concern for the south. The Persian figures exclude the hundreds of British civilian and military personnel associated with and paid for by the government of India and the Anglo-Persian Oil Company.

Persia and the Anglo-Russian Convention

It was probably Russia's defeat by Japan in 1905 that inspired some Persians to challenge Russian power in 1906. Persian nationalists appear to have expected the tsar to be too weak to protect the shah after upheavals within the Russian Empire itself. Sophisticated Persians may have viewed the victory of Japan (at that time the only constitutional power in Asia) over Russia (then the only major nonconstitutional power in Europe) as an encouraging sign for reforms in Persia. It was anticipated that London would oppose the pro-Russian shah in the light of British constitutional traditions, but hopes were dashed by the Anglo-Russian Convention of 1907, which divided Persia into a Russian sphere in the north, a British sphere in the south, and a neutral sphere in between. The Anglo-Russian settlement eventually enabled Russia to quash Persia's first experiment with constitutional government but failed to end the Persian practice of playing Britain off against Russia.[7]

Historians familiar with British sources alone have concluded that while the Persians were corrupt and the Russians expansionist, the British were more inclined towards reform. Recent historians have determined otherwise. According to the 1991 edition of *The Cambridge History of Iran*:

> On the whole the British desired those reforms that would facilitate trade and the security of foreigners and those connected with them in Iran. When really reforming nationalists appeared, as in the case of the Democratic Party during the Constitutional Revolution, who might have limited the privileges of foreigners in Iran, the British opposed them.[8]

St Petersburg provided direct subsidies and rebates to encourage Russian commerce and trade in Iran, promoted various banking schemes, and took a strategic approach to railways in Persia, as did London. Two British figures involved with Persia may be noted. Julius de Reuter (1816–99) was a German Jew who became a British citizen in the 1850s after founding a world news agency in the City of London. Pursuing financial ambitions during the 1860s, Reuter in 1872 secured from the shah a seventy-year concession that would have virtually controlled Persia's telegraph and transportation systems, minerals, banking and tobacco. His ambitions were not initially encouraged by the British government, but when Reuter was thwarted by a successful religious boycott of tobacco during the 1890s, the British government successfully demanded such high compensation that the shah's regime took its first large loan from Russia. The other example was William Knox D'Arcy (1849–1917), an Englishman who had made a fortune from Australian gold and who secured a mineral concession from the shah in 1901. The British legation in Tehran took an active part in the negotiations that led to the Anglo-Persian and later the Anglo-Iranian Oil Company (ultimately British Petroleum).[9]

Grey's memoirs recount how the shah, responding to a British minister who had urged him to confront the Russians, pretended a Russian rope was around his neck and asked: 'What can *you* do?'[10] The Qajar shah's regime was so feeble and Persia so fragmented that British officials in Tehran confessed that they did not know what was happening when revolutionary activity broke out in 1905 and the shah accepted a constitution, elections were held, and the first *majlis* (parliamentary assembly) convened in October 1906. The shah signed the Fundamental Law before he died at the end of 1906, and his stronger successor signed a Supplementary Fundamental Law early in 1907. Religious leaders rejected the secular form the revolution had taken and turned to the new shah, who viewed the *majlis* no more seriously than the tsar had recently viewed Russia's first duma.[11]

The Foreign Office was less concerned with the confusing situation in Tehran than with its impact on Anglo-Russian relations and British paramountcy in the Persian Gulf. During the final months of 1905, before Balfour stepped down as prime minister, Lansdowne explored the possibility of settling some of the imperial differences with Russia along the lines of the Entente Cordiale reached with France the year before. But he learned that the tsar was in no mind to pursue such talks in the wake of Russia's defeat by Japan, the Russian army being in no mood to compromise.[12]

Significant changes in London and St Petersburg diplomatic circles in 1906, however, improved relations between the nineteenth-century imperial rivals in central Asia. When Lord Hardinge left his ambassadorial post in St Petersburg to become permanent undersecretary at the Foreign Office, his place in Russia was taken by Arthur Nicolson. Both Hardinge and Nicolson had disliked their brief period of service in Persia and believed that Britain should come to terms with Russia over the country so as to keep a weak tsar from being dominated by a strong German emperor. When Nicolson arrived in St Petersburg, he encountered a less Anglophobic foreign minister and greater chance of constructive discussion.

Anglo-Russian negotiations were conducted in secret for fifteen months before being concluded in August 1907. Nicolson negotiated under the supervision of Grey and Hardinge.[13] In April 1907 Cecil Spring-Rice (1859–1918), the Foreign Office's minister at Tehran, expressed his concern about the impact the talks would have on Persians and Muslims. If Persia's new assembly was not somehow involved in the Anglo-Russian initiative, then he expected 'people will think that we are determined to override the popular will and will naturally turn to other countries such as Turkey and Germany for help and sympathy. There will also be strong agitation in all Mussulman countries and especially in India.' Grey himself countered with a minute which read: 'Our agreement with Russia is a mutual self-denying ordinance recognizing Persian independence. It may anger Persians who have lived on the enmity between us and Russia, but we cannot keep up agreements with Persia in order to curry favour with the Persians. E.G.'[14]

Early in September 1907, when Spring-Rice received his copy of the Anglo-Russian Convention, he feared London was still not taking Persia seriously: 'A child with a match box is not a serious person but he can be a dangerous one. That depends not on the child but on the matches. In this case the matches do burn.'[15] Spring-Rice correctly anticipated a negative impact not only on Persia but on other Muslim leaders who held London in greater suspicion because of the Russian company Britain now kept.

The British in India and the Middle East obviously did not share the Foreign Office's preoccupation with counterbalancing Germany at sea and in Europe. Grey sought to placate France, which favoured its Russian ally reaching an accord with Britain. In the Anglo-Russian Convention of 1907, Russia recognized British interests in Tibet and Afghanistan as well as its predominance in southern Persia. The convention mentioned neither Britain's special position in the Persian Gulf nor Russia's gaining access to the Mediterranean from the Black Sea via the Turkish Straits, but these matters appear to have been understood already in an informal trade-off between British interests in the Middle East and Russia's in central Asia and the Near East. The issue had stirred up much more than simply Persia.[16]

Once the Anglo-Russian Convention was made public, the debate in London began. Grey defended it as protecting Persia from German penetration, blocking Russian incursions from the north, and reducing the need for British military action. While he satisfied the Liberals in the House of Commons, Curzon fulminated in the House of Lords. Conservatives repeated their old fear of the Russian bear rolling across Asia while radicals reiterated their contempt for tsarist autocracy. Further criticism appeared in periodicals. Two articles in the *Fortnightly Review* opposed the Convention, attacking 'the gross ignorance of chiefs and clerks alike at the Foreign Office', and arguing that it would 'operate disastrously upon British interests in the Middle East'.[17] *Blackwood's Magazine*, concluded: 'There is not the smallest foundation for the supposition that the cause of permanent peace has gained one iota by the arrangement'.[18]

Some Radicals saw the Convention as a cynical imperialist pact that carved up Persia and spat upon the constitutional aspirations of Persians. Other critics included the Fabian Society, the Welsh District Council of the Social Democratic Federation, and the Oxford branch of the Independent Labour Party.[19] London's Persia Committee, modelled on the Balkan Committee and led by Professor E. G. Browne (1862–1926), launched a sustained attack against the pact with the tsar.[20]

PERSIAN REVOLUTIONARIES AT TABRIZ.
Parading before their leader, Satar Khan, at the Winter Palace.
Satar Khan performed wonders in licking his unruly followers into shape,
and towards the end of the siege, when famine threatened and discontent was
rife, he took the prudent course of drilling the whole male population in order to
divert their minds. His Nationalist troops certainly did him credit, giving a good account of
tnemselves on every occasion they came into contact with the Royalists. Photograph by Underwood.

THE FOREIGN OUTLOOK

15   1909 photo of discipline in the Russian sphere of north Persia, which was in disorder for years after the revolution of 1905 and despite the Anglo-Russian Convention of 1907.

None of the criticism impinged on Grey's Foreign Office, which held to its conviction that the Anglo-Russian Convention of 1907, like the Anglo-French Entente Cordiale of 1904, enhanced British security by helping to maintain the balance of power in Europe. As elsewhere, the Middle East was subordinated to European diplomacy.

THE REAY COMMITTEE

In the early nineteenth century Britain had secured its economic interests by negotiating with overseas regimes, but greater commercial competition led to increased private enterprise, which required a greater knowledge of foreign languages. Before steamships and railways improved mobility and communication, British merchants had stayed in the East, learned the languages, developed local ties, and formed trading dynasties as sons followed in their fathers' footsteps. By the latter part of the nineteenth century, however, they travelled home more frequently, worked for larger bureaucracies that relocated them more frequently, acquired less fluency with Asian and African languages and tended to rely on native-speaking intermediaries, or 'dragomans' in the Ottoman Empire.

In December 1906 a delegation in London petitioned the prime minister, the chancellor of the Exchequer and the secretary of state for India on behalf of improved facilities for the learning of Asian and African languages which were inferior to those in Berlin, Paris, Vienna and St Petersburg. The deputation, led by the vice chancellor of the University of

London, comprised representatives of organizations reflecting diverse commercial, cultural, economic, and religious interests in the Middle East: the British Academy, London Chamber of Commerce, Royal Asiatic Society, Central Asian Society, Japan Society, China Association, African Society, Anglo-Russian Literary Society, City of London College, Victoria League, Society for the Propagation of the Gospel in Foreign Parts, Church Missionary Society, London Missionary Society, Society for Promoting Christian Knowledge and British and Foreign Bible Society. [21]

Such concerns were not new. In 1800 the East India Company had trained its personnel in the subcontinent's languages mainly at Calcutta's College of Fort William. In 1806 it had established the East India College at Haileybury. But these colleges were abolished when India was transferred to the direct rule of the British government. Thereafter, British personnel received their training only after they had arrived in India, with less satisfactory results. The few British who tried to learn Indian languages relied upon native speakers rather than trained teachers. Poor linguistic training widened the gap between the peoples of India and the British, who increasingly depended on a new class of English-speaking Indians as intermediaries.

In 1857 Professor Max Müller, a prominent philologist, recommended the establishment in London of a School of Oriental Studies. Although he had the support of Prince Albert, the government's response was slight. Oriental studies were offered in London, Oxford, Cambridge or other universities, but focused more on the study of ancient texts than on modern languages. After more than three decades, the indefatigable Müller finally succeeded in establishing the London School of Modern Oriental Studies, its inauguration in 1890 being addressed by the prince of Wales. The privately funded Imperial Institute supported instructors in two London colleges to teach nine of the languages spoken in India as well as Burmese, Chinese, Japanese, Persian, Arabic, Turkish and modern Greek, and endowed an annual scholarship. It was a beginning, but a meagre one.[22]

The British and Indian governments made modest contributions: the Foreign Office paid £100 per year for each student at Cambridge University (with a £1,000 limit), the India Office provided grants of up to £2,000 per year to Cambridge and Oxford, Trinity College in Dublin, and University College in London, while the Colonial Office set aside £100 for the teaching of an African language at King's College, London. Even so, and including a £50 grant from the Hong Kong government, the University of London received only £450 per year for the purpose.

Much more was spent by other European governments: Germany allocated almost £10,000 a year for Berlin's Oriental school, with 42 teachers; France spent £7,000 on its main Paris school, with 26 teachers; Austria-Hungary and Russia each spent over £8,000 per year; while even Holland and Italy made bigger commitments than Britain. Some European capitals had Oriental institutes: Berlin's two schools had the largest number of students learning Oriental and African languages; Paris had nine Oriental schools, plus one in Algiers and another in Hanoi; Vienna had three; Budapest had two; St Petersburg's two schools were supplemented by two in Moscow and another in Vladivostok; the Dutch had two schools; and the Italians had four. All had better staffs, libraries and facilities, as well as more students, than London.[23]

In response to the 1906 delegation, the government appointed a committee to make recommendations for 'a thoroughly adequate scheme for the teaching of Oriental languages in London, and in what way the general organisation of a School for this purpose would most advantageously proceed'.[24] The committee was chaired by Lord Reay (1839–1921), a former governor of Bombay, and five others with connections with India, South East Asia and with education in general.

During 1906 and 1907 also, information was collected on the thirty languages spoken in Asia and Africa, the nature of each language, where and by whom it was spoken, how it contributed to literature and civilization, and – above all – each language's 'importance' to 'British interests'. Table 2 summarizes the conclusions:

Table 2
British Foreign Trade, 1906

Region & languages	Peoples (in millions)	British trade (in millions of £)
India (Assamese, Bengali, Gujarati, Hindi, Hindustani, Kanarese, Marathi, Panjabi, Pashto, Tamil, Telugu)	183	not given
China (Chinese)	400	15
Japan (Japanese)	47	13
S.E. Asia (Burmese, Malayan, Melanesian, Polynesian, Sinhalese)	68	32
Africa (Amharic, Hausa, Luganda, Somali, Swahili, Yoruba, Zulu)	92	65
Near/Middle East (Arabic, Armenian, Greek, Persian, Turkish)	67	30

Table 2 indicates also the relative volume of British trade throughout Asia and Africa, still of course much less than that with Europe and the Americas. In 1906 British trade with the Near and Middle East was roughly equivalent to that with Southeast Asia or with China and Japan combined, but much less than that with Africa. The figures for India were inexplicably omitted from the survey.[25]

According to the Reay Committee, the most important language of the Near and Middle East was Arabic, not simply because it was spoken by an estimated 35 million, but because it was 'one of the principal languages of the world', and the language of 'the religion of Mahomed', which in the early 1900s had 150 to 200 million followers in Asia and Africa. Other languages, such as Persian, Turkish and those of northern India included large numbers of Arabic words in their vocabularies. Modern Greek was spoken by 2.5 million in Greece, on the islands of Crete, Cyprus and Samos in the Aegean, as well as in Constantinople and Smyrna. The significance of Persian, apart from its ancient literature, was that it was spoken by over 10 million people across Persia, Afghanistan and Turkey. Turkish was spoken by over 15 million in southeastern Europe, the Anatolian peninsula and central Asia, but its importance was primarily as the official language of the Ottoman Empire – 'the greatest and most powerful independent Muslim State' of the time.

The Board of Trade provided the Reay Committee with seven tables on the importance of Asian and African trade for Britain and its European competitors. The commercial importance of more than thirty languages was considered by the committee. The 1906 figures for Arabic, Armenian, Greek, Persian, and Turkish were given in thousands of British pounds sterling (Table 3).

Table 3
Near and Middle Eastern trade, 1906

Language (by country)	Trade between countries speaking the same language	Trade with non-United Kingdom countries	Trade with United Kingdom
Arabic			
Egypt	40	28,301	21,819
Sudan	na	861	na
Tripoli	2	557	259
Tunis	352	4,772	575
Algeria	624	29,491	1,611
Morocco	239	1,399	1,570
Syria	897	5,101	3,295
Arabia			
Muscat	5	624	53

Bahrein	715	144	1,759
Yemen	552	926	na
Jeddah	na	858	na
Aden*	470	4,524	485
Mesopotamia	5	1,976	1,496
total	3,921	79,534	32,922
Armenian			
Turkey	186	1,633	378
Russia	667	3,262	800
total	853	4,895	1,178
Greek			
Cyprus	15	621	233
Greece	5	6,645	3,795
total	20	7,266	4,028
Persian			
Persia	—	9,288	1,385
Turkish			
in Europe & Asia			
(except Syria and			
Mesopotamia)	201	20,248	8,000
NW Persia	2	4,887	451
Trans-Caspia	—	3,036	na
total	203	28,171	8,451

*Excluding substantial government stores from India.

Based on the 1906 estimates of the Board of Trade, the British share of Near and Middle Eastern commerce represented 55 per cent of all trade with Greece, 40 per cent of that with Arabia, 27 per cent with Turkey, 24 per cent with Armenia and 13 per cent with Persia. Anglo-Greek commerce clearly had a dominant position within the eastern Mediterranean. The British handled the bulk of trade with Egypt, Mesopotamia and the Arabian peninsula and had economically dominated areas surrounding the Suez Canal, the Red Sea and the Persian Gulf even before the military occupation of them. While France was the leading European trader in North Africa and heavily involved in Syria, the British had the largest share of Morocco's Atlantic trade. Britain's trade with Turkey and Armenia was also substantial, but that with Persia insignificant before the discovery of oil. Despite growing competition, London was dominant in commerce from the Atlantic to the Mediterranean and around Africa to the Indian Ocean.

In addition to the statistical data, the Reay Committee heard evidence from seventy-three witnesses between February and July 1908. Apart from one German and two French professors, all were British, including professors such as Browne at Cambridge, lecturers such as Hartwig Hirschfeld of Jews' College, London, journalists such as Chirol of *The Times*; oriental travellers and authors such as Gertrude Bell, Sir Reginald Wingate, the sirdar of the Sudan, and Lord Cromer, recently retired from Egypt. Half the witnesses had connections with specific regions (sixteen with India, eleven with the Near and Middle East, eight with the Far East and five with Africa), while the others represented commercial, governmental, cultural and religious groups in London. A further nine sent memoranda supporting the call for a school within London University for the teaching not only of languages but also of the customs, religions and histories of Asia and Africa.

The report of the Reay Committee was presented to Parliament at the end of December 1908. The 156-page document concluded: 'As England is the country which above all others has important relations with the East, the fact that no Oriental School exists in its capital city is not creditable to the nation.' The Committee recommended that a single school, combining practical as well as scholarly training, be established within the University of London to teach the most important languages of the Near East, India, Further India (Malay Archipelago), the Far East, and Africa. It even specified an annual budget of £12,725, for a director, 5 professors, 9 readers and 16 native assistants, and recommended that funds from the Treasury be matched by the University of London. The remainder of the school's costs would be found from student fees and voluntary contributions from the London County Council, the London Chamber of Commerce and similar bodies.[26]

It took a further decade, and another committee – this time chaired by Lord Cromer – before the Reay Report was put into effect. In 1913 the government established a capital grant of £25,000 and promised £4,000 annually in appropriations. In 1914 Cromer's committee launched a fund-raising appeal for £100,000, but had raised only £36,267 by the end of 1916.[27] On 23 February 1917, King George V formally opened the School of Oriental Studies with the words: 'May God bless its labours in the advancement of learning, unity, and good government among my peoples of every race and language.'[28] The school was situated in a large building at Finsbury Circus, formerly the London Institute for the Advancement of Literature and the Diffusion of Useful Knowledge, a private institution founded in 1807.

Could Britain continue to dominate maritime trade between Europe and India without better knowledge of the customs, history, languages and religions of the region? The price of acquiring this knowledge seemed low given the profits London's traders and financiers had made throughout the nineteenth century, and expected to continue to make as Britain's imperial sway extended across the lands of the Middle East.

THE YOUNG TURKS

In 1908 a group of Turkish rebels – known as the 'Young Turks' to distinguish them from the 'Old Turks' who for years had been associated with maladministration and massacres – overthrew the regime of Abdul-Hamid, Ottoman sultan since 1876.

What historians call the Young Turk Revolution broke out in late July. The previous summer had seen drought and a bad harvest and, with decreased revenues, the government could not pay the salaries of its officials and soldiers. The revolution was stimulated by a military crisis in Macedonia, where Greek terrorism had been undermining the position of the Turkish Third Army. Turkish officers at Salonika believed their hands were tied and resented the sultan's sending a special commander to deal with the Macedonian situation. When the commander was killed, Abdul-Hamid turned to his Second Army in Anatolia; sympathizing with the rebel officers in Salonika, it refused to follow his orders. When demands came for the restoration of the 1876 constitution suspended in 1878, the sultan agreed to recall the Ottoman Parliament. Much like Russia's tsar creating a duma in 1905 and Persia's shah permitting an assembly in 1906, Abdul-Hamid's action bought him time, as did other concessions including press freedom, public debate and the right to strike. Elections at the end of 1908 returned a huge majority for candidates of the Committee of Union and Progress (CUP), an ethnically and religiously diverse group with varied agendas dating back to the 1870s.

In the winter of 1908–9 tensions mounted in the Balkans, in Constantinople and in southeastern Anatolia. Revolts in Bulgaria and Bosnia-Herzegovina, along with Crete's union with Greece in the latter part of 1908, heightened Turkish anxieties. The situation in the Ottoman capital worsened, and demonstrations and strikes by unskilled workers provoked the First Army in Constantinople, led mainly by Albanian Muslims loyal to the sultan, to overthrow the CUP government in April. Within a week the CUP and 25,000 soldiers had retaken the capital and exiled Abdul-Hamid to Salonika. Martial law was imposed and order restored, and the Young Turks were back in control.

A tragic consequence of the upheaval in Constantinople occurred in the southeastern Anatolian city of Adana, where Armenians refused to accept the sultan's military takeover. The refusal provoked a massacre of 20,000 by local Turkish soldiers and civilians, with arsonists destroying the offices of Armenian merchants and moneylenders. To protect Armenian lives and to avoid Russian wrath, Christian indignation worldwide and pressure from the Great Powers, the Young Turks ordered the temporary deportation of Armenians from Adana and held a funeral for fifty soldiers later buried in a common grave. One army officer emphasized that 'Moslems and Christians were lying side by side in token that they, living or dying, were henceforward fellow-patriots who would know no distinction of race or

16   The meeting of the Turkish parliament in 1908, a part of what London termed the 'Young Turk' Revolution, which reinstated the constitution the sultan had suspended four decades earlier.

creed'. While the Turkish military backed the CUP executive, members of the Ottoman Parliament passed military, legal, social, educational and municipal reforms. Conspicuously lacking, however, were fiscal reforms, since the Turkish Empire had lost its economic independence, its revenues and expenditures having for decades been under the control of European bondholders and managers of the Ottoman Public Debt.[29]

London's response to this complex situation will be indicated only briefly here. In July 1908 both politicians and the media initially appeared to approve the rebellion against the despotism of Abdul-Hamid, 'the terrible Turk'. Fleet Street did not mourn the last gasps of the 'sick man of Europe' when the Bulgarians declared their full independence from the Ottoman Empire in October. Neither did Westminster seem to mind Vienna's annexation of Bosnia-Herzegovina, and much less the island of Crete being united with mainland Greece. In spring 1909 there were reports of further massacres of Armenians, and British sermons, protest meetings and relief efforts proved powerless. The London Missionary Society's summer exhibition the previous year had featured a hundred tableaux in its 'Pageant of Darkness and Light'.[30]

That same summer Lord Grey, as foreign secretary, addressed the House of Commons on the issue of the Young Turks:

Our own sympathy must be with those who are trying to introduce reforms, and I should be the last to prophesy that they will fail. If they succeed, then they must succeed by their own efforts, but our sympathy is with them . . . while not relaxing our watchfulness, while not becoming slack in our desire to do all in our power to promote improvement in Macedonia, we shall for the present preserve an expectant and sympathetic attitude.[31]

A copy of Grey's parliamentary statement was sent to Constantinople with the new British ambassador, Gerald Lowther (1858–1916), with instructions that it should become 'as clearly and widely known as possible', short of a direct intervention in Turkish affairs. Grey feared the stirring up of nationalist resentment less than the upsetting of Anglo-Russian relations: 'We have now to be pro-Turkish without giving rise to any suspicion that we are anti-Russian.' Lord Hardinge, the permanent undersecretary, warned Lowther not to make any commitments to the new regime.[32] And both Grey and Hardinge were relieved when the British embassies in St Petersburg and Vienna confirmed that neither Russia nor Austria-Hungary would intervene in the Turkish revolution.[33]

The Foreign Office had immediately recognized Bulgaria's independence and Bosnia-Herzegovina's annexation by Vienna, Grey showing little sensitivity to Turkish loss of European territory that for centuries had been part of the Ottoman Empire. The foreign secretary was less hostile to the Turks than were Foreign Office mandarins who urged St Petersburg to renew its efforts to gain access to the Turkish Straits or those who believed the Young Turks should learn their lesson in Bulgaria if they were to avoid also losing Macedonia. Grey, unlike colleagues who sought to bring Russia and Bulgaria together at Turkey's expense, feared this might provoke war between the Bulgarians and Turks or, worse, push both into the arms of Berlin.[34]

By the beginning of 1909 the British embassy in Constantinople had begun to intensify the anti-CUP opinion already gaining ground in the Foreign Office. Lowther and his staff suspected that the CUP was 'under the inspiration of the German Embassy'.[35] The British embassy so disliked the CUP that it had endorsed the sultan's counter-coup in 1909. After the CUP regained command, Grey wired the embassy over its antipathetic stance: 'I think that during the last three or four months we have let ourselves slide too much into a critical attitude towards the Committee and the Young Turks . . . they have shown that there is real stuff in them, and we must be less critical and more sympathetic.' The permanent undersecretary added a few words of his own: 'Our only hope for a reformed Turkey rests now with the Young Turks, and if they do not meet with sympathy and cannot lean on us they will soon learn to lean on some other Power, and the splendid position which we had at Constantinople a few months ago will be lost.'

17   Sultan Abdul Hamid.

The British ambassador however never lost his paranoia about the CUP, whose leaders he considered 'wild chauvinists' ruled by a sinister cabal of 'Salonika Christians, Jews and freemasons'. Although, as he informed the Foreign Office, he would cooperate with 'mild chauvinists and moderates' in the CUP, he particularly loathed the Turkish army officers whom he called 'the Committee', and whose methods, he maintained, were 'those of Abdul-Hamid, only instead of being applied by one man, they are applied by a few'.[36]

A delegation of seventeen CUP parliamentary members visited Britain in late July 1909. On its first day the delegation visited the Foreign Office, lunched at the House of Commons, met the royal family at Buckingham Palace, and took tea with the London County Council. On the second day it visited the British fleet at Southend, lunched on board the *Lord Nelson*, and attended a banquet featuring a crescent-shaped dessert, Turkish music, coffee and cigarettes. The following day the delegation visited and had lunch at Westminster Palace, later meeting representatives of the Balkan Committee, the Overseas League, the Chamber of Commerce and Zionists, before departing on a week's tour of northern England. In his toast to the Turkish delegation, Grey was effusive: 'I have never seen anything more spontaneous, more genuine, more unanimous than the outburst of sympathy in Great Britain which greeted the change to a new order of things in Turkey last year.'[37]

Staged demonstrations of British goodwill however had little effect: the Turks denied Britain monopoly concessions in Mesopotamia. Nor did the Turks end their boycott of Greek traders. In August 1909 the Turkish constitution of 1876 was again revised in an attempt to bolster its empire; to gain greater control over Macedonia, non-Muslims were to be conscripted into the Turkish army. The Foreign Office remained sceptical, and suspicious of the Young Turks. Though initially more positive, Grey soon followed suit.[38]

FINANCE, TRADE AND *THE NEAR EAST*

There was, in the years before 1914, a dramatic increase in British investment abroad, especially in the United States and the British dominions. In 1902 John Hobson's influential *Imperialism* revealed and quantified how much more British surplus capital was being invested abroad than at home. In 1930 Herbert Feis published an award-winning book on British, French and German investment and the way it intersected with their respective diplomacies. While more recent authorities have amended some specifics, historians have largely corroborated Feis's impressionistic account:

> London was the centre of a financial empire, more international, more extensive in its variety, than even the political empire of which it was the capital. . . . The names of foreign lands and ventures vibrated unceasingly in the shadowy dimness of the London Stock Exchange, and the financial journals gave a panorama of the world's strivings in factory, mine, and field.[39]

Some 500 different London institutions were involved in British foreign investment, with long-term ventures and securities handled by such powerful issues houses as Barings, Rothschilds, Brown Shipley, Glyn Mills and Currie, and short-term financing being underwritten by smaller banks and investment companies. The larger firms were in broad agreement over government loans, but the market for securities was open, and individual investors went to brokers who bought and sold shares on London's Stock Exchange. Feis believed that precise knowledge about the City was impossible: 'Of that ever changing world of debts and balances, only approximate estimates can be made, only rough sketch maps.'[40] More recent historians, such as P. J. Cain and A. G. Hopkins, emphasize the importance of the financial and service sectors, which more than offset the decline in British industry and agriculture towards the end of the nineteenth century. They document the close relationship between the Foreign Office and the City of London before the war: Grey, for example, encouraged the founding of the British-owned Bank of Turkey, which opened in 1909 and closed in 1913.

The bank was established by Ernest Cassel (1852–1921), a German Jew with substantial interests, and connexions, in Sweden, North America and London. (Cassel was so close to the prince of Wales that, during the reign of Edward VII, gossips referred to Windsor Castle as Windsor Cassel.) With Rothschild bank, Cassel had financed Vickers, the world's largest arms manufacturer. When Rothschilds declined to finance the construction of the Aswan Dam on the Nile, Cassel accepted, much to Cromer's approbation. The Bank of Turkey initiative failed, however, when it proved unprofitable and investors turned elsewhere.[41]

Whitehall, with its traditional policy of free trade, adopted a hands-off approach towards foreign investment. Yet, as other European governments became increasingly linked with financial bodies, so both Conservative and Liberal administrations followed suit. And, as shipbuilders and arms manufacturers in France and Germany looked to their governments for support, so did their British counterparts. But in general British politicians subscribed to the view, long held by the City of London, that wars interrupted business: Britain had a vested interest in keeping the peace.

A new publication, *The Near East: A Journal of Oriental Politics, Finance, and Literature,* appeared in March 1908, a few months before the Young Turk Revolution. Its area of interest included the Middle East, before the term was current. The first issue declared: 'In addition to identifying itself with the Levant, *The Near East* will be actively concerned with the Balkan States, Egypt, Persia, and India.'

The Near East's opening editorial warned readers that 'the misguided policy of the British Government in regard to the Ottoman Empire will, if allowed to continue, create for this country a position at once humiliating and dangerous'. It recalled happier days after the Crimean War, when 'the British name was paramount all over the Balkan peninsula', and when Britain's 'friendly and intelligent understanding of Turkey' meant 'Christians regarded England as their natural protector, while Moslems acclaimed her as an ancient ally'. Those days had changed with Ottoman bankruptcy and defeat in the Russo-Turkish War in the 1870s, when successive British cabinets began 'muddling through in a policy of drift'. The press and religious zealots had turned the Turk into an 'unspeakable tyrant, a persecutor of Christians . . . who delighted in atrocities for their own sake'. *The Near East* was particularly indignant over the anti-Turkish tirades of those in London who championed the Armenians or backed Balkan nationalities. It believed British amity towards the Turks had been justified so long as the Russian Empire threatened the Ottoman Empire, but not after Russia's defeat by Japan in 1905.

The Near East was mainly concerned with declining British economic activity in the Near and Middle East. Since London had become a party to European 'exploitation of the Porte', many abuses remained through the old system of capitulations, which had placed European traders outside the jurisdiction of Turkish courts and exempted them from taxation. The system had worked satisfactorily until the nineteenth century, when capitulatory privileges (*barats*) began to be sold 'to all manner of persons'. Those who bought *barats* secured European passports and immunity from Turkish laws and taxes, which meant 'lost opportunities' for the British as well as for Muslims. Instead of using their trading advantage to develop railways and exploit oil resources, the British had allowed loathsome Levantines to take over.[42]

The editors of *The Near East* were gratified by the response of readers to their first issue.

> From almost every important quarter in Europe, Asia Minor, and Egypt we have received messages from our fellow countrymen complimenting us on our enterprise, and not the least prized of these encouraging communications are those which emanate from British subjects engaged in financial and commercial undertakings in the Near East.[43]

Readership – at sixpence per monthly issue or eight shillings for an annual subscription to the thirty-six-page periodical – was sufficient for it to survive until the 1950s; it became a weekly in the spring of 1911 and changed its name to *The Near East and India* in 1925 and again in 1935 to *Great Britain and the East*. It filled a gap left open by the Constantinople-based *Levant Herald* (known as the *Constantinople Messenger* in the late 1870s and early 1880s), which appeared between 1873 and 1913.[44]

The Near East offered its readership extensive coverage of trade and transportation. In May 1908 it reported that Britain still dominated commerce throughout the Turkish Empire, taking 35 per cent of Ottoman exports (wheat, sultanas, figs and olive oil) and supplying 32 per cent of the empire's imports (finished cottons, leather, woollens, hosiery, paint, and dyes). (Germany had only 4 per cent of exports and 6 per cent of imports.) In 1908, when Sir William Whittal stepped down as president of the British Chamber of Commerce at Constantinople, he noted that Britain's share of Turkish trade had declined from 45 to 35 per cent during his nineteen-year tenure. Whittal blamed the government's laissez-faire policies and failure to back investment, particularly in the Turkish railway.[45]

The Near East advocated greater support to British finance and trade in the eastern Mediterranean. It regularly opposed the policies of Grey's Foreign Office as insufficiently sensitive to the Turks, obsequiously deferential to the Russians or excessively pro-Bulgarian. For example, it criticized the entry on southeastern Europe in the Foreign Office's *1908 Blue Book* for being 'grotesquely one-sided, and calculated to misinform everyone who has the patience to study it'.[46] MPs who championed Balkan nationalism or Christian separatism at the expense of the Turkish Empire also came under attack, as did groups that championed Christian and Jewish minorities. That *The Near East* viewed Muslim and Islamic traditions much more sympathetically than did other London periodicals was evident in its extensive book review section, its brief commentaries on Parliament, and its comprehensive survey of press reporting of the Near and Middle East as well as of India.

The readers of *The Near East* included others than financiers and traders directly involved in the area. Though probably ignored by most politicians, journalists and officials, those genuinely interested in the Near and Middle East now had a publication that digested news and provided relevant comment.

The main advertiser was the Imperial Ottoman Bank, which indeed may have provided a subvention. The Ottoman Bank had been established in 1856 as an English joint-stock company; in 1863 the sultan had decreed the foundation of the Imperial Ottoman Bank, owned mainly by British and European investors. In 1865 the bank's capital had risen as investors rushed to buy bonds whose annual yields reached double figures.[47]

In the 1870s, however, matters worsened. In 1875, when the Turkish government acknowledged its bankruptcy, the Imperial Ottoman Bank absorbed the Austro-Ottoman Bank and became in effect the state bank of the Turkish empire. It won an exclusive right to issue bank notes and largely determined the finances of the imperial government. In 1878, after the defeat by Russia, Constantinople could not repay its loans. When bondholders failed to gain satisfaction at the Congress of Berlin, Britain initiated a naval demonstration at the Turkish Straits to ensure Turkish cooperation.

In 1881 the Turks agreed to control of the Ottoman Public Debt by London and Paris, along the lines recently established in Egypt. Although sovereignty was in effect lost, greater stability was achieved in Turkish finances, regular payments made to the public debt, and lower returns paid to European investors. Bank deposits also rose thanks to the growing number of accounts from Egypt after it came under British occupation. By the early twentieth-century the City's enthusiasm had cooled, and loans to the Turkish Empire 'attracted mainly French and German investors' and 'brought them more headaches than profits'.[48]

The Imperial Ottoman Bank's concession was extended until 1958, its headquarters located in Constantinople and its boards in Paris and London. By 1914 the bank had 80 branches, including 16 in European Turkey, 37 in Asia Minor, 11 in Syria, and 5 in Egypt.[49] The bank remained central to most economic activity in the Near and Middle East.

LORD CROMER'S EGYPT

Even before his retirement in 1907, Cromer was widely respected as an elder statesman on the Middle East. He had enjoyed the strong support of Balfour and, at the end of 1905, even been invited by Campbell-

18   Lord Cromer.

Bannerman to become Liberal foreign secretary. However, Cromer did not wish to be associated with what he expected to be the Liberal 'misgovernment' of South Africa and India.[50]

Shortly before his retirement, Cromer was able to test the new administration's commitment to the Suez Canal, Egypt and the Sudan in a dispute over the Sinai peninsula. In January 1906, when the sultan sent troops to an old Ottoman fort at the head of the Gulf of Aqaba, Cromer saw it as an attempt to reoccupy the Sinai, which Britain had long deemed vital to the defence of the Suez Canal. London immediately dispatched military and naval forces to Aqaba, and Cromer prompted the Foreign Office to make such forceful diplomatic protests that Constantinople recalled its troops. In the settlement of May 1906, boundaries were established and the Sinai peninsula became Britain's buffer for the Suez Canal and Egypt.

Although minorities and foreigners in Egypt applauded the British stand, the Turkish sympathies of Muslim newspapers irritated Cromer who, suspecting pan-Islamic fanaticism, wired London for military reinforcements. Egypt's population then numbered over eleven million, mostly Muslims but for about seven hundred thousand Copts and two hundred thousand Europeans, Jews and Greeks. The British numbered about 4,000 officers and troops, in command of some 16,000 Egyptian soldiers, so the addition of 1,400 British troops at the end of May 1906

19 Scene of four Egyptians hanged in Dinshawai, a village in the Nile Delta where a British soldier had died after an incident involving village panic over a party out shooting pigeons in 1906.

seemed — to the Foreign Office — a substantial reinforcement. Cromer was less reassured.[51]

The Egyptian view was soon tested by an incident that occurred at Dinshawai. In June 1906 five British officers left their camp to go pigeon shooting. Since pigeons represented a livelihood to some villagers, a dispute ensued in which five villagers were wounded. The officers were captured and beaten, one later dying of his wounds. The British rescue patrol that finally arrived on the scene fired at some villagers and clubbed one to death. Cromer supported the request that the accused villagers be tried by a special tribunal, established by the terms of the British occupation of 1882 but used only once before, in 1897. Grey, new to the Foreign Office, concurred.

The five-man tribunal met in mid-June. Its head was Butrus Ghali, a prominent Copt and senior official at the Ministry of Foreign Affairs since the 1890s; three of the judges were British officials, with little Arabic, and the fifth a Muslim closely associated with the British. The trial of the fifty-nine villagers lasted three days and resulted in harsh sentences: four villagers were condemned to death, two received life sentences, and others long periods of imprisonment or severe lashing. Without appeal, the executions and lashings were carried out the following day, in public. *The Times* briefly noted:

> The prisoners arrived at half past 1 o'clock. One man was hanged, and left hanging while two others were being whipped. Another was then

hanged and two were whipped. The remaining two men sentenced to
death were next hanged and the other culprit flogged. . . . The execution was over at half-past 4.

A correspondent for the *Egyptian Gazette* added that 'now and then a loud
wail from the women came from the village but save for this all was
strangely quiet'.[52]

The incident prompted widespread criticism in London: prior to
Dinshawai, in the first half of 1906, Egypt was mentioned in the House of
Commons on only twenty occasions. In the second half there were seventy
mentions, with Dinshawai as the principal topic. While Grey publicly
defended Cromer, the episode led to a reassessment of British policy: there
would be, at least, no more special tribunals. Cromer himself resigned in
April 1907, the brilliance of his reputation only marginally tarnished by
the Dinshawai incident, and in retirement he remained an influential figure
in London. In 1908 he published two volumes of memoirs, entitled
Modern Egypt, in which he revealed his thinking on the Egyptian
mentality:

> The mind of the Eastern is at once lethargic and suspicious; he does not
> want to be reformed, and he is convinced that if the European wishes to
> reform him, the desire springs from sentiments which bode him no
> good. Moreover, his conservatism is due to an instinct of self-preser-
> vation, and to a dim perception that, if he allows himself to be even
> slightly reformed, all the things to which he attaches importance will be
> not merely changed in this or that particular, but will rather be swept off
> the face of the earth. Perhaps he is not far wrong.[53]

Cromer was succeeded by John Eldon Gorst (1861–1911), who had
worked with him for eighteen years in Egypt's financial and interior
departments before being recalled to London in 1904 as an undersecretary
of state. Gorst therefore clearly understood that Grey wanted no further
incidents that might engage the House of Commons. In 1908, when a
British military officer was murdered by tribesmen in southern Sudan, the
Foreign Office forbade a retaliatory hanging and avoided another
Dinshawai.[54]

Unlike the autocratic Cromer, Gorst acquired a knowledge of Arabic.
Relations with Abbas Hilmi, the headstrong khedive who had succeeded
his more compliant father in 1892, were improved, and Gorst encouraged
his staff to mix more with Egyptians. While Cromer had ignored the
legislative council and general assembly, Gorst used both and decentralized
the administration so as to involve Egyptians more at the provincial and
municipal levels. The approach was approved of in London, but caused
unease among the British in Egypt itself.

In the spring of 1907 the fall in New York's stock market triggered a

20   Cromer's hand-picked successor as consul-general in Egypt, Sir Eldon Gorst, and Lady Gorst in the khedive's six-wheeled automobile, photographed near Cairo in 1908.

tightening of credit which effectively ended the boom that Egypt had enjoyed on the basis of its cotton exports since 1893.[55] The downturn contributed to nationalist frustration over British occupation. One protester was Mustafa Kamil, who in 1906, at the age of only thirty-two, had founded the nationalist party (al-Hizb al-Watani), and published a book, *The Rising Sun,* urging Egyptians to get rid of the British as the Japanese had defeated the Russians. Kamil died in 1908, reportedly from natural causes, and his funeral was attended by at least 8,000 people. One Egyptian writer observed: 'Mustafa Kamil's funeral day was the second time I saw the heart of Egypt throb, the first being the day of the Dinshawai executions.'[56]

Egyptian protests hardened the Foreign Office position, although Grey remained sensitive to Liberal Radicals in the cabinet and House of Commons. Since Gorst could not rely on the mixed courts to prosecute anti-British journalists, he was permitted to revive the tough Press Law of 1881. By the summer of 1909 concern about nationalistic agitation was such that a new Criminal Deportation Act was promulgated. Grey reassured Westminster that Gorst would control the act to avoid abuses: in 1909, of 12,000 Egyptians arrested, fewer than 300 were deported.[57]

As Egypt's recession worsened, the budget could be balanced only by reducing government expenditure, the value of the reserve fund having depreciated by almost £320,000. These fiscal constraints were such that Gorst might have hesitated before embarking in 1909 on an ambitious scheme for developing Sudan's railways as the best way of militarily securing the largest country in Africa. Gorst agreed with Wingate, the sirdar of the Sudan, that unless an extended railway provided greater mobility for Anglo-Egyptian troops, the number of forces would need to be substantially increased.

Failing to secure a loan in London, or convince the Foreign Office to provide funds by renegotiating the nineteenth-century Ottoman limits on Egypt's borrowing power, Gorst approached the Suez Canal Company in Paris, which wished to extend its concession for a further forty years from 1968 until 2008. In exchange, Egypt would receive four million Egyptian pounds over four years, a 4 per cent share of the company's profits, rising to 50 per cent in 1969 and three seats on the company's board of directors. Apart from being the main users of the Suez Canal, the British government was the largest single shareholder in the Suez Canal Company. Winston Churchill, then Liberal president of the Board of Trade, pragmatically argued that:

> On general grounds it would be better for the Canal to revert as speedily as possible into the hands of a weak military state, which would be allowed by international pressure to exact only a moderate toll for the upkeep of the water way.[58]

Grey reported to Gorst that the government reluctantly agreed to support the extension of the concession. The foreign secretary avoided raising the matter in Parliament by maintaining the fiction that the British members of the company's board of directors were independent of the government.

At that point, Gorst compounded his problems with a political blunder. After discussing the matter with Butrus Ghali, Egypt's prime minister and his chief financial adviser, Gorst decided to submit the draft proposal for the forty-year extension of the canal concession to the general assembly. While the prime minister, like the khedive, welcomed the prospect of a £4 million infusion of funds, virtually no one else did. When news reached the public, nationalists expressed outrage at the extension of foreign control over a canal that, in their eyes, had harmed more than it had helped Egypt. Gorst remained optimistic as the khedive introduced the measure to the general assembly early in 1910.[59]

In late February the Egyptian prime minister was assassinated. Butrus Ghali was killed by a young Muslim chemist who became an instant nationalist hero. The assassination of Britain's main Egyptian collaborator ended what little sympathy remained in the Foreign Office and Downing Street for liberalization. The possibility grew of Egypt slipping from British control.

21   Cover engraving of the former US president speaking at the Guildhall in 1910. Roosevelt had toured eastern Africa, the Sudan and Egypt, believing the British had a duty to rule Egypt.

Late in May 1910, Theodore Roosevelt, the former United States president, came to London. Roosevelt had been on safari in East Africa and briefly visited Khartoum and Cairo. Speaking at the Guildhall, he praised the British as guardians of civilization who should protect their imperial interests against an uncivilized and fanatical people prone to extremism and violence. Recent events in Egypt had demonstrated to Roosevelt that Egyptians were unfit to rule themselves. He exhorted the British to make up their minds: 'Either you have the right to be in Egypt or you have not; either it is or it is not your duty to establish and keep order. If you feel that you have not the right to be in Egypt, if you do not want to establish and to keep order there, why then by all means get out of Egypt.'[60] But he concluded:

You are in Egypt for several purposes, and among them one of the greatest is the benefit of the Egyptian people. You saved them from ruin by coming in, and at the present moment, if they are not governed from outside, they will sink into a welter of chaos. Some nation must govern Egypt. I hope and believe that you will decide that it is your duty to be that nation.

In June Balfour, as leader of the opposition, reminded the House of Commons that the Egyptians were not racially inferior, but had simply never known self-government. He believed the British in Egypt deserved London's strongest support. Grey thanked Balfour for his 'valuable contribution' and alluded to Roosevelt's words, since none had given him 'greater pleasure'. The foreign secretary responded to Roosevelt's challenge by saying 'we have gone on in Egypt doing more and more good work, year after year' and 'that good work depends on our staying there'. The British 'cannot abandon Egypt without disgrace to ourselves'.

Cromer, who may have used his considerable influence at the Foreign Office to promote the harder line, might have approved this patriotic vindication of his Egyptian career. But he admitted to having doubts about the continuation of British rule.[61] In his presidential address to the British Classical Association in 1910, he spoke of ancient and modern imperialism, asking whether modern imperialism could succeed where the ideal of 'self-government' at home conflicted with the requirements of 'good government' abroad.[62]

Cromer recommended that Kitchener succeed Gorst when the consul-general died from cancer in 1911. He was convinced that Kitchener, the greatest soldier of the British Empire, could silence Egyptian nationalism. King George V also supported the nomination, and Kitchener was appointed. Apart from a few Liberal MPs and journalists, who doubted the soldier's suitability for the diplomatic post, London was enthusiastic at the prospect of so commanding a figure taking control of Egypt.[63]

Chapter 4

Anticipating War: 1911–1914

A GERMAN GUNBOAT sent to Agadir, Morocco, during the summer of 1911, precipitated the most acute military crisis Britain encountered before 1914. The Liberal government stood publicly with France and secretly prepared for war. The anti-German posture brought it welcome and much needed support: it had survived two general elections and a constitutional crisis as well as facing militant strikers, angry suffragettes and mutinous army officers in Ireland.

While the British press focused its attention on domestic crises, Italy declared war on Turkey in the autumn 1911. No sooner was there peace, in 1912, than the Turks were attacked and defeated by Bulgaria, Serbia and Greece. Within weeks of the conclusion of the First Balkan War in 1913, a further, month-long war broke out.

As Fleet Street applauded the defeat of the Turks, Whitehall weighed British options. For the Foreign Office, Anglo-Turkish relations mattered less than Anglo-Russian amity. Prolonged negotiations with both Constantinople and Berlin finally allayed misgivings over building a railway from Baghdad to the Persian Gulf. The government was persuaded to buy control of the Anglo-Persian Oil Company in 1914.

After the assassination of the heir to the Austro-Hungarian Empire at Sarajevo in June 1914 led to a continent-wide war early in August, a naval crisis erupted at the Turkish Straits. When Germany pressured the Turks into bombarding Russian ports on the Black Sea, Britain declared war on the Ottoman Empire, as it had against Germany and Austria. While Downing Street waited for the Turks to strike the first blow, Whitehall ordered elaborate precautions at the Suez Canal and the Persian Gulf. In barely three months the Balkan crisis that had widened into a European war reached the Middle East.

LLOYD GEORGE'S BUDGETS AND CHURCHILL'S NAVY

The weather was warm for the coronation of George V in June 1911; indeed London basked in record temperatures throughout July and August. But during the months in which an outbreak of war between Germany and France was feared, the government faced a plethora of domestic problems. Over Ireland, the House of Lords threatened to veto a reform bill passed by the Commons, and the prime minister, Asquith, persuaded the king to create new peerages in order to pack the chamber.

During the summer, anxieties grew over increasing worker militancy. When rioting broke out during a seamen's strike in Liverpool, Churchill, the home secretary, called in the army. The troops were stoned by the strikers, two being killed and twenty wounded. The country also experienced its first general railway strike in August, after Churchill had suspended civil regulations in order to send the forces to Merseyside. Workers, like the suffragettes, now adopted direct action.

At this point, in July 1911, a German gunboat appeared off Agadir. The popular Fleet Street papers printed rumours that the German fleet had been mobilized and German battleships surrounded the British Isles, unopposed by the navy and undetected by Admiralty Intelligence.[1] Sensation and scaremongering by Germanophobic newspapers had become common, but in 1911 the anxieties spread more widely, to Grey's Foreign Office, to Churchill and to Lloyd George.

Winston Churchill (1874–1965) was born at Blenheim Palace, given by Queen Anne and the grateful British nation to John Churchill, first duke of Marlborough. Winston's father, Randolph, was a prominent Tory, and his mother, Jennie Jerome, had been born in the United States. Neglected by his parents but dazzled by his Marlborough ancestry, Churchill showed little flare until he entered the military academy at Sandhurst. While there his father died, at the young age of 46 and of syphilis, without having achieved his political goals, factors which stimulated Winston's own ambition. After graduating from Sandhurst, Churchill was commissioned as a cavalry officer and saw action on the northwest frontier of India. In 1898 he served with Kitchener's army at Omdurman in the reconquest of the Sudan; in 1899, having resigned from the army, he travelled to South Africa to cover the Boer War as a newspaper correspondent.

Churchill entered the House of Commons as a Conservative Unionist in 1900, but joined the Liberal Party in 1904. In 1906 he was elected Liberal MP for Manchester North-West, but subsequently rejected in an election required of MPs named to the cabinet, before winning the safe Scottish seat of Dundee. When Asquith became prime minister and Lloyd George chancellor of the Exchequer, Churchill succeeded Lloyd George as president of the Board of Trade.

David Lloyd George (1836–1945), however, had significantly different origins. After the death of his father when only an infant, he moved with his mother, sister and brother into the humble household of his bachelor uncle, a Welsh shoemaker who combined Baptist fundamentalism with temperance, Welsh pride and radical liberalism. Growing up in a household that centred around himself, Lloyd George acquired a firm sense of his own importance that was enhanced by his gifted oratorical performances in churches and political platforms in north Wales. Elected MP for Caernarvon while in his mid-twenties, he first made a name for

22   Churchill chats with Lord Northcliffe, the most powerful newspaper proprietor in Fleet Street. The scene is a meeting to promote the development of aviation, held at Hendon in 1911.

himself by attacking the Boer War and characterising Dutch farmers as the victims of British capitalism and imperialism.

Lloyd George's effective attacks on Tory warlords, pub owners, landholders and protectionists led Campbell-Bannerman to appoint him president of the Board of Trade in 1905. The Welshman enjoyed strong support from evangelicals, particularly the editor of the *British Weekly*, a Scottish parson known as 'the man who made Lloyd George.'[2] As chancellor of the Exchequer in 1908, Lloyd George provoked the resentment of the wealthy for his 'People's Budget' of 1909 and welfare initiatives of 1911. Yet, despite his commitment to attack poverty, he readily accepted the hospitality of the rich, often neglecting his wife and children.[3]

Lloyd George and Churchill realized how useful they could be to each other, and there was a rapport between the two men.[4] Churchill disliked golf and Lloyd George detested drink, but each smoked cigars and talked more freely with the other than with those members of Asquith's cabinet that were products of public schools, Oxford and Cambridge. Churchill's aristocratic and Lloyd George's humble backgrounds differed, but both defied middle-class conventions. Each needed to raise money for his political career – Churchill through writing and Lloyd George through

23 Lloyd George, chancellor of the Exchequer, and Churchill walking to Westminster Palace on budget day, 1910, accompanied by Lloyd George's wife and private secretary.

law. Both knew the value of good public relations, and cultivated their connections with people who could help them. Although the prime minister held the key to their political future, Churchill and Lloyd George relied on each other to determine how best to approach Asquith over the crisis in summer 1911.

The British could not be indifferent to the crisis over Agadir. The Anglo-French Entente of 1904 had first been tested in the earlier Moroccan crisis of 1905. In 1906 Britain and the other powers had guaranteed Morocco's political and financial independence, yet France had used its police force and banking power to maintain a grip on the country as it had on Algeria and Tunisia. The French bombardment and occupation of Casablanca in 1907 further strained relations with Germany. Then, in the spring of 1911, following the arrival of a French military expedition in Fez, Germany dispatched a small gunboat, the *Panther*, to Agadir on 1 July.[5]

Britain declined to send troops to Agadir, although the incident confirmed the Foreign Office's worst anxieties about Germany. Grey protested to the German ambassador, but the British were not invited to the talks that resulted in Germany's climb-down in Morocco in return for French territorial acquisition in the Congo.

The crisis pushed Churchill and Lloyd George into line with their colleagues in Asquith's cabinet. On 19 July Grey declared that if the Foreign Office had not heard from Berlin by 21 July, the British would send a battleship to Agadir. That evening, the chancellor of the Exchequer had agreed to speak to the Bankers' Association at the Mansion House. As Lloyd George brooded over the diplomatic crisis, he began to fear that France would cede to German military superiority unless Britain defied Germany publicly. He spoke with Churchill and with Asquith and showed the text of his speech to the Foreign Office, where Grey poured over the sensitive passages for so long that Lloyd George was half an hour late for the dinner. Much of his speech was delivered without notes, but Lloyd George read the conclusion:

> I believe it is essential in the highest interests, not merely of this country, but of the world, that Britain should at all hazards maintain her place and her prestige amongst the Great Powers of the world. . . . I can see that nothing would justify disturbance of international good will except questions of the gravest national moment. But if a situation were to be forced upon us in which peace could only be preserved by the surrender of the great and beneficent position Britain has won by centuries of heroism and achievement, by allowing Britain to [be] treated where her interests were vitally affected as if she were of no account in the Cabinet of nations, then I say emphatically that peace at that price would be a humiliation intolerable for a great country like ours to endure.[6]

The Mansion House audience knew the culprit, even if Germany was not named. The speech was well received by bankers and the press in both London and Paris, but Berlin was furious and soon afterwards announced an increase in German naval construction and a buildup of its army.

The threat of a German attack on the British fleet was real. On 23 August the prime minister convened the Committee of Imperial Defence, inviting Lloyd George and Churchill for the first time, along with officials from the Foreign Office, War Office and Admiralty, and army and naval personnel. This fateful meeting laid the foundations for the linking of British and French expeditionary forces in the event of war with Germany, and for the further buildup of the British navy.[7]

Lloyd George made no further excursions into foreign affairs before the 1914–18 war. Politically he risked alienating the Radical Liberals and Evangelical Christians who had turned against Grey. Within the cabinet, however, Lloyd George maintained a hard line. In October Asquith announced the appointment of Churchill as first lord of the Admiralty, a post he had sought the year before: at the age of only thirty-five, he held one of the most powerful positions in the world. Given the newly-passed Official Secrets Act, too, he was a party to Britain's most confidential diplomacy.[8]

The Agadir crisis not only hardened attitudes within the government, but strengthened those Conservatives and Unionists who wanted tougher Tories at the head of their own party. Balfour was blamed for the loss of the 1910 general elections, and stood down as Conservative leader.

Cross-party support was vital for the ambitious naval programmes that characterized the years before the Great War. Between 1912 and 1914, growing naval demands necessitated higher taxes in successive budgets, particularly in 1908 and 1914, through income tax, death duties, taxes on all sales and stock transactions, real estate capital gains, and luxury taxes. The increased revenue met not only defence but also social welfare provisions. Between the fiscal years 1908–9 and 1914–15, Britain's annual net expenditure (expenditure chargeable against current revenue) on welfare increased by 900 per cent, compared with an increase for the navy of 60 per cent and the army of only 8 per cent. In real terms, however, the welfare total of £74.8 million was exceeded by combining the respective allocation to the navy (£70.7 million) and the army (£6.9 million). And of course these figures reflect only the net increase in expenditure. The overall naval budget was enormous, not counting the substantial naval contributions from the Dominions, which underwrote the costs of further battleships.[9]

Lloyd George succeeded in raising sufficient funds wholly through taxation and without the necessity of borrowing. Germany, by contrast, needed to borrow at least 25 per cent (and in some years as much as 50 per cent) of the cost of naval construction; its shipbuilding programme in fact declined in the years before 1914.

TURKISH DEFEATS

Some historians have argued that the Agadir crisis led inexorably to war in 1914, and the debate will doubtless continue. They do agree, however, on the immediate impact of the second Moroccan crisis on the Turkish Empire in North Africa, the eastern Mediterranean and, especially, the Balkans. Yet few acknowledge how inflexible was the diplomacy adopted by the British, French and Russians, on one side, and the Germans and Austro-Hungarians, on the other. Acquiescence in the defeat and humiliation of Turkey between 1911 and 1913 helped propel the Great Powers towards war, well before the assassination of the heir to the Austro-Hungarian throne in June 1914.

While the diplomatic, strategic and political consequences of Agadir were being digested in London, Italy declared war on the Turks at the end of September 1911. Within a week, Italian forces invaded Tripoli, the main Mediterranean port of what is now Libya. Britain and the other Great Powers protested publicly, but all had secretly approved the Anglo-French-Russian diplomacy, while the German-Austro-Hungary axis had

24 'Oyez! Oyez! Oyez!' The royal proclamation of strict British neutrality over war between Italy and Turkey, read by Colonel Kearns on the steps of the Royal Exchange, London.

already sanctioned Italy's eventual acquisition of Tripoli. None appeared concerned for the Turks, who appealed in vain for help against the Italian aggression. When Italy launched a naval demonstration at the Dardanelles in spring 1912, the Turks closed the straits, much to Russia's dismay. Italy then occupied the Dodecanese islands, off the coast of Anatolian Turkey, which London and Paris refused to concede. Paris loaned no further funds to Constantinople, although Whitehall did permit a British firm to build new ships for the Turks, provided they were paid in advance, a stricture which involved some Turkish women in selling their own hair to meet the cost.[10]

The very day Turkey concluded peace with Italy in October 1912, it found itself facing declarations of war from Bulgaria, Serbia and Greece The Balkan states, moreover, were well prepared, as is clear from the swift successes won by the Bulgarians and Serbs, restrained only by Austria-Hungary and Russia.[11]

Although the Near East was of much less concern to the British than the Middle East, Grey convened a Great Power conference on the Balkans in London in January 1913. He urged the Turks to cede Adrianople to Bulgaria and the Aegean islands and Crete to Greece. In March, when the Bulgarians secured Adrianople, they concluded peace with Turkey. The conference reopened in May and culminated in the Treaty of London, by which Turkey ceded Crete but left the status of both Albania and the Aegean Islands open.

The Second Balkan War lasted a month, in July 1913. It was precipitated by a reckless Bulgarian commander who attacked advance positions held by the Serbs and Greeks. They retaliated, aided by Turkey and Rumania. Treaties provided the victors with territory at Bulgaria's expense, and the Turks regained Adrianople. The second round of war in the Balkans intensified resentments and stiffened resolve.[12]

At the end of 1913 the Turks appointed a German military officer to reorganize the Turkish army, starting with the corps at Constantinople. Paris supported St Petersburg's insistence that the officer be stationed elsewhere than at Constantinople. Early in 1914 Berlin too exerted pressure, and Turkey agreed the German should become inspector-general of the Turkish army. The Foreign Office already knew that Russia expected to take over the Turkish Straits in the event of a European war, and when George V and Grey visited Paris in April, an Anglo-Russian naval convention was concluded. Further Anglo-French-Russian diplomacy continued in the weeks immediately preceding the fateful assassination at Sarajevo.[13]

The cumulative effect of military defeat and diplomatic humiliation was to embitter militant Turkish nationalists: losing in the Balkans was bad enough, but being abandoned by Britain, ally of the Turks since the Crimean War, was infinitely worse. While Turkish diplomats regretted the passing of the alliance, army officers began to look to Berlin.

Since the 1880s the Great Powers had become so accustomed to compensating each other with territory in Africa and Asia that they assumed they could do the same in the Near and Middle East. Nothing dispelled the prevalent and dangerous illusion that Turkey no longer mattered. Great Power diplomats scarcely mourned the death of the sick man of Europe, so why should the foreign secretary concern himself over the loss of the Turkish Straits, or the marginalization of Turkey in northern Africa and western Asia? Between 1911 and 1913, Turkish requests for support from Britain were rejected by Grey on the grounds that 'the time was not opportune'.[14]

KITCHENER IN AND BEYOND EGYPT

Herbert Horatio Kitchener (1850–1916), the self-made soldier of Anglo-Irish descent, became the British Empire's greatest military hero of the early twentieth century. Kitchener was thirteen when he moved with his father, a colonel, and his ailing mother from Ireland to Switzerland, where he was educated at a French school. In 1870 he graduated from the Royal Military Academy at Woolwich and served four more years with the Royal Engineers. Kitchener's first, longest and most famous postings abroad were in the Middle East. In 1874 the army loaned him to the Palestine Exploration Fund for four years of surveying. In 1878, when Britain acquired Cyprus, Kitchener first surveyed the island and then served as a British vice-consul in Asia Minor. After the occupation of Egypt in 1882, Kitchener commanded the Egyptian cavalry, surveyed the Sinai peninsula and parts of eastern Africa, patrolled the Sudanese frontier, reorganized the Egyptian police, served as adjutant-general of the Egyptian army, and became its head or sirdar. In 1898, after two decades in predominently Muslim countries, Kitchener led the reconquest of the Sudan, raised the Union Jack over the ruins of Gordon's palace in Khartoum, and returned to London in triumph. Standing over 6 feet, 2 inches tall, with dark eyes, a full moustache, and dark-hued cheeks and jowl, Kitchener had an imposing appearance that exuded power and determination.[15]

Kitchener's reputation was further enhanced by his successful, if ruthless, command over the British army in the latter half of the South African War. Since there seemed little more for him to achieve militarily, he contemplated crowning his career with the viceroyalty of India, but instead had to content himself with the command of the Indian army between 1902 and 1909. Thereafter he aspired to the British ambassadorship in Constantinople, but the fierce opposition of Liberal Radicals thwarted his ambition. Instead he took a fifteen-month tour of Australasia and, planning retirement, bought land in East Africa, where he planned to winter, having already purchased an estate in Kent as his main residence.

In the tense atmosphere following the Agadir crisis, however, Asquith set aside Liberal suspicions and invited Kitchener to tackle the troubles in Egypt. Reporting to the Foreign Office, he took up the post of consul-general in early September, only weeks before Italy invaded Tripoli. Kitchener was given free rein, and quickly imposed autocratic controls: he summarily closed five Egyptian newspapers and ordered the arrest of nationalist agitators. He diminished the influence of Khedive Abbas, removing his power to confer titles, decorations and patronage, and compromising his control of religious charities (*waqfs*) by placing them under a ministerial department. Kitchener also took on Egyptian politicians associated with the Legislative Council and General Assembly. His Organic Law abolished both institutions and created a new body that, like its predecessors, remained a consultative chamber with powers to discuss, but not prevent, taxation. Drawing on his experience of India, Kitchener did institute modest schemes to improve the welfare of Egyptian farmers, the *fellahin*, without raising land taxes.

Meanwhile Kitchener monitored London politics closely. Upset by a

25 At Port Said, en route to the ceremonial durbar in India in 1911, King George V and Queen Mary received the khedive of Egypt and Kitchener on the *Medina*, a new P & O vessel of 13,000 tons.

critical article in the *Fortnightly Review,* he wired the Foreign Office with characteristic severity:

> From the local German paper you will see what advantage our enemies are taking of the lying statements the Fortnightly has published . . . . I hope that you will be able to wash the editor's head well, and perhaps take other measures to contradict his article. Possibly a question in the House might be arranged and give the opportunity.[16]

Grey and Asquith regularly consulted Kitchener on matters of Middle-Eastern importance. In May 1912 he was authorized to participate in a Committee of Imperial Defence meeting convened on Malta to determine whether the British navy, concentrated in the North Sea, could be adequately replaced by the French navy in the Mediterranean. Before the conference, Grey communicated his own thoughts:

> It may be contended that, if we were at war with Germany, we could let things take their course in the Mediterranean for the first two or three months, and after having established unquestioned superiority [in] the

Mediterranean Sea, or won the war, we could then recover everything in the Mediterranean. But this raises very serious questions for Egypt. For, if the prospect were admitted, it seems to me that it would, here and now, very materially affect the investment of capital in Egypt and the Soudan. We could not, I suppose, hold Egypt and the Soudan against an attack by Turkey or any Great European Power unless we had command of the sea in the Mediterranean. Apart from this have we force sufficient to control native risings in Egypt or the Soudan, that might be the consequence of our being involved in war elsewhere? And, if the answer is in the negative, how can we reinforce the British army in Egypt unless we have a considerable fleet in the Mediterranean to insure the safe transport of troops from Malta or elsewhere?[17]

Grey's ramblings highlight his expectation of war with Germany, his fear of Muslims disturbing British economic interests and military influence, and his concern that Britain should retain their naval predominance in the Mediterranean. At the Malta meeting, the CID decided not only to maintain British battle squadrons at Gibraltar and Malta but also to strengthen naval defences at Alexandria.[18]

Kitchener's view did not always prevail. In November 1912, after the defeat of Turkey by the Italians, Serbs, Bulgarians and Greeks, Kitchener proposed that Egypt cease paying suzerainty to the sultan. It was not the time, Grey replied:

At present all the Great Powers are practically sworn to 'disinteressement' so far as Turkey is concerned. Our position would be very much weakened if we were trying to get anything for ourselves, and there would be a general scramble. There may be other opportunities of some deal with Turkey. I do not see how they are to arise, but we are living in a world of surprises.[19]

RAILWAY SETTLEMENTS

Germany's projected railway through Anatolia to Baghdad and the Persian Gulf raised familiar issues for Grey's Foreign Office. Having encountered the opposition of the Conservative administration, Turkey approached the Liberal foreign secretary in the hope of raising custom duties to subsidize the railway. Grey countered that monies derived from the so-called kilometric guarantee, which required British approval, should be used for reform in Macedonia rather than railway development.[20] Grey was influenced by Russia's suspicions over the railway; even after the Young Turks had loosened Abdul-Hamid's control, Grey refused to cooperate on the Baghdad Railway despite the fact that a meeting between the kaiser and the tsar in Potsdam at the end of 1910 decisively altered the diplomatic situation. Without informing the Foreign Office, Nicholas II had agreed to end Russian opposition to the German railway in exchange for German recognition of Russian paramountcy in northern Persia.

In 1911, Turkey once again approached the Foreign Office over the question of customs duties. To allay British anxieties about possible German control over the railway beyond Baghdad, Constantinople proposed that a Turkish company build and operate the railway between Baghdad and Basra, with Britain, France and Germany having equal representation and influence. Before responding to the proposal, the Foreign Office asked the India Office, the Board of Trade, the Admiralty and the War Office for their view, and received detailed demands as to the number of British governmental and non-governmental directors to serve on the board of the proposed Turkish railway company, the administration and duration of the company's concession, rate exemptions for British passengers on other parts of the Anatolian-Baghdad Railway, and the use of existing British resources in the Persian Gulf for the development of the railway. British officials agreed that the extension of the railway from Baghdad to the head of the Persian Gulf should neither compromise British paramountcy in the waterway nor permit any other Great Power a foothold along the coastline. Only when these conditions were approved did the Foreign Office open further negotiations: one Turkish official spent over a year in London routinely calling on the Foreign Office.

Foreign Office approval came in the spring of 1913, once the head of its Eastern Department reached agreement with the Board of Trade and the India Office. Grey then brought the matter to the cabinet, which added three further provisions guaranteeing British dominance of the Persian Gulf: British navigation rights on the Tigris and Euphrates rivers, British management of the Shatt-al-Arab waterway, and British operation of the port of Basra. When Paris and St Petersburg expressed no reservation, the Anglo-Turkish Convention needed approval only from Berlin.

The railway issue was settled – and an agreement signed by Britain and Germany – in June 1914. Having informed Berlin of the terms of the Anglo-Turkish agreement regarding the building and operation of the proposed railway, the Foreign Office added further guarantees prohibiting British economic discrimination against the other Great Powers, German encroachment in the Persian Gulf, or Russian and French claims in Asiatic Turkey. Berlin approved the Convention but ignored the additional matters, and requested that the construction of other railways between the Mediterranean and the Persian Gulf be prohibited. Britain insisted that its short southwestern Anatolian railway from Smyrna to Aidin become part of the larger railway system and that British irrigation projects in lower Iraq operate without interference. Still hoping to persuade the City of London to invest in its railway to Baghdad, Berlin agreed, provided London did not challenge German irrigation activities in Anatolia.[21]

It had taken Grey three years to settle the question of the German

A FACTOR WHICH MAKES FOR PEACE: THE COST OF LETTING LOOSE THE DOGS OF WAR.

DRAWN BY A. LANOS.

THE ALCHEMY OF MARS: TORRENTS OF GOLD POURED INTO THE WAR GOD'S CRUCIBLE FOR THE CREATION OF A "FIGHTING MACHINE."

26   The expectation that huge expenditure on defence would serve as a deterrent to war in Europe was proved false with the outbreak of a continent-wide conflict in 1914.

railway through Asiatic Turkey. By 1914, only about 20 per cent of the railway had been finished. It was not completed until 1940.

Britain was also slower than France to come to an agreement on Turkish finances. While Paris supplied 60 per cent of the loans and concluded successful negotiations with the Turks on the French-controlled Ottoman Bank and Deutsche Bank, the British foreign secretary seemed almost supercilious about the Turkish financial situation. Late in 1913, Grey wrote to the British ambassador in Constantinople:

Finance is going to be a great difficulty for the whole of Europe except perhaps ourselves, for we do not live on loans. . . . [Finance] is a market over exploited already and countries that cannot get along without borrowing from the outside may collapse. Whether Turkey is such a country I am not sure. On paper she is bound to collapse without loans, but Eastern countries can do without money in a way of their own, and the French have invested so much in Turkey that they will strain many points to keep her on her feet.[22]

PERSIA AND THE ANGLO-PERSIAN OIL COMPANY

Persia's revolutionary upheaval in 1906, the Anglo-Russian Convention of 1907, the Russian-backed coup led by the shah in 1908, and the escape of the shah in 1909 contributed to what the Foreign Office increasingly regarded as a civil war. After ridding the country of the shah and his Russian-trained Cossack brigade, Tabrizi nationalists from the north and Bakhtiyari leaders from the south came together in Tehran to give a new lease of life to the parliamentary assembly. What historians call the second *majlis* of 1910 needed to restore financial order before resources could be found to reestablish control over the provinces, where many refused to pay taxes and banditry was rife.

The Tehran assembly, wanting nothing to do with either Russia or Britain, turned to a young American, Morgan Shuster. Arriving in May 1911, Shuster was appointed treasurer-general with wide powers to put the country's finances in order. He soon proposed the establishment of a tax-collecting gendarmerie, which infuriated St Petersburg. In the autumn, when Shuster's financial and tax-collecting plans began to take effect, and some disgruntled landowners took refuge in foreign legations to avoid taxes, the gendarmes confiscated property in the name of the *majlis*. Since some of the properties had been pledged as collateral for its loans to Persia, Russia issued an ultimatum that called for the dismissal of Shuster, the replacement of his gendarmes by Cossacks, and a Persian apology. As Shuster recalled in his memoir, *The Strangling of Persia,* the *majlis* defied the ultimatum and Russian forces entered Persia. The *majlis* appealed to Washington, but the US government disassociated itself from Shuster. In public Grey defended Russia's use of force, but privately urged restraint.

At the end of 1911 Russia issued a further ultimatum, requiring the *majlis* to dismiss Shuster, hire no other foreign advisers without the consent of Russia and Britain, and reimburse Russia for the costs of its latest military operations in Persia. The *majlis* again rejected the ultimatum. Grey reminded St Petersburg of the possible consequences of Russian action in Persia: that he himself might be forced to resign, or the government fall, either of which could disrupt Anglo-Russian relations and push Britain towards rapprochement with Germany. But he did concede the need to restore order in Tehran. Persian state government virtually ceased to exist as Russian troops imposed tough military rule throughout the north, and Britain continued its indirect rule through cooperative tribal leaders in the central and southern parts of the country.[23]

After 1911, as the situation deteriorated, Grey wrote to the head of the British legation in Tehran in fatalistic mood:

> It may be that the task of establishing order without partition is an impossible one. But even if you think it is, I am sure that you will continue to do your best to accomplish it and if you fail, or rather, if we

fail: for it is our instructions from home which you are carrying out, I shall be very ready to admit the causes of the failure was no fault of yours, but the inherent impossibility of the task.[24]

Grey, having been associated with the 1907 Anglo-Russian arrangement, could apparently regard his Persian policy as working, so long as no Persian territory was formally annexed either by Russia or by Britain.

Three London views of the events in Persia in 1911 demonstrate the lack of consensus over Britain's involvement in the Middle East. The January 1912 issue of the liberal *Nineteenth Century* stated: 'It cannot be said that the part played by the Government of Great Britain was a very heroic or creditable one.'[25] But sympathy for Persia was atypical. The February 1912 issue of the more middle-of-the-road *Fortnightly Review* was also critical, noting that London seemed less interested in Persia than it had been a few years earlier, but observing that 'Russia has given assurances that the occupation of Persian soil by its troops is provisional and temporary', and reminding readers that the British had given 'similar assurances with respect to Egypt' almost thirty years previously.[26] The October 1912 issue of the more conservative *Edinburgh Review* observed of Britain and Russia that: 'Not in the interests of Persia, but rather in their own interests, both powers are compelled to take an active and vigilant share in deciding the future of the Persian race.' Yet, since Persia would fall into anarchy without European help, the 'aims of Great Britain, at any rate, are absolutely beyond reproach'.[27]

While the British press was only mildly concerned about the Russian military occupation of northern Persia, Whitehall became highly involved in the issue of oil in southwestern Persia. Secret negotiations that had begun in London in 1912 were to lead to the British government purchasing the majority of the shares of the Anglo-Persian Oil Company. News of the purchase was made public only in the spring of 1914.

In 1901, William Knox D'Arcy, an Australian oil prospector, negotiated a sixty-year concession from the Persian government. D'Arcy had not intended to exploit the oil himself, but float a company to extract it. After spending £250,000, D'Arcy turned to the Burma Oil Company, later the Anglo-Persian Oil Company (APOC), the consortium involved in the discovery of oil in Khuzistan, the southwestern province of Persia, in 1908. Given the weakness of the government in Tehran, APOC simply negotiated with Arab chiefs in Khuzistan and arranged for Bakhtiyari tribal leaders to guard the company facilities. From the Khuzistan oilfields, APOC then constructed a 140-mile pipeline to Abadan, an uninhabited mudflat island in the Shatt-al Arab waterway flowing into the Persian Gulf, which the oil company leased from an Arab sheik. The building of a refinery and support facilities on Abadan had driven APOC heavily into debt.[28]

Such was the position in the summer of 1912. With oil replacing coal in the British navy, Winston Churchill asked Fisher, the former first sea lord, to preside over the Royal Commission on Oil Supply for the Navy, instructing him bluntly: 'You have got to find the oil; to show how it can be stored cheaply; how it can be purchased regularly and cheaply in peace; and with absolute certainty in war.'[29] APOC would service the need, but not until the Foreign Office had complicated the situation.

In September 1912 Mallet, assistant undersecretary and head of the Eastern Department, contacted APOC to inquire about its participation in the Turkish Petroleum Company (TPC), a consortium that had recently been formed to explore and exploit oil throughout Asiatic Turkey. APOC's chief executive officer, Charles Greenway, was familiar with the diplomacy of oil and interested in TPC, although he considered it more sensible for Britain to concentrate on Persia, where there was oil, instead of becoming involved in Asiatic Turkey. Nonetheless, APOC preferred to secure the concession in Iraq rather than let this fall to foreign control. Mallet agreed with Greenway, but eventually resented his threat to sell out to Shell unless the Admiralty gave APOC a contract.

What mattered more to Greenway was that the British government should strengthen APOC, which needed £2 million for further development. Given APOC's debt, Greenway boldly asked for an annual subsidy of £100,000 from the British or Indian governments. He also sought exemption from duties on Persian oil imported into India, and asked the Admiralty (for the navy) and India (for its railways) to guarantee an annual order of 500,000 tons of oil. In return Greenway was willing to accept one or two government representatives on APOC's board.

Churchill approved Greenway's proposals, but they raised fundamental difficulties and were opposed by both the India Office and the government of India. Churchill seized the opportunity offered by revolutionary turmoil in Mexico, which threatened to cut off the supply of oil from Lord Cowdray's Mexican Eagle Oil Company, to strike a deal with APOC.

By spring 1913 the Admiralty was already doing business with APOC. The first lord concluded a single contract for 30,000 tons of fuel oil in 1913–14, and then considered a long-term contract for larger quantities. The Treasury, however, did not favour long-term contracts, arguing that the navy's need for fuel hardly justified 'an expedient unbusinesslike and so unsound'. Churchill saw them as a hedge against increased oil prices. When the cabinet failed to reach agreement, Churchill proposed that the government itself supply the £2 million and become a shareholder of APOC, following the precedent of the purchase of stock in the Suez Canal Company in 1875. He observed, moreover, that APOC profits might enrich the Exchequer in the longer term. With the approval of the governor of the Bank of England, the cabinet agreed to Churchill's proposal.[30]

The case for collaboration between government and business still had to be made in Parliament. In July 1913 Churchill argued it on the grounds

27 View of the Anglo-Persian Oil facilities beside the Tigris River at the head of the Persian Gulf. In 1914, the British government became a substantial shareholder in the company.

that the Admiralty needed to find dependable sources of oil. He did not propose that the government finance a particular company but envisaged the Admiralty becoming:

> the independent owner and producer of its own supplies of liquid fuel; firstly, by building up an oil reserve in this country sufficient to make us safe in war and be able to override price fluctuations in peace; secondly, by acquiring the power to deal in crude oils as they come cheaply into the market.

More controversially, Churchill imagined the Admiralty being able 'to retort, refine, top . . . or distill crude oil of various kinds until it reaches the quality for naval use . . . and dispose of its surplus products'.[31] His performance was warmly received by the House of Commons and the press, *The Times* praising him for his authoritative defence of the national interest.[32]

To Churchill's dismay, however, Admiralty experts began to express reservations. One pointed out that the government should at least send its own geological experts to the Persian oilfields before making such a huge investment. By September 1913 a commission had been formed, consisting of a former director of Naval Intelligence, a colonial adviser on oil affairs, a professor of mining from Birmingham University and two geologists. While Churchill waited for a report, the financial situation of APOC grew so grave that it could not even meet its current expenses: the company was on the brink of financial ruin, even after borrowing £150,000 from D'Arcy and another director and running its cash balance to £3,806.[33]

In November a bill authorized the purchase of £2 million worth of APOC stock. How the money was to be raised had not been determined: the government had one idea, and APOC another. The most divisive issue involved a governmental veto. Whitehall's chief negotiator feared the company might adopt a policy of profit maximization, prejudicial to Admiralty interests, yet recognized that the company's ordinary business should not be hampered by government interference. It was finally agreed that, in matters of naval and foreign policy, an Admiralty and Foreign Office veto should apply, and the contract was approved in May.[34] Subsequently, however, the Admiralty tested the fuel oil and discovered it was below naval specification: its viscosity was too high. This property presented no difficulty in warm climates, but in cool temperatures the oil would have to be heated.

None of these revelations undermined Churchill's support for government ties with APOC. But the House of Commons debate of June 1914 has been characterized as 'conspicuous for emotion rather than reason'.[35] Britain was so preoccupied by naval security that MPs barely noted the oil coming from south Persia. Some newspapers criticized Churchill, and *The Times*, reversing its position of the year before, now described the government's investment in APOC as an 'impetuous and careless undertaking'.[36]

WHITEHALL'S WAR AGAINST THE TURKISH EMPIRE

The assassination of the heir to the Austro-Hungarian throne, in Sarajevo at the end of June 1914, precipitated a further Balkan crisis and led, in early August, to the outbreak of war throughout Europe. Although there were immediate repercussions for Anglo-Ottoman relations, Britain did not officially declare war on the Turks until early November. During the preceding three months, however, the Admiralty, Foreign Office, War Office and India Office anticipated war against the Turks and prepared for its extension into the Middle East.

At the end of July, Churchill, as first lord of the Admiralty, prevented Turkey from taking possession of two battleships commissioned from a British shipyard. The Turks had paid £3.7 million for the two ships, the *Reshadiye* and *Sultan Osman,* and a crew of 500 was already preparing to sail to Constantinople. British sailors boarded the vessels to prevent the hoisting of the Turkish flag, and despite official protests the ships were requisitioned by the Admiralty without compensation.[37]

Churchill's rashness was matched in Constantinople by that of Enver Pasha, the pro-German minister of war. Enver's negotiations led to the signing in early August of a secret treaty with Germany by which Berlin agreed to support the Turks if they declared war on Russia. Since Enver did not speak for the Turkish government as a whole, and since his treaty had not committed Turkey to war, the Turks were free to announce their official neutrality once Russia, France and Britain had declared war on Germany and Austria-Hungary.

A naval incident soon provoked the British. In mid-August the German ships, *Goeben* and *Breslau*, escaped into the Turkish Straits while pursued by the British Mediterranean fleet. Under the conventions of war, enemy ships could not remain in neutral waters for more than twenty-four hours without giving cause for war, so the German ambassador in Constantinople immediately announced that the ships had been 'sold' to the Turks. On hearing the news, Churchill ordered a British blockade of the Mediterranean entrance to the Dardanelles. Grey demanded the expulsion of the German crew while Enver defiantly gave the ships Turkish names, designated the chief German officer 'commander of the Ottoman fleet', and had the German sailors don fezzes.

Once again the Foreign Office did nothing to ease the crisis. When it was discussed in cabinet, Churchill's action was opposed by Kitchener, now at the War Office, and Lord Crewe (1858–1945), at the India Office. Asquith noted that:

> Winston, in his most bellicose mood, is all for sending a torpedo flotilla through the Dardanelles to threaten if necessary to sink the *Goeben* and her consort. Crewe and Kitchener were very much against it. In the interests of the Mussulmans in India and Egypt they are against our doing anything at all which could be interpreted as meaning that we are taking the initiative against Turkey. She ought to be compelled to strike the first blow. I agreed to this.[38]

If Turkey were to 'strike the first blow', the extension of the war would be easier to justify.

Churchill then embarked on some personal diplomacy. Having met Enver in 1910, he wrote to him of his 'personal regard' for the Turkish war minister, but reminded him of the 'overwhelming superiority' of the Allied navies: 'If they were forced into a quarrel with Turkey, their blow could be delivered at the heart.' Enver did not reply, and Churchill then proposed to accept the support of the Greek army in attacking the Dardanelles. Lloyd George approved, but Grey feared Russian opposition and Kitchener had reservations.[39] In late August, Asquith noted the various positions of his cabinet colleagues: 'Winston violently anti-Turk'; 'Kitchener strong that Rumania is the real pivot of the situation'; 'Lloyd George keen for Balkan confederation'; and 'Grey judicious and critical all round'. Noting that the rest of the cabinet was mostly 'silent and bewildered', Asquith passed the responsibility to his foreign secretary.[40]

28 Germany's *Goeben* flying the Turkish flag after escaping its British pursuers, entering neutral waters at the Turkish Straits, and being 'sold' to the Turks in August, 1914.

29 Churchill, first lord of the Admiralty, with General Ian Hamilton during army manoeuvres in 1913. Two years later, many Londoners would blame the Gallipoli disaster on these two men.

Grey adopted an uncompromising stance in discussions with the Russian and French ambassadors. Russia, already pressed by the German army, did not wish to face Turkey as well and urged that its neutrality be encouraged by guaranteeing its territory, modifying the capitulations as a first step towards abolition, rescinding Germany's economic concessions (including the Baghdad Railway), and returning an island Greece had recently acquired from Turkey. To strengthen Russia's resolve, Grey promised it Constantinople, as formalized in the Declaration of London, signed secretly at the beginning of September. Later that month Turkey announced it was closing the straits. British ships were patrolling the Mediterranean and Russian the Black Sea. When Churchill authorized a British warship to stop and search a Turkish vessel, the diplomatic and naval breach between the British and Turkish empires was complete.[41]

Whitehall's officals prepared for war against the Turks. But so long as Muslim pilgrims could reach Mecca, Britain appeared unconcerned about the threat of pan-Islamic action. Some officals preferred to think that war would open new options in relation to the Arabs and allow the settling of old scores with the Turks in the Persian Gulf.

Early in September Churchill dispatched three ships to protect the oil refinery at Abadan. At the same time officials in the India Office began devising plans for the Indian army to occupy the port of Basra. 'Of the various objects to be attained by sending a force up the Gulf, I have always regarded the moral effect on the Arab chiefs as the primary and the protection of the oil stores as the secondary,' wrote the Secretary of State for India to the viceroy.[42] The viceroy's initial reluctance was overcome when Lord Crewe permitted the government of India full discretion over operational details, and promised full support from the Admiralty. By mid-October an Indian expeditionary force, originally destined for France, landed on the island of Bahrein and, once war broke out, proceeded to the head of the Gulf.

To supplement military preparations, the India Office initiated closer diplomatic ties with Arab chiefs in the Gulf, including the sheikh of Kuwait, the first openly to sign a treaty of alliance with the British. An Indian political officer, William Shakespear, was instructed to persuade Ibn Sa'ud, the leader of Nejd and head of the puritanical Wahhabis, to ensure that no Arabs sided with the Turks against Britain. Captain Shakespear did his duty, but in 1915 was killed by a swordsman identified with Ibn Rashid, a pro-Turkish rival of Ibn Sa'ud.

While the tactics of the Indian government were to negotiate individually with Arab chiefs, Kitchener proposed a more ambitious approach. In September he initiated secret talks with Abdullah, one of the sons of Husayn, the eldest of the Quraysh descendants of the Prophet seen by some as the founder of the Hashemite dynasty. In this case Grey deferred to Kitchener's experience, approving a letter to Husayn – to be delivered upon the outbreak of war with Turkey – offering support to Arabia provided 'the Arab nation assists England in this war, that has been forced upon us by Turkey'. The letter even held out the possibility of Husayn succeeding to the caliphate: 'It may be that an Arab of true race will assume the Caliphate at Mecca or Medina and so good may come by the help of God out of all the evil which is now occurring.'[43]

By early autumn Whitehall too was preparing its Egyptian officers for war with Turkey. Naval patrols in the Suez Canal were increased, and a deliberately defensive posture assumed on the west side of the canal. In August the Egyptian Council of Ministers had decreed that, since Egypt was deemed to be at war, Egyptian citizens were prohibited from activities on behalf of Britain's enemies. The khedive remained at Constantinople, and the Egyptian Legislative Assembly, due to meet in November, was proprogued.

When war broke out in Europe, the British ambassador to Constantinople had been at his post for under a year. Mallet, a bureaucrat rather than a diplomat, and formerly Grey's private secretary, warned in mid-October that the impulse towards a Turkish war might simply be a German tactic to divert Russia and Britain from the war in Europe. But the insight came too late to make any difference: London had, for months if not years, been geared up for war against the Turks.

WARTIME CENSORSHIP

After £(T)2 million in gold had reached Constantinople from Berlin in mid-October 1914, Enver Pasha ordered the German commander of the Turkish fleet to commence naval manoeuvres in the Black Sea. On 29 October the Turkish navy bombarded the Russian port of Odessa. Within two days telegrams were dispatched to officers in the Middle East, and a week later Britain officially declared war against the Turks.[44]

The navy took steps immediately to demonstrate its paramountcy throughout the eastern Mediterranean, Persian Gulf and Red Sea. On 3 November Churchill ordered British and French battleships to fire on the outer forts of the Dardanelles in order to test the range of Turkish guns on the Gallipoli peninsula. On 5 November British ships forced their way past the only Turkish fort guarding the entrance to the Shatt-al-Arab, preparing the way for a British expedition which captured Basra in only two days.

Anglo-Indian troops easily overcame the Turkish irregulars, whom they outnumbered almost ten to one; the Turks had only one gunboat on which to retreat up the River Tigris. On 22 November British troops hoisted the Union Jack over Basra. A proclamation, read by Sir Percy Cox (1864–1937), the chief political officer of the expedition, blamed Germany for tricking the Turks into war, reassured the residents that Islam would be respected and that they were 'at full liberty' to pursue their lives 'as usual', something of an impossibility given the presence of 10,000

30 Immediately upon the outbreak of war with the Turks in 1914, the British occupied Basra, the small port at the head of the Persian Gulf. This view is of Basra's shipping quarter.

Anglo-Indian troops. On 23 November Cox urged the British to proceed immediately to Baghdad, though they lacked the troops, transport and supplies for the 350-mile journey to be feasible.[45]

Much more was involved in maintaining British interests at the Suez Canal and in Egypt than in protecting its assets at the Persian Gulf. On 1 November British troops marched through the streets of Cairo; the following day Egypt was placed under martial law; and on 5 November Britain declared it would bear 'the entire responsibility for the war without calling on the aid of the Egyptian people'.[46] The country was not proclaimed a protectorate until late December, when the khedive had been deposed and his pro-British uncle installed as the sultan of Egypt. No such ceremony took place when the British annexed Cyprus. The colonial secretary in Whitehall simply issued a formal order in council to this effect on 6 November.[47]

In London, censorship had been imposed upon the outbreak of war in Europe, and all references to Turkish neutrality had been prohibited since early September. The news embargo abruptly ended at the end of October, however, when in its 30 October issue, *The Times,* under the headline 'Turks Enter the War', declared that 'the opinion of competent judges of Ottoman affairs' was that 'the clique of Judaeo-Ottoman desperadoes known as the C.U.P. has, for a year past, been bent on war'. Dark hints of a 'Judaeo-Turco-Austrian-German plan' were also floated. The

31   A Poy cartoon of Churchill, at the Admiralty, Kitchener at the War Office, and Lloyd
George, chancellor of the Exchequer, singing confidently of the war in November, 1914.

next day the paper told its readers not to be concerned about the Turkish
army, for which 'immense deductions' should be made because of its
'lethargy, want of money, intrigues, and every sort of embarrassment'.
Such propaganda helped prepare public opinion for the formal British
declaration of war on Turkey of 6 November.[48]

The first public statement about the extension of the war to the Middle
East came from the prime minister on 9 November, when he spoke at the
annual banquet of the City of London at the Guildhall. This civic ritual
had survived the Napoleonic, Crimean and South African wars, and there
seemed no reason for it not to take place in 1914.[49] After an elaborate
dinner came the toasts. Balfour, member of parliament for the City of
London, proposed the first: 'To our Allies', which was followed by toasts
for Japan, Russia, France and Serbia, the loudest cheer being for Belgium.
After the French ambassador responded briefly for the Allies, toasts were
then proposed to 'the imperial forces of the Crown' and 'his majesty's
ministers'.

In his address, Asquith passed quickly over the events of the first
hundred days of the war, and the crisis in the Balkans that had precipitated
it. He took time to voice his disappointment with the Turks for allowing
'their true interests to be undermined and overborne by German threats,

by German ships, by German gold'. Criticizing the 'lawless bombardment of Russian ports' and Turkish 'intrusion into Egyptian territory', which had forced Britain and her Allies into war, Asquith added that it was 'not the Turkish people' but its government that had 'drawn the sword' and 'rung the death knell of Ottoman dominion, not only in Europe, but in Asia'. The conclusion of his speech was dramatic: 'The Turkish Empire has committed suicide.'[50]

Two days later, on 11 November, the opening day of the new session of Parliament, the government released a white paper entitled 'Correspondence Respecting Events leading to the Rupture of Relations with Turkey'. The document consisted of 184 telegraphic messages exchanged between Grey, as foreign secretary, and Mallet, ambassador in Constantinople, carefully selected to highlight the deterioration in Anglo-Turkish relations since August, and the patient and conciliatory attitude of the Foreign Office in the face of provocative action by the German-dominated Turks. There was no reference to Grey's secret diplomacy with the French and Russian ambassadors in London, nor any indication of the extensive military and political preparations initiated by Churchill, Kitchener and others.[51]

At two o'clock that afternoon the king read his address to Parliament. The queen and her ladies-in-waiting were dressed in mourning for the war casualties, and khaki made its first appearance in the House of Lords. The central paragraph of the unusually brief speech referred to the recent extension of the war into the Middle East:

> Since I last addressed you, the area of the war has been enlarged by the participation in the struggle of the Ottoman Empire. In conjunction with my Allies, and in spite of repeated and continuous provocations, I strove to preserve, in regard to Turkey, a friendly neutrality. Bad counsels, and alien influences, have driven her into a policy of wanton and defiant aggression, and a state of war now exists between us. My Mussulman subjects know well that a rupture with Turkey has been forced upon me against My will, and I recognise with appreciation and gratitude the proofs, which they have hastened to give, of their loyal devotion and support.[52]

The speech seconding the motion to approve the king's speech was delivered by Lord Bryce (1838–1922), the historian, statesman and former ambassador to Washington. Bryce was one of the country's greatest living jurists, and had championed the Armenians and other Ottoman minorities since the 1870s. Noting the extension of the war that he correctly predicted would be remembered as 'the World War', Bryce declared that the peoples of the Ottoman Empire envied those who benefited from British imperial administration. While he regretted the extension of the war on humanitarian grounds, he foresaw 'some compensations':

The Allied powers will now be able to deal more fully with the resettlement of South Eastern Europe and of Western Asia when the end of the war arrives and when the time comes for endeavouring to extinguish forever the oppression and maladministration from which both Mussulmans and Christians have alike too long suffered.[53]

Such sentiments would be shattered before Bryce's death in 1922.[54]

Chapter 5

The Empire Adrift: 1914–1916

BEFORE THE WAR British diplomacy had revolved around a careful balance between the Great Powers, each power maintaining its own defence establishment, cooperating with its allies, and compensating other countries with concessions outside Europe. The unprecedented scale and technological advance of the war between 1914 and 1916 set the British and other empires adrift.

At the end of 1914, with a military stalemate on the western front, Britain decided to strike in the east where the enemy was presumed to be weaker. Churchill led the argument for the unsuccessful Dardanelles naval expedition of 1915 which turned into the disastrous military campaign on the Gallipoli peninsula. The extent of British losses against the Turks, and Bulgaria's decision to ally with the enemy, caused panic in Downing Street. The Cabinet supported a French-inspired expedition to Salonika, an Anglo-Indian advance on Baghdad, and a Cairo-conceived Arab revolt against the Turks. All these efforts failed. By 1916 the army was led by General Robertson, who brought order to the War Office. The tactics of General Haig, however, failed to defeat the enemy at the Somme, and further bloody offensives were required. Lloyd George replaced Asquith as prime minister at the end of 1916.

British policies in the Middle East reflected the course of the war. Expecting to defeat the Turks, Britain, along with Russia and France, provisionally partitioned the Turkish Empire and offered Turkish territory to Italy and Greece as an inducement to join the Allies. In the event, the Foreign Office supported an Arab revolt against the Turks. Reports of the massacre of Armenians made little impression in Britain where war censorship and propaganda screened the news presented to a public far more preoccupied with the enormous casualties of the western front.

ASQUITH, LLOYD GEORGE AND THE WAR POLICY COMMITTEES

The war brought Asquith, and from December 1916 Lloyd George, unprecedented problems in relation to the Middle East. Neither man had military experience, but even those who did were unprepared for the enormous size of the forces and equipment, the modern shelling of the artillery that made offensives so costly, and the tactics that pitted huge

32   Asquith, prime minister, watching soldiers adjust fuses near the western front in August, 1916. Asquith failed to steer an effective course between Westerner and Easterner war strategists.

armies against each other in a grotesque stalemate which lasted until 1918, when the Allies finally pushed through German lines. Asquith and Lloyd George were also unprepared for the huge demands on the economy and the social pressures generated by the war. Neither prime minister favoured increasing state power, but in practice both greatly extended wartime controls. Both led coalition governments but gained advantage over the City, Parliament and the press. Neither however could dictate to the army, in particular the general staff and the commander of the western front.

The effectiveness of Middle Eastern policy depended not only on winning the war but on broader issues involving Britain's place as a global economic force, an imperial power in Asia and Africa, and a state with ties to the dominions. Such questions were debated by war policy committees in Downing Street, by interdepartmental committees in Whitehall, and by Allied conferences in London and abroad.[1] The first of the war policy committees was set up by Asquith in November 1914. By the time he ceased to be prime minister at the end of 1916, the committees had supplemented, and virtually displaced, the cabinet. Modelled on the CID (Committee of Imperial Defence), established by Balfour in 1902, Asquith's committees were run along very similar lines.[2] He used them, as he had used the CID before the war, to explore options and consolidate support. Where a committee could not agree, Asquith would postpone consideration to a later meeting or find a way, outside the conference room, to achieve his goal. Policy decisions were often phrased vaguely so as not to offend members who disagreed. And when problems arose, Asquith deftly engineered a solution, working through other committee members to achieve a consensus. His mental agility might perhaps have prompted more searching questions about the actual conditions in the field; he might also have demanded more of his ministers. But his caution as a war leader may indeed account for his political survival: in the spring of 1915 Asquith withstood a crisis, precipitated by a shortage of shells and the resignation of Admiral Fisher, by forming a coalition with the Conservative and Liberal parties, while during the winter of 1915–16 he survived disastrous campaigns in the Near and Middle East initiated by his committees.

The effectiveness of the war policy committees improved after Kitchener was replaced at the War Office by General Robertson, the commander of the general staff. Asquith's War Committee met six or seven times a month during 1916, often enough to keep members abreast of the military and political situation, but not so often as to distract ministers from their departmental duties. The meetings themselves were well organized: an agenda and background papers were distributed in advance, and individual members alerted when items specifically relevant to them were to be discussed. The prime minister usually opened meetings by asking Robertson to report on the latest military position. Discussions then focused on the five or six core items of the agenda, covering specific military, naval, financial, diplomatic and political problems. After the meeting, copies of relevant conclusions were circulated to appropriate departments, the heads of which were held accountable to the War Committee.[3]

The operation of the war policy committees favoured politicians over military officers more accustomed to action than to debate. Admiral John Fisher, commenting on his own experiences in 1915, when he resigned as first sea lord, observed that: 'When sailors get round a Council Board they are almost invariably mute. The politicians who are round that board are not mute; they never would have got there if they had been mute.'[4] Kitchener in particular felt at a disadvantage, and his 'loud, staccato voice' and 'that remote look in his eyes' bothered Lloyd George.[5]

The behaviour of other leading figures can be characterized briefly. Churchill and Lloyd George were bold, but sometimes naive, in committee. In a diary entry at the end of February 1915 Asquith noted: 'Our two rhetoricians, Lloyd George and Winston, . . . have good brains of different types, but they can only think talking; just as some people can only think writing. Only the salt of the earth can think inside and the bulk of men cannot think at all.'[6] Grey, in failing health, was often absent, and

Lord Crewe generally deputized as chairman when the prime minister was away. Balfour, detached from the new Conservative leadership, contributed cogent commentary on the Middle East, yet lacked the influence and the will to persuade the committee to heed his advice.

William Robertson (1860–1933), the first chief of the general staff to rise from the ranks, was son of a Scottish villager. After six years in India, building a reputation as a military administrator, he served in France until recalled to London. Though supported by Asquith, Robertson's stubborn concentration on the western front angered Lloyd George, who conflicted with him also on Middle Eastern policy.

When, towards the end of 1916, Asquith refused to let him chair the war policy committee, Lloyd George gathered sufficient Conservative support to form a new coalition and handpick a new war cabinet. Until then, however, Asquith's War Committee had avoided glaring error. Asquith avoided the mistakes that Lloyd George's war cabinet would make in 1917 and Curzon's Eastern Committee in 1918 and 1919. Lloyd George and Curzon often bypassed Whitehall and allowed excessive discretion to British officers and officials in the Middle East. Instead of drifting and then suddenly overreacting to events – as in 1914 and 1915 – or letting the war in the Middle East generate its own momentum – as would happen from 1917 to 1920 – Asquith's Middle East policy was limited to defending British wartime interests.

WESTERN VERSUS EASTERN STRATEGY

Since the defeat of Napoleon in 1815, Britain had aggressively protected its overseas empire and cautiously sought a balance of power in Europe, both policies presuming British naval and economic superiority. According to the so-called 'blue water' school of strategy, naval power could make Britain virtually unassailable. Britain hence took sides in Continental diplomacy, but tried to avoid committing troops to Europe. No British expeditionary forces had been sent to the continent since the Crimean War.

Most military leaders in Britain, particularly those involved in the western theatre, argued that the defeat of Germany required victory in western Europe. Other theatres of war were less important, and some even dismissed the British battles in Asia and Africa as 'side shows'. In the view of Admiral Fisher, any attempt to destroy Germany by defeating the Turks would merely represent cutting off a German toe.[7] Strategists consistently argued that operations in the east created logistical problems, overburdened shipping, drained the empire of its manpower, and distracted war leaders from the enemy's main thrust on the western front. British politicians, on the other hand, were more concerned about the stalemate on the western front and the mounting casualties arising from outmoded tactics. They sought less costly breakthroughs in other theatres.

33 Aerial view of the pyramids south of Cairo, showing a German aircraft on the right. Britain maintained overwhelming aerial, as well as naval and military, superiority in the region.

Some historians have described all opponents of the Western strategy as followers of an Eastern bloc policy, but there was in fact no unanimity among Britain's Easterners: Balkanists favoured the isolation of Germany from Austria and Turkey by gaining allies in the Balkans; Indianists believed that an Anglo-Indian defeat of the Turks would ease pressure on Russia in the Caucasus and on other fronts; Hellenists were confident that the allies and Greece would take Constantinople; Arabists believed the Arabs could harry the Turks and free Britain from war in the Middle East; and Zionists anticipated Jewish support for the allies in Russia and the United States. To these disparate strategies would be added a variety of Eastern agendas later urged by Imperialists, Dominionists and Internationalists. Conspicuously absent from Britain's Eastern strategists were the Russianists, despite the fact that Germany directed its main campaign in the East against the tsarist empire.

Historians will continue to debate the war strategy, but during the 1914–18 war, British policymaking shifted from a Western to an Eastern orientation in response to the actual war situation. By the end of 1914, with the stalemate on the western front, Asquith agreed to initiate operations in the East. But after the failure of the Dardanelles/Gallipoli and Salonika expeditions in the last half of 1915 and of the Baghdad offensive early in 1916, Asquith agreed to the concentration of resources on the western front.[8]

DISASTERS AT THE DARDANELLES AND ON GALLIPOLI

The failure of the naval expedition to the Turkish Straits and the disastrous campaign on the Gallipoli peninsula during 1915 is a well-known chapter in the history of the First World War. Historians have generally applauded the strategy and condemned the execution. Churchill's political career was very nearly ruined by the episode. The focus here will not only be Churchill, but also the role of various members of Asquith's war committees.

Frustration in Downing Street over the military situation on the western front surfaced at Christmas 1914, when some members of the cabinet began to concede that the war would last longer than all but Kitchener had anticipated. Proposals for strategic alternatives proliferated. Lloyd George wrote a memo in favour of a military offensive in the Near East as a prelude to a Balkan Confederation in association with the Allies, or for a direct attack against the Turks on the coast of Syria. Sharing some of his Balkanist enthusiasms, Maurice Hankey (1877–1963), the naval officer who served as the secretary of the CID, produced an extended paper recommending that joint naval and military operations be undertaken at the Dardanelles. Balfour agreed with Hankey that, while subsidiary to the main Western theatre, such an attack could have 'very valuable results'. Hankey's suggestion rekindled Churchill's interest in the Dardanelles, hitherto closed to the British navy.[9]

Early in 1915 Churchill pursued the issue with support from the tsar and from Admiral Sackville Carden (1857–1930), commander of the Mediterranean entrance to the straits. On 2 January he learned that the tsar had personally appealed to Kitchener for help against the Turks in the Caucasus. He discussed the tsar's request with Grey and Kitchener, who agreed to inform Russia that Britain would initiate some kind of diversion against the Turks. Aware of Kitchener's reluctance to commit troops, Churchill wired Admiral Carden the same day, asking if the British navy itself could force the Dardanelles. The next day Carden responded: 'I do not consider the Dardanelles can be rushed. They might be forced by extended operations with large numbers of ships.' That afternoon, at Asquith's War Council, and again at a dinner hosted that evening by Churchill for Asquith at Admiralty House, the first lord discussed the Dardanelles. 'Your view is agreed with by high authorities here,' Churchill wired Carden, requesting him to make a detailed proposal. The admiral's plan, which arrived on 12 January, recommended the bombarding of the outer and inner forts of the Gallipoli peninsula and then, once the minesweepers had done their job, advancing through the narrows to the

34 Churchill, first lord of the Admiralty,
and Fisher, former First sea lord, leaving a
meeting of the Committee of Imperial
Defence in 1913, before differing on the
Dardanelles and Gallipoli.

Sea of Marmara. Delighted with the possibility of such a brilliant stroke,
Churchill urged the War Council to approve the naval bombardment of
the Gallipoli peninsula in February.

By the end of January, however, the War Council had become divided
over the Dardanelles expedition. Fisher had second thoughts about
Carden's plans; he submitted a long memo, and excused himself from
further War Council discussions. The Council, however, agreed that the
navy should begin operations in mid-February and that, later in the spring,
British troops should be sent to Salonika to support Serbia and induce
Bulgaria to join the war against Turkey. Dissension then emerged between
Lloyd George and Churchill, the latter wanting British soldiers for the
Dardanelles expedition and the former preferring to retain troops for
Salonika in the event that Carden's plan failed. Meanwhile, Kitchener
resented the interference of politicians in what he felt was a military
matter. When he advised delay, the prime minister agreed.[10]

From the first the expedition made very disappointing progress: in late

35 The Allied naval expedition at the Dardanelles, which the Turks mined, and the campaign for the Gallipoli peninsula, where Turkish gunners shot at landing troops. London gave up in 1915.

February two British ships were destroyed and another severely damaged, yet more and more troops were dispatched to the scene. What had begun in the winter as an auxiliary force to support a naval expedition had turned into a complicated peninsular campaign. The pivotal responsibility was that of the commander-in-chief, General Ian Hamilton (1853–1947), whose campaign in Gallipoli achieved even poorer results than Carden's Dardanelles expedition: the number of army casualties reached thousands during the spring and tens of thousands by summer.[11] The Gallipoli operations had been hastily planned, ill-coordinated, inadequately supplied, and badly led. Hamilton had been inadequately briefed by Kitchener, with little intelligence and an incompetent staff. Unaware of enemy dispositions, he drew up elaborate arrangements for British troops to land simultaneously at several points along the shores of Gallipoli, while French forces were to land at the same time on the Asiatic side of the straits. Disembarkations went well, but too many men landed at Cape Helles, on the southern tip of the peninsula, and far too few were sent to the western coasts of Gallipoli. Moreover, Turkish soldiers positioned in the peninsular hills held defensive advantages.

Downing Street remained confident despite heavy casualties and calls for reinforcements. But on 13 May the *Goliath*, with its crew of 600 men, was sunk. Asquith convened a meeting of the War Council at which Fisher demanded retrenchment and the recall of other naval vessels. The same afternoon Fisher confirmed detailed arrangements for the withdrawal with the Admiralty, but discovered the following morning that Churchill had subsequently amended the naval lists, adding ships and supplies. Infuriated, Fisher resigned.[12]

36 Anzac troops photographed on board ship before landing at Gallipoli on 25 April 1915, a date commemorated annually in Australia and New Zealand in memory of the men lost.

Fisher's resignation prompted criticism at Westminster, but Asquith and Lloyd George made a shrewd political move. Forming a coalition with the Conservatives on a minor Admiralty issue to head off a full-scale attack on the government, Asquith appointed Lloyd George to head a new Ministry of Munitions, and invited the leader of the Conservatives, Andrew Bonar Law (1858–1923), to join a coalition government. Bonar Law secured Churchill's dismissal from the Admiralty and replacement by Balfour. Conservatives were also appointed to the Colonial and India Offices, but the main portfolios remained in Liberal hands.[13]

Far from altering the course of British operations in the Dardanelles, the new coalition endorsed the existing policy. Asquith established a new war policy committee, the Dardanelles Committee, the first meeting of which was held not at Downing Street but in the prime minister's room at Westminster, a gesture to accommodate the Conservatives.

During the summer of 1915 Asquith continued to support Kitchener, who had outlined the alternatives facing the British at Gallipoli: withdrawal, the immediate commitment of further troops, or the continuation of Hamilton's present course. Under pressure from generals on the western front and lacking sufficient forces for a major assault on Gallipoli,

Kitchener recommended the third option. Churchill, demoted to the post of Chancellor of the Duchy of Lancaster, but still on the Dardanelles Committee, favoured a major offensive at Gallipoli. Lloyd George remained concerned for the Balkans, where he felt Allied military force would keep Bulgaria out of the clutches of the Central Powers. While the Dardanelles Committee debated, Kitchener sent five further divisions to Gallipoli. Hamilton refused a Turkish request to bury their dead, a needless barbarism that only increased the hideousness of a sweltering battleground rife with insects and disease. Sick soldiers were transported to Egypt, where they were jammed into overcrowded hospitals and hastily converted hotels.

With the failure of the spring offensive in France, the Dardanelles Committee authorized the transfer of troops from the Western Front to the East. By August casualties had reached close on 100,000. Blaming London for underestimating the Turks, Hamilton requested 40,000 further men to replace those lost in August, as well as an additional 50,000 reinforcements to continue the campaign.[14]

SALONIKA AND BAGHDAD

Downing Street was shaken from its stupor over Gallipoli when Bulgaria joined the enemy at the end of the summer. Bulgaria was the missing link that joined the German, Austrian and Turkish empires – the *Drang nach Osten* that Fleet Street had dreaded before the war. Given the seriousness of the Allied war situation and the removal of Asquith's direction – through ill health – in the autumn of 1915, differences sharpened, with politicians, soldiers, and bureaucrats blaming each other for past failures. Along with the Admiralty, Balfour and Churchill favoured the maintenance of a military presence in the Dardanelles, while the general staff sought a withdrawal from the peninsula. By the time Asquith had sided with the evacuationists, other disagreements had surfaced. Balkanists regarded the Allied position in the Near East as so precarious that they pushed for an immediate military offensive to be launched from Greece. With his earlier hopes for a Balkan Confederation blocked by Grey's Great Power diplomacy, Lloyd George persuaded Asquith to overrule Whitehall and support a French-led expedition from the port of Salonika. At the same time, Indianists proposed an Anglo-Indian advance to Baghdad, a step encouraged by the India Office and the Foreign Office.

To understand the proliferation of committees that produced such divergent opinions on the Near and Middle East, the sheer variety of meetings that took place in Downing Street and Whitehall during the latter part of 1915 should be considered. Apart from the cabinet, there were Asquith's high-level war policy committees, and the unwieldy Dardanelles Committee, renamed the War Committee in October. There were also special cabinet subcommittees on the general war effort, various interdepartmental committees set up in Whitehall to deal with specific problems in the East, and military and diplomatic conferences with the Allies before and after the formation of the new French government at the end of October. In addition, there were meetings held within the War Office, Admiralty, Foreign Office and India Office where departments might pursue their own policies without cabinet approval. The volume of information coming from officials in the Near and Middle East and the level of discussion within Whitehall reached fever pitch.[15]

The Balkanist case remained closely linked to the Gallipoli campaign. The war policy committee met at the end of September to consider the announcement of Bulgaria's mobilization, the Greek prime minister's request for Allied troops to support its own and Serbia's defences against Bulgaria, and the French plan for an Allied landing at Salonika. Lloyd George had seen his hopes for a British-backed confederation of Balkan states ignored by Grey's diplomacy early in 1915, and his worst fears about Bulgaria were confirmed in the autumn. In a combative cabinet perfor-mance, he voiced his fears of the future, not only in the Balkans but throughout the East, unless something was done. Grey agreed that an Allied landing would bring Greece into the war but once again repeated a Great Power argument that the British could hardly refuse to support the French in Salonika after the French had joined the British Dardanelles project earlier in the year. Asquith's committee eventually authorized 'the temporary diversion' of British troops from Gallipoli to Salonika. The Balkanists thought Asquith lukewarm, while the Indianists, Dardanelles diehards and Gallipoli evacuationists all believed that he had made a serious blunder in transferring British soldiers from the Gallipoli peninsula to Salonika.[16]

Before the French and British could land at Salonika, the Greek alliance evaporated as the pro-Allied prime minister faced a showdown with the pro-German king. Ignoring the king, the Anglo-French landing in early October brought down the Greek premier. No amount of diplomatic pressure, or threats, or the offer of the island of Cyprus, mollified the Greek king. Bonar Law and Edward Carson (1854–1935), the leading Conservative critics of Gallipoli, were so enraged by the Balkan situation that they found themselves, with Lloyd George, attacking Grey for not having forced Greece's hand, and blaming Asquith for abandoning the Serbs to a Bulgarian onslaught.

The embarrassment at Salonika provided diehards such as Churchill, Kitchener and Balfour with others to blame. Balfour criticized the French for having foolishly abandoned the Dardanelles for the Balkans, proposing instead that France be responsible for the defence of the Balkans while Britain guarded Gallipoli. Churchill and Kitchener predicted a collapse in British prestige in the East as British troops were drained from Gallipoli to Salonika. Churchill offered a novel suggestion to the war policy committee, that he hoped 'the unreasonable prejudice against the use of gas upon the Turks' would cease, for the 'winter season is frequently marked by south-westerly gales, which would afford a perfect opportunity for the employment of gas by us'.[17]

The Salonika disgrace empowered the general staff within the War Office to press for the replacement of Hamilton by Charles Monro (1860–1929), an officer who shared their view of eastern operations as distractions from the main theatre on the western front. Monro proceeded at once to Gallipoli and soon made recommendations congenial to the military strategists.

At the beginning of November Asquith took decisive steps on the Eastern and Anglo-French dilemmas, as well as on the heated issue of conscription and the general criticism of his conduct of the war. He forfeited the support only of Carson (the most impatient Gallipoli evacuationist in the coalition) and Churchill (the most stubborn Dardanelles diehard). Kitchener remained within the government, despite his reluctance to evacuate Gallipoli, and after a strong performance in the House of Commons at the beginning of November, was sent on a special mission to the Mediterranean. Asquith himself took over the War Office, and established a small new War Committee, which would meet regularly and frequently throughout 1916, and which would eventually authorize the successful evacuation of Gallipoli. At the end of 1915, when the Greek king demanded the withdrawal of Allied troops from Salonika, most members of the War Committee would have been happy to comply. But the idea of evacuation was adamantly resisted by the French, supported by Russia, and Asquith was compelled to acquiesce once again by the constraints of Great Power diplomacy. The significance of such political manoeuvring was lost on the troops, stationed in the mountains north of Salonika, who froze in their summerweight Gallipoli uniforms under tents without poles.[18]

The single bright spot on the eastern horizon for Downing Street during the latter part of 1915 was Anglo-Indian success at the head of the Persian Gulf. The government of India had transformed the Basra expedition into the Mesopotamian campaign – the British in India replacing 'Iraq', the Arabic name for the province, with the biblical term 'Mesopotamia'. The government of India ordered General John Nixon (1857–1921) to secure oil pipelines, take control of 'the whole of Lower Mesopotamia', and plan for a 'subsequent advance to Baghdad'.

Lord Hardinge, the Foreign Office mandarin who had become viceroy of India in 1910, staked India's security on the campaign in Mesopotamia. In April 1915 he wrote to his Foreign Office colleague, the permanent undersecretary, Arthur Nicolson, anticipating a Russian belt through Armenian territory and the acquisition by Britain of the lion's share of Asiatic Turkey. In September Hardinge responded to Nicolson's 'gloomy reading' about Gallipoli, but anticipated good news from Kut, the last stop before Baghdad:

37   Lord Kitchener at Sedd–el–Bahr, on the south tip of Gallipoli, late in 1915, before evacuating the peninsula. McMahon, the high commissioner in Egypt, is the tall man on the right.

38   Troops from India aboard a Persian Gulf transport en route to the Mesopotamian campaign in 1915. India's soldiers, workers, and taxpayers had played a major part in the war in the Middle East.

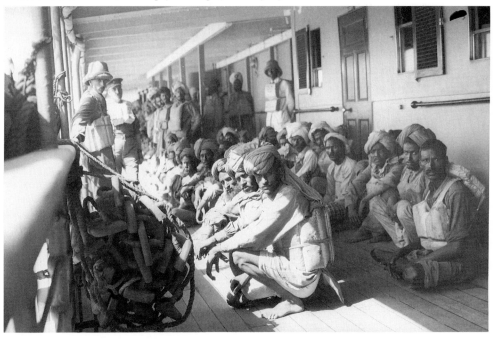

39 General Townshend at Kut.

The capture of Baghdad would, from our point of view and that of
Persia and Afghanistan, have a far greater effect than the capture of the
Straits and Constantinople, and I am not sure that it will not be done.
Had the Dardanelles and Constantinople fallen, I always counted on
Baghdad falling like a ripe plum into our lap.[19]

Support for the advance to Baghdad was virtually unanimous within
London, although some raised questions about what the soldiers would do
once they arrived. An interdepartmental committee in Whitehall
considered whether such an advance was 'strategically and politically
expedient'. It met on three occasions early in October, considering
submissions from General Nixon which ignored the misgivings of General
Charles Townshend (1861–1924), the officer deputed to lead the Baghdad
offensive. The committee urged Nixon to go ahead with the troops he
had, acknowledging that he might require reinforcements if he were
expected to hold Baghdad.[20]
   Kitchener supported the advance to Baghdad on the grounds that
British forces could raid the city for anything of military value. Indignant,
Lord Curzon, the former viceroy of India who had resigned after a
showdown with Kitchener in 1905, expressed dread at the 'spectacle' of
British soldiers in retreat from Baghdad. Curzon declared he was 'nervous'
about holding Baghdad: 'If the Germans and Turks pushed eastwards, our
position would be precarious, and retirement would counteract our

momentary advantage.' Curzon's misgivings were ignored by Downing Street, desperate to recover the prestige squandered in the Dardanelles and Gallipoli.[21]

In the event the Anglo-Indian advance to Baghdad did not live up to expectations. General Townshend's division encountered strong opposition at Ctesiphon, the ancient capital of the Sassanid Empire, whose ruins lay between Kut and Baghdad, which had been reinforced by a Turkish division. Having lost more than a third of his division in casualties, Townshend retreated to Kut early in December 1915. When three Anglo-Indian rescue missions dispatched early in 1916 had failed to reach Kut, Nixon resigned for reasons of 'ill-health'. After being besieged by the Turks for several months, Townshend and his men ran out of food, fuel, and medicine. In April Britain surrendered Kut. Townshend and his officers were transported to Constantinople, while the remaining soldiers were left to reach Baghdad on foot.

THE ARABS AND ALLIED SECRET DIPLOMACY

Britain's war with the Turkish Empire introduced the possibility of an Arab rebellion against their imperial overlords. The Arabs, who since the death of the prophet Muhammad in the seventh century had rarely been united, were dominated by the Turkish military for over a thousand years. British political officers of the Government of India had made treaties with Arab chieftains along the eastern coast of the Arabian peninsula, and more recently the British in Egypt and Sudan had made contact with Arab leaders in the western part of the peninsula and Arab army officers in Syria and Iraq. While officers in Egypt and Sudan were eager to involve Arabs in the war, the Anglo-Indians remained sceptical.[22]

Kitchener was the first major figure in London to be clearly identified as an Arabist. After he had moved to the War Office, he maintained communication with British officers in Cairo and Khartoum who saw him as their spokesman in London. During the autumn of 1914, as we have seen, Grey approved Kitchener's suggestion that Cairo should make overtures to Husayn, the sharif of Mecca and a leader of the Hashemite clan.

In April and May 1915, while Britain anticipated success at the Dardanelles and Gallipoli, Asquith established an interdepartmental Whitehall committee to consider strategies for the future of Turkish Asia. The committee was headed by Maurice de Bunsen (1852–1932), former British ambassador to Vienna, who presided over thirteen meetings with representatives of the Admiralty and Foreign, India and War offices. The committee produced voluminous papers, maps and a final report of 20,000 words.[23]

Mark Sykes (1879–1919), as Kitchener's representative, assumed an important role in the committee and indeed influenced Arab affairs, Allied

40   Mark Sykes.

diplomacy and Middle Eastern policy for the remainder of the war. Sykes
was a restless man in his mid thirties, heir to a baronetcy and a large estate
in the north of England, a military officer and a Conservative MP since
1911. He had travelled throughout the Ottoman Empire, ridden horseback
through much of Anatolia, Syria and Iraq, learned Arabic and Turkish, and
published a number of articles and books on the Middle East. Sykes much
preferred the traditional religious and tribal leaders he had encountered in
the Asiatic countryside to the cosmopolitan Levantines he met in eastern
cities. He argued that Britain should not abandon the Ottoman Empire,
where 'Turco-German' agents had fomented trouble, and he disliked the
idea of partitioning the empire – or dividing it into spheres of interest –
because this would bring Russian paramountcy in the northern Asiatic
belt, French predominance in the middle area, and leave the British
confined to the south.[24]

Sykes' recommendation to the de Bunsen Committee envisaged the
end of the Ottoman Empire in southwestern Asia. To replace Ottoman
rule Sykes proposed five 'historical and ethnographical provinces', namely
Turkey, Syria, Palestine, Mesopotamia and the Arabian peninsula, which
he saw as free from 'the vampire-hold' of Constantinople and the 'competition' of European powers. Once his work for the committee was

completed, Sykes undertook an intelligence mission for Kitchener. At Gallipoli, Egypt, India and Mesopotamia, he interviewed deserters from the Turkish army as well as captured prisoners and war refugees.[25]

The Foreign Office, meanwhile, maintained communication with the sharif of Mecca. In July Husayn asked the British to recognize what he called 'the Arab nation', specifying it as the territory between the Mediterranean and the Persian border from the Anatolian peninsula and along the 37th parallel south to the coasts of the Arabian peninsula. In return 'the Sharifian Arab Government' would 'grant Great Britain preference in all economic enterprises in the Arab countries'. With London still contemplating victory over the Turks at Gallipoli, the Foreign Office was unreceptive to Husayn's demands and declared that negotiations over 'frontiers and boundaries' appeared 'premature'.

By autumn 1915, however, when Britain faced failure at Gallipoli and had seen Bulgaria join the enemy, Kitchener and Grey reassessed the position in the hope that an anticipated British military victory at Baghdad might induce Husayn to join the Allies. Grey authorized Cairo to accept his terms, apart from districts along the coast of Syria which the French had long claimed, and the British sphere in the Persian Gulf up to Baghdad. Husayn however refused to concede any of Syria and expected compensation from the British for their claims in the gulf.[26]

In November 1915 Nicolson convened a committee at the Foreign Office made up of representatives of the Admiralty, India Office and War Office. At its second meeting, a French representative was invited to present his country's territorial demands and to react to Cairo's correspondence. François Georges-Picot, who had served as French consul in Beirut before the war and then worked on Syrian and Palestinian affairs for the French foreign ministry, disliked the Arab scheme. The Foreign Office had stressed in communications with Mecca that Syria required 'careful consideration' since 'the interests of their ally France are involved', adding that British recognition of Arab claims after the war would be contingent upon assistance in defeating the Turks. Sykes, having returned to London, was invited to attend the committee's meeting with Picot, learning that Paris was receptive to the Arab scheme provided the French had complete control over the Mediterranean coast and exclusive administrative influence over the Arabs in the Syrian and Palestinian hinterland. Nicolson asked Sykes and Picot to work on the Arab scheme in detail.[27]

Sykes, the amateur, supplied the rhetorical and geopolitical flourishes to the partnership, while Picot deftly protected French interests. France demanded, and obtained, the island of Cyprus, occupied by the British since 1878, in exchange for Britain's acquisition of the Palestinian port of Haifa. The Sykes-Picot memo envisaged a 'confederation of Arab States', under the 'suzerainty' of an unnamed 'Arabian prince'. Area A, along the Mediterranean coast of Syria and Palestine, would come under direct French rule. Area B, from the head of the Persian Gulf to Baghdad and beyond, would come under British control. In a Blue Area adjacent to A and a Red Area next to B, France and Britain would respectively 'establish such direct or indirect administration or control as they desire'. Dividing the French A and Blue areas from the British B and Red areas was a diagonal line running northeasterly from the port of Haifa to Baghdad, along which the British could build a railway. Finally, a Brown Area around Jerusalem was set aside for 'an international administration', in the light of specific 'requirements':

(a) that the Latin and Orthodox religions receive equal consideration in Palestine.
(b) that members of the Jewish community throughout the world be permitted a conscientious and sentimental interest in the future of the country.
(c) that the mosque of Omar represents, next to Mecca, the most holy and venerable shrine in Islam, and . . . should be under the sole control of Moslems; and that the chief of the Arabian confederation should have an equal voice in the administration of Palestine.[28]

Sykes and Picot's memo was handed to Nicolson, who sought to allay Whitehall's misgivings that the proposals unduly favoured the French. At the final meeting of his committee in January 1916, Nicolson reminded British officials: 'If the Arab scheme fails, the whole scheme will also fail and the French and British Governments would then be free to make any new claims.'[29] In February the scheme was submitted to Asquith's cabinet, and referred to a cabinet subcommittee chaired by Lord Crewe that made no further changes and authorized the Foreign Office to proceed to gain Russia's consent.[30]

Sykes, seconded from the War Office to the Foreign Office, proceeded with Picot to St Petersburg. Despite having met Herbert Samuel (1870–1963), the Liberal home secretary, who, as a prominent Jew, had explained Zionist aspirations in Palestine to Asquith's cabinet, Sykes was unreceptive to Zionism. But in Russia, the fate of the large, downtrodden Jewish population impressed him deeply. When Sykes observed that Zionism could be 'something with which to dazzle Jewish opinion', Nicolson requested him to keep such thoughts to himself. At the end of April the French ambassador in St Petersburg and the Russian foreign secretary exchanged formal notes dividing Asiatic Turkey between the two countries.[31] The final exchanges between the French and Russian ambassadors were handled by Grey in May 1916, though the agreement between the Allies remained secret until the end of 1917.[32] But when, in autumn 1916, the Italian ambassador in London learned of the agreement, he demanded Allied recognition of Italian territorial ambitions in the Turkish Empire. At that point, neither Britain nor Russia wanted to negotiate with the Italians, while France was strongly opposed to Italian claims on the

41   T. E. Lawrence with Arabs at Akaba. He needed a guard since the explosion of Turkish railways and other acts funded by Cairo's Arab Bureau led Turkey to put a price on his head.

Anatolian peninsula which conflicted with French interests in the coal-rich areas of Asia Minor. Grey informed the Italian ambassador that if Italy expected to be treated as a Great Power, then it would have to fight like one against Germany.[33]

In June 1916, supporters of the sharif of Mecca took up arms at Medina and openly declared war against the Turks. Although these rebels had been armed and subsidized by the new Arab Bureau, set up in Cairo by the British earlier that year, the rebellion took London by surprise. Husayn demanded and received a monthly subsidy of £125,000, approved by Asquith's War Committee but paid for by the government of Egypt. In October, when Husayn declared himself 'king of the Arabs', Grey met the French ambassador in London and approved only the more limited designation of 'king of the Hejaz'.[34]

THE GENERAL STAFF'S OPPOSITION TO 'SIDE-SHOWS'

When Robertson became chief of the general staff at the end of 1915, he insisted that all military orders should go through his office. He not only corrected Kitchener's maladministration of the War Office but also resisted demands from Asquith's War Committee to take more action in the East. Although successful in restraining interference in the Middle East, he failed to halt continued British military participation in the Balkans. To facilitate Allied cooperation, Robertson sent his personal representatives to leading commanders in France, Russia and Italy. And, before agreeing to lead the general staff, Robertson insisted that he, rather than the secretary of state for war, should appoint all leading commanders. Asquith agreed, having already named General Douglas Haig (1861–1928), a man with a tough reputation in the army, to command British forces in France. Haig's appointment turned out to be one of the most critical of the war.

In the spring of 1916, Robertson recommended that the British concentrate on a western offensive, discontinue operations in Salonika, and maintain military activities in all other active non-European theatres. Asquith's War Committee, however, deferring to French wishes, disagreed, and postponed Haig's spring offensive. Robertson criticized the Foreign Office for 'taking too modest a view of our own powers and abilities, while exaggerating those of our Allies', and recommended several further diplomatic initiatives, such as the signing of a peace agreement with Turkey at Russia's expense and detaching Bulgaria from Germany at the cost of Greece and Turkey, each a suggestion of breathtaking boldness.[35]

Resistance to Robertson was shaken at the end of February when Germany attacked Verdun. The development made the War Committee acutely conscious of the vulnerability of the French Briand government, which had initiated the Salonika expedition the previous autumn, and for which the expedition was, in Asquith's words, 'a question of life or death'. Robertson had to content himself with Haig's plans for the Somme in the summer of 1916.

Early in 1916 Robertson appointed a new commander for Egypt, General Archibald Murray (1860–1945). Murray refused to panic over rumours that Turkey would dispatch 300,000 men against Suez and that Senussi tribesmen would threaten Egypt from the west. Two small Turkish demonstrations in Sinai early in 1916 were easily crushed, and Senussi raids were also stopped later in the year. To avoid having to station large numbers of men on the west side of the Suez Canal, Murray sent small sorties into Sinai to destroy wells that the Turks would need if they were to attack Egypt. These and other changes in Egypt enabled six divisions to be sent to France in March and four more in June. In addition to the troops transferred to Salonika, the number of British soldiers in Egypt was cut from over 400,000 to fewer than 200,000.

Following the failure to capture Baghdad, the War Committee agreed that the Anglo-Indian operations should come under War Office control. Robertson attached no importance to Kut or Baghdad, but India's Mesopotamian fiasco had resulted in over 40,000 casualties. Despite the protests of Indianist strategists, Robertson ordered Anglo-Indian forces to remain on the defensive and, in the event of Turkish attack, to retreat.

Robertson consistently opposed large-scale operations in the Middle East. Learning that Russia was able to police northern Persia by means of small, well-equipped tribal bands, Robertson proposed that the British do the same in south Persia. The War Committee approved the recommendation, leading to the formation of the South Persian Rifles, eventually numbering 11,000 troops. This innovation was later copied in Baluchistan and on the Afghan border, in what was called the Eastern Persian Cordon. Robertson subsequently took control of operations in Mesopotamia by placing General Stanley Maude (1864–1917) in command. And Robertson named General Monro, who had led the evacuation of Gallipoli, commander of the army in India. None of the three new commanders would exaggerate the threat in the East. Nor would they allow the British army to be distracted from the critical western front.

Kitchener was drowned en route for Russia in June 1916. Asquith appointed a reluctant Lloyd George to take his place as secretary of state for war. Asquith hoped Lloyd George's distrust of soldiers would diminish as he worked more closely with the chief of the general staff and that Robertson would learn to cooperate more readily with politicians. The hopes, however, remained unfulfilled.

Beyond the War Office, Robertson's power depended on the prime minister. Asquith trusted him and took his policy recommendations seriously, but never allowed Robertson to dictate to the War Committee. The mutual respect and understanding between the two men were necessary, if not sufficient, conditions for the successful prosecution of the war.[36]

In the latter part of September 1916, Haig's offensive on the Somme proceeded with awful slowness and brought enormous British, and in particular Canadian, casualties. Asquith's most brilliant son, Raymond, was killed, and another was invalided during the Gallipoli campaign.

During Asquith's brief absence from the War Committee, Bonar Law took the chair. Eastern strategists bristled when Robertson submitted a memo noting that, since the British did not have enough men to occupy Baghdad, they should confine their operations to Basra. Nor could he understand why 100,000 British troops should be tied up holding back only 40,000 Turks. Austen Chamberlain (1863–1937), secretary of state at the India Office, and Lord Curzon, former viceroy of India, now directing the Air Board, took the Indianist line, Curzon reversing his position of the year before and urging the taking of Baghdad. Asquith was back as chairman when the War Committee next discussed the Middle East at the end of September. Robertson's opposition to a British expedition to support the Arab Revolt was strengthened when the Hashemite's forces successfully defeated the Turks at Taif, a town in the mountainous heights south of Jeddah. In addition, officials in Egypt and the Sudan reported that the mere presence of British troops in the Arabian peninsula would identify Husayn so strongly with the British that the Arabs might turn against him, and the government of India repeated its reluctance to send

Europeans near the Muslim holy places. Finally, the British naval commander in the Red Sea reported that he could handle the situation there without British troops. Robertson, however, was less successful in his attempt to reduce further the British presence in Mesopotamia, where the War Committee preferred to keep the door to Baghdad ajar.[37]

The compromises between Robertson and the Eastern strategists, so grudgingly agreed in September, soon became impossible to sustain. Frustration mounted in the War Committee after the bloody battle on the Somme and after the Anglo-French effort in Macedonia had failed to rescue Rumania from Bulgarian attack. In October Robertson infuriated Lloyd George by stubbornly resisting his demand that reinforcements be sent to the Balkans, and in November Lloyd George declared Robertson personally responsible for British casualties on the Somme, which had exceeded 400,000 men.

Asquith and his fellow members of the War Committee were unable or unwilling to reduce the animus between Lloyd George and Robertson. All shared some of the responsibility for destroying the most effective policy-making body of the coalition, but Lloyd George was the most aggressive member to force the strategic issue and the one most willing to circumvent the committee itself. In mid-November Robertson attended the long-awaited conference with Allied military representatives at Chantilly, which merely called for the renewal of the Somme campaign early in 1917. At the same time, Asquith and Lloyd George met French politicians in Paris and commiserated over their generals. Lloyd George returned to London determined to find supporters for the establishment of a smaller war policy committee, over which he was to preside even while Asquith remained prime minister.

At the next meeting of the War Committee, an acrimonious debate erupted over whether the British should agree to the sending of a French brigade to Rabegh, the Red Sea port where most of Husayn's stores were located. Arabist and Indianist strategists tried to use the presence of the French troops to force Robertson to allow British troops on the Arabian peninsula. Robertson was supported by a young officer attached to the Arab Bureau, one T. E. Lawrence (1888–1935), the future 'Lawrence of Arabia', who argued that the presence of either British or French forces would turn the 3,000 to 4,000 Arabian tribesmen against Husayn. Chamberlain, then head of the India Office, questioned Lawrence's evidence, and subsequent discussion of the issue set the individual members of the War Committee at each others' throats. Chamberlain and Curzon refused to let the French send a brigade to Rabegh; Lloyd George attacked them for their 'dog-in-the-manger policy to keep the French from going, if we did not go ourselves'. Robertson said that if the British 'had to send one brigade, he would rather send our brigade alone, after the Salonika experience'. This was to be the last time the War Committee discussed the Arabs.[38]

If Asquith's war policy committee could not agree on a minor matter such as Rabegh, it was difficult to see how it could deal with more fundamental and pressing questions such as future operations in France, reverses in Russia and the Balkans, German submarines menacing the British navy, and indeed the entire campaign against Germany. Many memoirs, biographies and histories have provided detailed accounts of the fall of Asquith and rise of Lloyd George in late November and early December 1916. It is clear, however, that much depended upon the strategic dilemmas that divided Western and Eastern strategists, the feud between Lloyd George and Robertson, and the inability of Asquith to settle such differences after the horrors of the Somme.

Lloyd George's request to chair a new war committee offered one solution to the crisis in war policy. Asquith at first acceded but then withdrew his support in the belief that the Liberals had more political support than in fact they did. It was a profound miscalculation by the consummate manager of parliamentary and cabinet politics. Lloyd George, seeking Conservative support both inside and outside the coalition, destroyed Asquith's premiership. The irony was that Lloyd George displaced neither Robertson's general staff nor Haig's command. As prime minister, he would find himself making many of the same compromises with Western strategists that he had previously refused to accept when minister of munitions and war.

NORTHCLIFFE'S PRESS AND WARTIME COVER-UPS

The newspapers owned by Lord Northcliffe (1865–1922) included the establishment *Times* and the popular *Daily Mail*. Both publications reduced their criticism of the conduct of the war while, in the summer of 1915, seeking to recover some of the prestige lost after the unpatriotic exposure of the shells shortage on the western front. That autumn *The Times* criticized Asquith's leadership in Gallipoli, and the *Daily Mail* outspokenly blamed him for the confusion in the Balkans, although war censorship, in line with the Defence of the Realm Act, kept the worst of the eastern embarrassment from public awareness.

British hostility towards the Turks was greatly reinforced by reports of the Armenian massacres of 1915. In the autumn, Lord Bryce announced that as many as 800,000 Armenians were reported killed.[39] But since there was little precise information, the general response was muted. Fleet Street, in any case, had a good deal of other material to use as war propaganda. Of the terrible plight of the Armenians, *The Economist* observed, cryptically: 'It is, we trust, the last crime of an expiring Turkey – an atrocity on a scale which even this war will hardly reproduce.'[40] In general even the fate of the Armenians and the evacuation of Gallipoli did not move public opinion as deeply as the growing lists of war casualties on the Western Front, lists

42   Emaciated Armenian victims of the Turks during World War I, the first genocide of the twentieth century. This photograph was taken from the kit of a captured Turkish soldier.

which appeared in such fine print in the newspapers that readers needed a magnifying glass to spot the names of individuals.

When the British had been forced to surrender at Kut in the spring of 1916, Parliament pressed for the publication of government papers on Mesopotamia. The release of selected papers on that campaign prompted a parliamentary demand for a similar publication of documents relating to the Dardanelles. In June Bonar Law announced that these would be released, except for those of 'so confidential a character that they ought not to be published' or those which were 'still going on'.[41] To counter further suspicion, Asquith appointed commissions on Mesopotamia and the Dardanelles, which were to conduct their investigations in secret and report back to Westminster. Witnesses would appear on a voluntary basis and their testimony kept confidential. Asquith's manoeuvre avoided a full parliamentary enquiry, for which there were two unsettling precedents: one during the Napoleonic Wars, which had preoccupied Parliament for several months, and the other, during and after the Crimean War, which had brought down Aberdeen's government.

As the Dardanelles Commission was beginning its investigation in September 1916, Hankey, as secretary of the War Committee, reported that the commissioners had requested minutes of the war policy committees. Hankey informed the commissioners that since his minutes 'had not been checked by the members and were in fact only his impressions', he did not see that they 'had much value as evidence'. Curzon thought that releasing the minutes was 'out of the question'. Lloyd George suggested that the commissioners might be permitted to see Hankey's minutes and curtly observed that the Dardanelles Commission was 'a Court of Enquiry which was going to pillory them all'. He added that he would like to see Hankey's minutes before appearing before the commissioners in order 'to refresh his memory'. When Grey remarked that he was 'not going to refresh his', Balfour observed that it was 'probable that the commission would ask him to do so'. By the next War Committee meeting, Asquith had drafted the government's refusal to disclose Hankey's minutes on the grounds that this would compromise the principle of collective cabinet responsibility.[42]

The non-controversial report of the Dardanelles Commission was published only in March 1917. Meeting only twenty times and calling few witnesses, the commissioners readily accepted Hankey's explanation of the expedition. The report accepted his argument about the higher organization of the war, his narrative of events, and his disingenuous account of British diplomacy toward Russia and Bulgaria, and differed from Hankey only in its more critical assessment of Churchill and Fisher. The horrors of Gallipoli were not included in the report, although John Masefield's *Gallipoli,* published in October 1916, was reprinted three times before the end of the year.[43]

The report of the Mesopotamian Commission was issued in July 1917. Meeting sixty times and calling over a hundred witnesses, the commissioners made a more comprehensive study of the Anglo-Indian campaign than the Dardanelles Commission had undertaken. Hankey allowed it sufficient information to criticize errors of judgement and faulty organization. But it failed to query the justification for the Baghdad offensive any more than commissioners had questioned the rationale for the Dardanelles expedition. In the midst of war, few dared to question what their leaders were doing.[44]

After the death of Kitchener, London needed a new hero. When Lloyd George succeeded him as secretary of state for war in June 1916, Northcliffe's newspapers were happy to turn him into their man of the hour since no British generals seemed about to fill the void. The morning after Lloyd George had formed his new coalition, in early December 1916, *The Times* led with an editorial celebrating 'the new determination of a united people to secure an efficient Government for war and the belief he can give it to them'. The same piece applauded the departure of Asquith: 'The exclusive regime of Tadpole and Taper is no more.'[45] Fleet Street rallied the country around the new prime minister in the expectation that he was the only man in London who could lead the British to victory.

Chapter 6

War Imperatives: 1916–1918

LLOYD GEORGE TRIED but failed to wrest power from the generals by concentrating policymaking in his new smaller War Cabinet, special committees, and the Supreme War Council at Versailles. The new prime minister was more attuned to the dominions and the United States than to Great Power diplomacy. Since the United States was not at war with the Turks, this limited Lloyd George's plans for the Middle East; nevertheless, he backed the Balfour Declaration in the expectation that it would increase support from American Jews for the Allied war effort. After the British reached Baghdad and Jerusalem in 1917, Lloyd George was unable to ensure that these victories were followed by a routing of the Turks to force them out of the war. Russia's withdrawal from war and the Bolsheviks' publication of secret agreements created new imperatives for British wartime diplomacy. Persisting with the Middle East campaign, Lloyd George declared new war aims and encouraged propaganda in line with the ideology of national self-determination. Secretly he authorized two abortive attempts to bribe the Turks into making a separate peace.

Lloyd George was as frustrated as the generals by the continuation of the slaughter in France and Belgium, the collapse of Russia in 1917, the five German western offensives during the spring and early summer of 1918, and the massive fighting on the western front in the last months of the war. In the autumn of 1918 the French-led victory in the Balkans caused Bulgaria to surrender and proved more decisive than any British operation against the Turks. With Lloyd George severely critical of French leaders as the war ended, severe armistice terms were imposed on the Turks, which Constantinople quickly accepted. What kind of Middle East would emerge from the defeat of the Turks could not be foreseen.

GROWING DEPENDENCE ON THE UNITED STATES

As the power of Russia and France declined during the course of the war, Britain increasingly relied on the United States while making even greater demands on the Empire and its own resources. US supplies had become vital even before April 1917 when the United States declared war against Germany. Although the United States did not participate in the campaigns of the Near and Middle East, Britain's increased economic, naval and military dependence on it still affected Allied war aims and propaganda in the Middle East.

Only after the United States entered the war could the Treasury obtain war loans directly from the US government rather than relying upon American private investment. For the Admiralty, the end of US neutrality meant fuller Anglo-American cooperation in resisting German submarine warfare, the most obvious common threat. Although American troops were not absorbed into Allied armies or commanded by Allied officers as those of the British dominions had been, and although American soldiers were not engaged in combat on the western front until 1918, most of London's policymakers believed that American involvement in the war effort would ultimately lead to an Allied victory.[1]

It is important to appreciate how commercially and financially dependent on the United States Britain and the Allies became during the war. In the autumn of 1914 the British began purchasing goods, including rifles, from US manufacturers eager for the business. The neutrality of the US government did not block purchases by any belligerent state since such sales were regarded as purely commercial and distinct from US diplomatic relations. American brokers and agents offered their services for high fees. Purchasing became so chaotic that Downing Street determined that all Admiralty and War Office ordering in the United States should be funnelled through a single purchasing agency and that all financing should be concentrated in one banking firm.

In January 1915 Asquith's government selected J. P. Morgan in New York, the banker's banker and a Wall Street leader, for this purpose. New York Morgan was linked to Morgan, Grenfell in London and to Morgan, Harjes in Paris. Downing Street had confidence in New York Morgan because of the Anglophilia of the Morgan family and because the senior partners in New York and London owned stock in the other two Morgan companies. In May 1915, when the Ministry of Munitions was established, the ties between the British government and New York Morgan strengthened. By the end of 1916 Lloyd George's new department had placed munitions orders exceeding $20 billion in the United States. The funds New York Morgan realized from these sales helped the British government finance its war purchases, because New York Morgan advanced funds to Britain with a 2 per cent interest rate for loans on demand.[2]

Since the British government received no loans or grants from the US government while America remained neutral, London had to depend on the private money market in New York, particularly New York Morgan. Having to purchase US munitions, food and other supplies for Britain as well as for its allies, the British Treasury took out loans at 5 to 5.5 per cent interest, borrowing on collateral that was being rapidly depleted. By the autumn of 1916 the Treasury recognized that of the £5 million then required daily for the war, £2 million had to be found in North America.

When Britain issued unsecured treasury bills and the US government disapproved of them, the bills found few American buyers. New York Morgan was able to slow runs on the British pound, but this led Britain to accumulate such immense bank overdrafts that London had to cease placing orders in America. A 1916 agreement required all British-owned securities in the United States to be deposited with the US Treasury. Such stiff new terms on further British loans immediately attracted many more American subscribers.

Critics in the City of London blamed New York Morgan for precipitating the crises and some Fleet Street journalists suspected US financiers of profiteering from Allied vulnerability, but in fact the huge cost of the war had simply overwhelmed British financial resources. Although the crisis had passed by early 1917, Britain's financial situation remained precarious. In February, when Germany threatened unrestricted submarine warfare and Washington almost immediately severed diplomatic relations with Berlin, Lloyd George's coalition sighed with relief. Downing Street knew it needed to survive financially only until the entry of the United States into the war, when it would start to make public loans to meet British and Allied war needs.

In April and May 1917 Britain sent the first of a succession of missions, led by Balfour and Northcliffe among others, to North America to highlight the importance of North America to the British Isles and Europe. By the end of 1917 virtually nothing could be purchased in the United States or paid for by the British government without the permission or aid of the US government. 'The implications for the relationship between the two governments was soon obvious,' noted Kathleen Burk in 1985: 'The British were now very much dependent on the Americans, rather as the French, Russians, and Italians had been on the British.'[3]

British economic dependency can be demonstrated statistically, and simply. The British public debt in the United States soared between 1915 to 1920, with the amounts outstanding at the end of each financial year expressed in millions of pounds, as follows:

1915–16	1916–17	1917–18	1918–19	1919–20
£61.7m	£303.6m	£757.3m	£1,027.3m	£1,036.9m

During 1917 and 1918 the US government advanced over $4 billion in cash and almost $5 billion in materials to Britain. Yet, there were huge deficits in the Exchequer from 1914 to 1919, which are shown here in millions of pounds:

1914–15	1915–16	1916–17	1917–18	1918–19
£333.8m	£1,222.4m	£1,624.7m	£1,989m	£1,609.3m

43 The US entry into the war in April 1917 gave the Allies an immediate financial boost, though no Americans fought in Europe until 1918. The US never declared war on the Turks.

Although the Exchequer went increasingly into debt, Anglo-American financial circles never allowed the pound/dollar exchange rate to drop more than a few cents, from a high of $4.85 3/4 in 1915 to a low in 1918 of $4.76 7/16. Thus, while the City of London lost its financial pre-eminence to Wall Street in the last years of the war, international capitalism survived the war quite well.[4]

LLOYD GEORGE'S WIZARDRY

The political dexterity of the 'Welsh Wizard', his openness to innovations at the Ministry of Munitions and his success in swaying public opinion, have been well recognized by historians. Less attention has been paid, however, to his policymaking failures and his administrative blunders during the last two years of the war.

Lloyd George was far less experienced in foreign affairs and defence matters than his Conservative colleagues, who remained committed to prewar assumptions about the balance of power. Less tied to the past, Lloyd George tended to deal pragmatically with the present. The strengths and weaknesses of the prime minister and his predominantly Conservative colleagues are evident in their handling of British policy towards the Near and Middle East.

Lloyd George kept the ministers within his coalition and the premiers of the British dominions unified despite their many differences. He remained far more convinced of the importance of Anglo-French operations in the Balkans than his colleagues, most of whom preferred to leave the Near Eastern theatre to the French in order to concentrate British resources in the Middle East. More quickly, if not more willingly than most of his colleagues, Lloyd George adapted British war aims to the new internationalism established by the US president, Woodrow Wilson. In 1917 Lloyd George launched a National War Aims campaign, and in 1918 set up a new Department of Information to supplement the task of censorship undertaken by the Press Bureau since 1914. He persuaded public opinion at home and abroad that the British were liberating the world from the menace of 'the terrible Turk' and were supporting Arabs, Armenians, Greeks and Zionists. Yet, as Whitehall sometimes warned, propaganda aroused expectations that the British might find impossible to fulfil after the war.

Lloyd George's persistence as an Eastern strategist has already been observed in his exasperation with those who supported the western front, his support of British operations in the Dardanelles, Salonika and Mesopotamia, and his lack of attention to the Russian sphere.[5] His strategic thinking sprang not simply from his wartime experience but also from his ignorance of war strategy and disgust for most of the generals. He did not subscribe to prewar assumptions about the balance of power, neither was he a Germanophobe, Francophile or Russophile, as were some in the Foreign Office. And, unlike army officers, Lloyd George had not been 'toughened' by battlefield experience. The more the casualties mounted in Flanders and France, the more the whisky-drinking generals from privileged backgrounds offended the teetotal prime minister.

Lloyd George's impatience with the unimaginative and costly tactics used on the western front contributed to his personal determination to find ways to defeat the enemy in the East. Assuming that the enemy should be attacked where it was most vulnerable, Lloyd George failed to appreciate that the axiom is not universally applicable. Mistakenly regarding the enemy front as a more or less continuous line stretching from Belgium through the Balkans to the Middle East, Lloyd George concluded that the enemy should be confronted wherever weakest along that line, that is in Austria-Hungary, Bulgaria or Turkey. Lloyd George's Easterner strategy – in all its Balkanist, Arabist, Zionist, Imperialist, Dominionist and Internationalist variations – was mistaken in that Germany was not as militarily dependent on its allies as Austria-Hungary, Bulgaria and Turkey were on Germany. He was not alone in this mistake, but he also underestimated the geographical obstacles of the mountainous Near East and the arid Middle East, failed to grasp the enormous logistical problems and costs that made Allied military advances in these regions so difficult and slow, undervalued the fighting determination of the Turks and Bulgarians, and gave too little consideration to the political problems that arose from war in the East. He assumed that such matters would not be settled until after the war had been won, when he expected them to be valuable bargaining items at the peace conference rather than merely grist to the British imperial mill.[6]

Lloyd George grew so inflexible over war strategy that he became increasingly intolerant of any officer, official or politician who disagreed with him. So blinded did he become to any faults in his plans for the Middle East that when the operations there consistently failed to make the Turks sue for peace, he blamed those who carried out his plans, rather than reconsidering the strategic assumptions upon which they were based. But others too were inflexible. Lloyd George at least recognized the importance of the Balkans rather more than his colleagues, most of whom were sceptical of the French-inspired expeditions based on Salonika and Lloyd George's own closeness to the Greek premier. However he, like most of his cabinet, never acknowledged that by consuming scarce resources in campaigns in the Near and Middle East during 1917 and 1918, the British were diverting resources from the more important theatres in Russia and France. Lloyd George would of course have been less adamantly opposed to the Western strategists if Allied military performance in France and Flanders had been more successful and less costly, or if there had been victories sooner than the late summer of 1918. The army suffered from its failure to break through German defences in 1917, with Haig sticking to his original tactics and Robertson clinging to the western strategy as tenaciously as Lloyd George clung to his.

By the final two years of the war, the Eastern-Western strategic deadlock had become a topic of London gossip and a matter of grave concern to the few military journalists who backed Haig and Robertson against Lloyd George. Personal and professional animosities between Lloyd George and Haig-Robertson heightened civilian-military rivalries. London's principal policymakers became so closely identified with what happened in the eastern and western battlefields that, despite wartime censorship, their careers and reputations depended integrally on military success.[7]

British policy towards the Middle East was also conditioned by the centralization of power during the war and by the personal style of Lloyd George's wartime leadership. The prime minister managed to exclude generals from cabinet and committee meetings, circumvent Whitehall offices through the use of interdepartmental ad hoc committees, gain the support of dominion politicians by consulting with them on a more regular basis, back Allied generals against British generals, countermand Haig and Robertson by setting up the new Supreme War Council at Versailles, undermine the Foreign Office through personal diplomacy, and deceive Parliament and the press. His machinations put himself and others under considerable stress. Too many important decisions were made by too few men.

Lloyd George initially appointed four others to the War Cabinet, within which he was the only Liberal member. Arthur Henderson (1863–1935) was chairman of the Parliamentary Labour party until he resigned in the summer of 1917, amid socialist demands for the revision of Allied war aims. Henderson's seat in the War Cabinet was eventually taken by George Barnes (1859–1940), who provided a continued token Labour presence. Lloyd George also appointed three Conservatives: Bonar Law, Milner and Curzon, who by and large supported the Middle Eastern thrust he gave to war policy.

Andrew Bonar Law, leader of the majority Conservative party, was also leader of the House of Commons and chancellor of the Exchequer. Born in Canada and educated in Glasgow, he had made a fortune in iron before entering Parliament and was staunchly committed to the union of Ireland with Great Britain. Neither aristocratic nor an old Tory, Bonar Law had powerful allies in Fleet Street, such as Max Aitken (later Lord Beaverbrook) who became London's leading press baron after Lord Northcliffe died in 1922. The Conservative leader usually agreed with Haig and Robertson, but concurred with Lloyd George over the need to defeat the Turks and Bulgarians before taking on Germany.

Alfred Lord Milner (1854–1925), high commissioner in South Africa during the Boer War, may have seemed a curious choice for the War Cabinet, especially since Lloyd George had censored Milner for using Chinese 'coolie' labour after the war finished in 1902. Yet Lloyd George appreciated that Milner was a hero to powerful financiers in the City and imperialists in Fleet Street. Moreover, throughout the dominions, Milner's name was familiar to the influential subscribers to *The Round Table*, the premier journal of the British Empire. As Milner had no political ambitions for himself, Lloyd George could count on his loyalty. The prime minister would find the former proconsul's shrewdness about generals helpful in critical showdowns with Haig and Robertson, and the military case Lloyd George put forward for British offensives in the Middle East was supported by Milner's imperialism.

Lord Curzon suffered from a spinal complaint and, wearing a brace, his stiff posture and strict formality made him appear pompous to those who did not know him. Distant from Balfour and Bonar Law and lacking popularity among Conservatives, Curzon accepted positions in Asquith's and Lloyd George's war coalitions because they provided opportunities his ambition for high office could not resist. With his extensive experience in the East, Curzon naturally took a special interest in the war against the

Turks but always gave way to Lloyd George. A workaholic, he was ever willing to go over the administrative problems that arose from British military occupation of so much of the Middle East during and after the war. Through his diligence Curzon expected to become indispensable to British efforts in the Middle East.

To facilitate the work of his War Cabinet, Lloyd George relied on machinery that had been established for the Committee of Imperial Defence before the war and further developed for Asquith's war policy committees in 1915 and 1916. Secretary Hankey remained at the head of the War Cabinet Secretariat but enlarged his staff, adding Mark Sykes, Tom Jones (1870–1955), a Welshman put up by Lloyd George, and Leopold Amery (1873–1955), a disciple of Milner. All three became assistant secretaries, with Sykes handling foreign affairs, Jones dealing with domestic problems, and Amery concentrating on the empire. Sykes edited the weekly *Eastern Report*, while Amery's *Western and Imperial Report* dealt with the rest of the world. When Professor 'Persian' Browne of Cambridge heard that Sykes and Amery were advising the War Cabinet, he warned the editor of the *Manchester Guardian* that the influence of these 'two ambitious young officers' was 'most dangerous'.[8]

Besides the War Cabinet Secretariat, Lloyd George had a personal staff, dubbed by the press the 'Garden Suburb' because their offices were located in temporary quarters on the lawn behind Downing Street. Lloyd George's staff mixed Welshmen with George Adams, Gladstone Professor of Politics at Oxford, Waldorf Astor, a millionaire newspaper proprietor, and Philip Kerr, another figure close to Milner. Kerr was the only member of Lloyd George's personal staff involved with Middle Eastern policy. Having travelled in the region before 1914, Kerr penned *Round Table* articles that envisaged a future world state which, like the British Empire, would supersede racial, national and geographical differences. Such high-minded views led Kerr to regard British expansion in the Middle East as a step towards a world state.[9]

Lloyd George was more contemptuous than confident of Whitehall, which seemed ineffective in waging war against the Turks. Prewar bureaucrats had done little for the massacred Bulgarians and Armenians, but the Foreign Office, India Office, Admiralty and War Office remained the instruments for executing British policies in the Middle East. With so strong-willed a prime minister, the Conservative ministers heading these departments often had their loyalty severely tested.

As foreign secretary, Balfour enjoyed considerable prestige at home and abroad. But on the most critical issues of war and peace, Lloyd George kept his own counsel and preferred himself to represent Britain at major wartime conferences. Balfour was nearly seventy when he took over at the Foreign Office, increasingly lacking both the energy and the inclination to confront the prime minister.

The India Office was at one point presided over by Austen

44   The Imperial War Cabinet posed in the garden behind 10 Downing Street in 1918. In the front row, third from left, is Bonar Law, with Lloyd George and dog in the centre; third from right is Balfour. Curzon, General Smuts and Chamberlain are at the centre of the second row, while Montagu is third from the right. Hankey and Amery are fourth and fifth from the right in the back row.

Chamberlain, second of the three Conservative leaders whose family fortune came from manufacturing screws in Birmingham. He resigned after publication of the scathing Mesopotamian Commission report in July 1917, his place being taken by Edwin Montagu (1879–1924), a Liberal partisan of Asquith who, as an assimilated English Jew, opposed Zionist aspirations in Palestine and, as head of the India Office, reiterated the government of India's fear of offending Muslims.

The service departments in Whitehall during the last two years of the war posed a nightmare for Lloyd George. The Conservatives who headed the Admiralty and the War Office duly issued War Cabinet orders to the first lord and the general staff, but the complex administration of naval and military operations was beyond the grasp of any one civilian.

OCCUPYING BAGHDAD AND JERUSALEM

At his very first meeting with the War Cabinet, on Saturday 9 December 1916, Lloyd George told General Robertson that he wanted British operations in Sinai accelerated in order to mount a great military offensive into Palestine and Syria. Lloyd George believed such an offensive would propel the Arabs outside the peninsula to rebel against the Turks. The following

45 The British officially entered Baghdad on 11 March 1917. This success encouraged Lloyd George and London's other Easterners to intensify efforts to force the Turks out of the war.

Monday Lloyd George returned to the general theme, leaving the details to the general staff.[10]

General Robertson had put Maude and Murray in charge of British expeditionary forces in Mesopotamia and Egypt. Both generals realized Robertson was opposed to taking troops from the western front for advances on Baghdad and Jerusalem, and both knew that London's Eastern strategists remained committed to recovering prestige lost in the Turkish capture of the British at Kut. By the end of 1916, Maude had organized the Mesopotamian Expeditionary Force into 150,000 fighting men, backed by 100,000 Indian forces at Basra. While Robertson had reluctantly agreed to an advance on Baghdad, he resisted a Palestine offensive. Murray reported that he would require two divisions from Mesopotamia, mounted troops from India and cavalry from France in order to push from the Sinai peninsula into Palestine.

At a post-Christmas conference in France and a subsequent meeting in Rome, Lloyd George failed to convince the Allies to back a Palestine-Syrian offensive. In turn, he opposed Haig's plan for a February campaign in Flanders and instead supported an April attack proposed by General Robert Georges Nivelle, the dashing French general who had recently succeeded General Joseph Joffre. Lloyd George thought he had got his way on the Nivelle offensive, but the War Cabinet agreed with Robertson that not only should Palestine be postponed, but also that one British division should be transferred from Egypt to France.

General Maude's early 1917 success in Mesopotamia rekindled Lloyd George's enthusiasm for eliminating the Turks from the war. The British incurred light casualties while pursuing the Turks up the River Tigris, capturing Kut in late February and advancing to Baghdad in early March. When the War Cabinet ordered Maude to 'exploit the recent operations to the fullest possible extent', his divisions moved so swiftly that British river-craft could scarcely keep up with them. The outnumbered Turkish forces withdrew to the north of Baghdad.[11]

The capture of Baghdad convinced some junior officers at Murray's headquarters in Cairo that the British should immediately engage the Turks in battle at Gaza and thus keep the Turks from withdrawing further into Palestine and being reinforced from Syria. In mid March, a British political officer from Egypt met Milner, who immediately wrote to Lloyd George that the young man had 'converted into a certainty a feeling wh[ich] has been so strong in me the last few days, that I have almost burst out with it several times, but felt that, with no jumping off place, I could not expect attention'. Urging the prime minister to spare half an hour to talk with this man 'straight from the spot', Milner asked rhetorically: 'Having got the Turk on the run, should we not keep him on the run?' As Milner might have anticipated, Lloyd George's War Cabinet immediately endorsed an advance into Gaza.[12]

Murray, moving his headquarters from Cairo to Sinai, authorized two mounted and one infantry division for the advance. His operations on Sinai had proceeded slowly throughout 1916, using forced Egyptian labour and pack animals to lay railway tracks and pipelines to supply the three British divisions in Sinai. But as caution was thrown to the wind, haste and faulty intelligence brought failure. At the end of March 1917 the British broke through all but one section of the Turkish line; but heavy fog and poor British communication allowed the Turks to destroy almost half a British division the second day. The First Battle of Gaza upset Robertson, but the War Cabinet ordered Murray to push onwards. In the three-day Second Battle of Gaza, the British lost 6,500 men – more than three times the number of Turkish casualties.

Lloyd George immediately decided to replace Murray with someone he thought more able. In the words of the War Cabinet, 'the moral and political advantages to be expected from an advance in Palestine, and particularly from the occupation of Jerusalem', would relieve 'the strain on the people of this country due to the War' and counteract 'the depressing influence of a difficult economic situation'.[13] The War Cabinet was alluding to German submarines that had destroyed so much British and Allied shipping that food shortages caused severe rationing early in 1917. Disappointment over Gaza, however, was soon lightened by the entry of the United States into the war.

Lloyd George's hopes of defeating the Turks were raised even higher during the spring meeting of dominion leaders, designated the first Imperial War Conference, and the first such meeting since 1911. In addition to the South African troops in southeast and southwest Africa, the dominions had sent two and a quarter million men to Europe and the Middle East (one and a quarter million from India and a million from Australia, Canada and New Zealand). War Cabinet meetings were scheduled on alternate mornings to those of the Imperial War Conference, while Lloyd George and members of the War Cabinet spent much of their afternoons and evenings speaking and dining with dominion leaders.

The discussion was frank. A subcommittee, named 'Territorial Desiderata in the Terms of Peace', and chaired by Curzon, included representatives from Canada, Newfoundland, New Zealand, Nova Scotia and India as well as relevant Whitehall officials. Curzon informed his subcommittee of the secret Allied agreements the Foreign Office had negotiated and stated that the 'French were very jealously attempting to peg out claims'. He believed that 'the only safe settlement was that Palestine should be included in a British Protectorate'. Curzon concluded that the British had to emerge from the war paramount throughout the southern part of the Ottoman Asiatic provinces and must also retain the island of Cyprus and control as much of Persia as possible. South Africa's General Jan Smuts (1870–1950) agreed with Curzon about the importance of Palestine for defending Egypt, protecting the Suez Canal and securing British communication, and Curzon's committee was willing to pursue a separate peace with Bulgaria or Austria, but not with Turkey.[14]

There could be no operations against the Turks during the heat of the summer, but the War Cabinet did not alter its outlook towards the Middle East despite historically significant developments in Russia, France and the Balkans during the spring of 1917. In March, widespread strikes and riots in Russia had encouraged mutinies throughout the ravaged army, leading to the creation of a provisional government and the abdication of the tsar. At this time the upheavals in Russia were of less immediate concern to London than the situation in France. By May 1917 the French government had dismissed General Nivelle, whose spring offensive had failed disastrously, with mutinies in over half the 112 divisions of the French arm, 629 soldiers being court-martialled, and 75 executed by firing squads. The Balkan crisis arose from the failure of a spring Allied offensive against Bulgaria. The Allied naval blockade imposed on Greece, the confiscation of Thessaly's harvests since 1916, and a French ultimatum issued to Greece in June 1917 had, however, forced the abdication of the pro-German king, Constantine. The pro-Allied Elutherios Venizelos then took power and led Greece into the Allied camp.

In May Curzon chaired a further War Cabinet subcommittee to consider the effect of a Russian withdrawal. In the light of recent failures in the Balkans and at Gaza, General Robertson recommended that the Macedonian campaign be completely turned over to the French, that Maude remain in Baghdad and that British forces remain in Sinai. As first sea lord, John Jellicoe (1859–1935) protested against the heavy demands being made on British shipping in the eastern Mediterranean. Since the

British had lost 875,000 tons of shipping to German submarine attacks in the Atlantic and North Sea during the month of April alone, Jellicoe insisted that the British navy concentrate in home waters so as to meet the civilian as well as the military needs of Britain and France.[15]

Curzon acknowledged such military and naval considerations but argued that the British would be in 'extreme danger' if Palestine were not secured, since a

> teutonised Turkey, left in possession of Asia Minor . . . and of Syria and Palestine even if the British remained in occupation of Mesopotamia, would involve a perpetual menace to Egypt, the disappearance of the Arab Kingdom of the Hedjaz, and the grave peril of the British position at Baghdad. If Russia went out of the war in the course of the summer, the danger in Palestine would become one of immediate urgency, since but little time would be left to defeat the Turkish army now in Palestine, before it was powerfully reinforced, and the last chance of coming to terms with Turkey on conditions favourable to ourselves, would have disappeared.[16]

Aside from his exaggeration, Curzon knew that Lloyd George had already made up his mind that the British would take Palestine.

War Cabinet members were under great stress in 1917. The diary kept by Frances Stevenson, Lloyd George's secretary, mistress and later wife, is revealing. On 19 May she wrote: 'D. [David]is seriously contemplating some changes in his Ministry. He says he wants someone in who will cheer him up and help & encourage him, & who will not be continually coming to him with a long face and telling him that everything is going wrong.' Her entry a week later stated: 'D. has been very, very tired this week – more tired I think than I have ever seen him before, and he has been working unceasingly from morning till night.'[17] In the last week of May Hankey noted in his diary how 'cruel' he had felt when he had to insist that the War Cabinet sit two days from 11:30 a.m. to 6:00 p.m., adding that even the ever diligent Curzon told him that he feared that he was on the verge of a nervous breakdown.[18]

Lloyd George established a new War Policy Committee in June. Curzon, Milner and Smuts were its only members. Smuts, the victorious South African general, had agreed to stay on in London as a permanent member of the War Cabinet after refusing Lloyd George's offer to take command of the Palestine campaign. Hankey took the minutes of the new committee, which were so secret that only he possessed the key to the box in which they were filed. That summer Lloyd George used the War Policy Committee to make changes at the Admiralty and increase the use of convoys to protect Allied shipping from German submarines as well as ensure sufficient naval support for military operations in the Near and Middle East. He failed, however, to convince his colleagues that Haig should postpone further offensives on the western front until 1918, when American forces would be available. Since Haig's prestige had risen after the rescue of Nivelle's disastrous campaign, Lloyd George needed to acquiesce to War Policy Committee support and War Cabinet authorization for Haig's major offensive planned for the late summer of 1917.[19]

General Robertson appointed Edmund Allenby (1861–1936), a cavalry officer who had distinguished himself in France during the spring of 1917, to take command of the Palestine campaign. Before Allenby left in June, Lloyd George promised him virtually everything he requested. Allenby telegraphed London of his plans for a September offensive, asking for and receiving two more divisions and sufficient cavalry to carry on where the Sinai railway had left off.

Lloyd George called a meeting of the War Policy Committee to explore the line he should take at a forthcoming Allied conference in Paris intended to secure agreement to the transfer to Allenby of further British troops from Salonika. The prime minister reminded Milner, Curzon and Smuts that the French and Russian representatives 'would undoubtedly press for an offensive' against Bulgaria, with the French obtaining support from the Italians and the Russians arguing that 'we were out for loot' in the Middle East. His political sensitivity remained acute.[20]

Allenby's requests were reviewed by Robertson, who believed that the British were already prepared for Russia's collapse and the movement of Turkish troops from the Caucasus and Syria against either Mesopotamia or Egypt. Robertson recommended that Allenby postpone his advance to Gaza and Jerusalem until later in the autumn.[21] He estimated enemy and Allied forces in the Near and Middle East in July 1917 as follows:

Troops	Enemy	British	Allied
Balkans	300,000	200,000	400,000
Palestine	60,000	270,000	
Mesopotamia	60,000	280,000	

While historians may not agree on the numbers of troops in the principal theatres of war, the British clearly enjoyed overwhelming superiority in the Middle East.

Lloyd George ensured that Allenby secured a division from the Balkans and another from India, with Royal Flying Corps units for intelligence purposes. Allenby was also offered extra non-British regular forces, a 'Jewish Regiment', which was eventually given a number rather than a name out of respect for the 40,000 Jews who had already enlisted in the British army and did not want their war record associated with the performance of a single regiment. Similarly, the small number of regulars in the so-called Arab Legion was of more political than military significance. Allenby was authorized to distribute propaganda among Arabs to facilitate his advance, with planes dropping cigarettes and pictures of Husayn, the

46 The Turkish sultan greeting the German kaiser upon his arrival in Constantinople in October 1917. As the Allied war against the Turks escalated, the Turks demanded more support.

king of the Hejaz, behind Turkish lines, while Lawrence, brought to Allenby's attention for the role he had played in capturing the port of Aqaba at the beginning of July, encouraged the Arab revolt on the right flank.[22]

By September Lloyd George was concerned that Allenby's slowness would make it impossible to knock the Turks out of the war that winter. Hankey visited the prime minister in northern Wales, finding him 'ill' and 'despondent' over the narrowness of view of the general Staff and the inability of his colleagues to agree with him.[23] Lloyd George revived his 1914 proposal for an Allied amphibious attack on the north Syrian port of Alexandretta. His hopes for an Italian summer and autumn offensive against Austria-Hungary were disappointed.

The prime minister's fury with Robertson was magnified by Haig's failure to break through German lines in his four-month-long offensive in Flanders, which ended in the muddy slaughter history remembers as Passchendaele. Almost 400,000 British and Imperial troops were killed, including a large number of Canadians. The losses at Passchendaele created an acute shortage of military manpower for Britain, which strengthened Lloyd George's hand in opposition to Haig and Robertson. With the carefully orchestrated support of British and Allied leaders, Lloyd George established a new Allied Supreme War Council at Versailles.

At the end of October Allenby launched his offensive with 75,000 infantry and 17,000 cavalry, twice as many infantry as the Turks and ten

47   The official British entry into Jerusalem took place on 11 December 1917. General Allenby here receives various Christian, Jewish and Muslim notables in what was called Barrack Square.

times the number of their cavalry. Beersheba was taken and Gaza fell after heavy fighting in early November, with half the Turkish force escaping up the coast and the other half retreating into the Judaean hills near Jerusalem. The British suffered 5,000 casualties, while Turkish losses were heavier, with many taken prisoner. Although Allenby's line was overextended, with gaps as long as five miles, he ordered his right flank into the mountains east and north of Jerusalem to sever Turkish communications. Since Jerusalem surrendered to Allenby without a fight on 6 December, the city sacred to Jews, Christians and Muslims did not become a battlefield. However, the military occupation of Jerusalem would be fraught with administrative and political problems for Britain and her allies.[24]

THE BALFOUR DECLARATION AND WAR AIMS

As Allenby's forces were advancing in Palestine, Balfour as foreign secretary made public his communication to Lord Rothschild (1868–1937), a prominent British Jew who, like his father before him, sought official backing for Zionist aspirations in Palestine. What has become known as the Balfour Declaration was no Jewish conspiracy, no outpouring of wartime humanitarianism, no hasty improvisation, but rather the result of months of calculation and deliberation on the part of Balfour's Foreign Office and Lloyd George's War Cabinet. The first drafts were produced during the summer, amendments made in the autumn, and the document approved by President Wilson before being released in early November 1917.[25]

In the spring of 1917, when the initial advance on Gaza had failed, several prominent Zionists in London met Lloyd George, members of the War Cabinet, its secretariat and the 'Garden Suburb'. Although the Zionists found individuals sympathetic, Balfour himself was unable to make an official commitment because of secret inter-Allied wartime agreements involving Palestine. Balfour realized that Lloyd George, like his colleagues, disliked the Anglo-French Arab scheme of 1916 that had specified an international 'Brown area' around Jerusalem. The best that Balfour could do for the Zionists was to hold out the possibility of an Anglo-American protectorate in Palestine.

Balfour's 1917 mission to North America put him in touch with prominent US officials and Zionists. The foreign secretary found President Wilson sympathetic to Zionism but unwilling to endorse an Anglo-American protectorate since the United States remained neutral towards the Turks. A secret US mission to Switzerland was proposed in the early summer by Henry Morgenthau, the former US ambassador to Constantinople. The mission was intended to explore the possibility of the United States brokering a separate peace with the Turks, under the cover of Morgenthau facilitating American relief efforts to his Jewish coreligionists in Palestine. When the Foreign Office heard of Morgenthau's intentions, however, the Zionist leader Chaim Weizmann was sent to Gibraltar to abort Morgenthau's mission and the preservation of Turkish sovereignty over Palestine.

Given Weizmann's success at Gibraltar, Mark Sykes of the War Cabinet Secretariat met the Zionist leader Nahum Sokolow at the Foreign Office to draft an exchange between Lord Rothschild and Balfour. The foreign secretary found it too long and detailed, so Sykes and Sokolow prepared a shorter version: 'His Majesty's Government accepts the principle that Palestine should be reconstituted as the National Home of the Jewish people' and 'will use its best endeavours to secure the achievement of this object and will discuss necessary methods and means with the Zionist Organization'. Balfour amended the draft slightly and turned the matter over to the War Cabinet.[26]

Milner prepared an alternative form which did not commit the British government so fully to supporting a Zionist state in Palestine. Edwin Montagu, the Liberal secretary of state for India, speaking as an English Jew, protested that British support of Zionism would prejudice those Jews who were non-Zionists. Montagu also believed that the majority of Jews in England were unsympathetic to Zionism. On 3 September, when 'The Zionist Movement' appeared on the War Cabinet agenda, and neither

Lloyd George nor Balfour was present, Montagu reiterated his opposition. Robert Cecil (1864–1958), acting as foreign secretary in the absence of his cousin Balfour, emphasized that US Zionists were very impatient for British endorsement. Zionism did not reappear on the War Cabinet agenda for another month, however, while speculation increased about the propaganda advantages to be gained by the British in Russia by openly supporting the Zionists. Some officials believed that an Allied commitment to Zionism would counteract left-wing antiwar elements in Russia and that even if Russian Jews would not stay in the war for the sake of the tsar, Zionists might nevertheless fight on for their national home.[27]

On 4 October the War Cabinet again discussed Zionism, with the prime minister now in the chair and the foreign secretary leading the discussion. Cabinet members had before them the Milner-Amery amendment – 'nothing shall be done which may prejudice the rights of existing non-Jewish communities in Palestine'. Balfour announced that the Foreign Office had reports that Germany was now out 'to capture the sympathy of the Zionists'. As to Montagu's concerns that Zionism jeopardized those Jews who lived in England and outside Palestine, Balfour stated: 'Just as English emigrants to the United States became, either in the first or subsequent generations, American nationals, so, in future, should a Jewish citizenship be established in Palestine, would Jews become either Englishmen, Americans, Germans, or Palestinians.' What was 'at the back of the Zionist Movement', Balfour stated, was 'the intense national consciousness held by certain members of the Jewish race'. He appreciated that the views of successful Jews who had been assimilated into Britain and the United States differed from the passionate aspirations of most East European Jews. Unconvinced by Balfour, Montagu raised two 'practical questions': 'How was it proposed to get rid of the existing majority of Mussulman inhabitants and to introduce the Jews in their place? How many would be willing to return and on what pursuits would they engage?' Balfour did not answer Montagu. Curzon doubted that large numbers of Jews would be involved since he dismissed Zionism as 'sentimental idealism, which would never be realised'. Lloyd George concluded the War Cabinet's discussion by instructing the Foreign Office to send the draft of the Balfour Declaration to President Wilson for his approval and by ordering Hankey to report on the opinion of Anglo-Jewry.[28]

When Lloyd George's War Cabinet returned to the matter on 31 October, Balfour once again led the discussion and reported that President Wilson had agreed to the draft, but had nevertheless refused to do so publicly. Hankey reported that most British Jews supported Zionism. Since Montagu had gone to India, Curzon was the only one left to express reservations. Speaking 'from a purely diplomatic and political view', Balfour repeated that by making 'a declaration favourable to such an ideal, we should be able to carry on extremely useful propaganda both in Russia and America'. When Curzon expressed doubts about Jewish immigration into

Palestine. Balfour predicted that 'a very much larger population could be sustained' if Palestine were 'scientifically developed'.

When Curzon asked what was meant by the term 'national home', Balfour stated that it meant

> some form of British, American, or other protectorate, under which full facilities would be given to the Jews to work out their own salvation and to build up, by means of education, agriculture, and industry, a real centre of national culture and focus of national life. It did not necessarily involve the early establishment of an independent Jewish State, which was a matter for gradual development in accordance with the ordinary law of political evolution.

Curzon still 'feared that by the suggested declaration we should be raising false expectations which could never be realised'.

Overruling Curzon, Lloyd George authorized Balfour to send Rothschild the following declaration:

> His Majesty's Government views with favour the establishment in Palestine of a national home for the Jewish people, and will use its best endeavours to facilitate the achievement of this object, it being clearly understood that nothing shall be done which may prejudice the civil and religious rights of existing non-Jewish communities in Palestine, or the rights and political status enjoyed by Jews in any other country.[29]

On 9 November *The Times* printed the declaration, without comment, under the heading 'Palestine for the Jews. Official Sympathy', on page seven at the top of the fifth column, sandwiched between headlines on Lenin deposing Kerensky and Colonel House's mission to the United Kingdom. Like *The Times,* the rest of the press gave the declaration scant attention. and British support for Zionism had little or no effect in revolutionary Russia, which left the war soon afterwards.[30] Neither did the British occupation of Jerusalem lift morale in London as much as Lloyd George had expected; Allenby's success was completely overshadowed by the war gloom evoked by the losses at Passchendaele, the collapse of Italian defences at Caporetto, and anarchy in Russia.

In late November the *Daily Telegraph* published a letter from Lord Lansdowne, the Tory foreign secretary from 1900 to 1905, that specified terms on which the Allies might negotiate with Germany. The letter from so distinguished an elder statesman would have had greater impact if other Conservative papers and Northcliffe's empire had not immediately condemned it. Lloyd George, in a widely publicized after-dinner speech to barristers at Gray's Inn in mid-December, pointedly attacked Lansdowne: 'The danger is not the extreme pacifist . . . but I warn the nation to watch the man who thinks there is a halfway house between victory and defeat.'

48   Chaim Weizmann, chairman of the Zionist Commission, reading a 1918 memorial of appreciation from the Jews to General Allenby in Jerusalem, following the Balfour Declaration of November 1917.

Unwilling to negotiate when British and Allied fortunes were so low, the prime minister predicted a better day in the new year, thanks to US military participation and the establishment of the new Supreme War Council at Versailles. Claiming that humanity, history and God were on the side of the British and the Allies, Lloyd George declared that 'untold generations of men will thank God for the strength which He gave us to endure to the end'.[31]

Lloyd George, having taken on right-wing criticism at the end of 1917, then faced a campaign from the left that called for the revision of Allied war aims or even an end to the war. When the Bolsheviks published the secret Allied war agreements that the tsar had concluded with Britain and France, including the prospective Russian annexation of Constantinople, Lloyd George initially dismissed the news as war propaganda. Then the British Labour Party Executive and the Trades Union Congress Parliamentary Committee organized a special post-Christmas conference in Westminster Hall. The conference attacked Allied war aims in the light of the Bolshevik demand that all belligerent governments repudiate their imperialist ambitions. The ideological challenge coming from the Bolsheviks in Russia was echoed not only by labour leaders in Britain, but by supporters of a new liberal internationalism that was soon to be articulated in Wilson's Fourteen Points.

Lloyd George's immediate problem was the shortage of British manpower and the need to transfer men from industry to the battlefield. Because industrial workers had been exempted from service, he would violate the pledges the government had previously made to the trade unions at a time when the home front was weary from its fourth winter of war. The prime minister appeared before the Trades Union Congress (TUC) to explain why the government was asking workers to sacrifice yet more for the war. Lloyd George once again stirred his audience, but only after he had spent several days discussing his text with members of his coalition and his allies in Westminster and Fleet Street.[32]

The prime minister delivered what *The Times* called 'the most important State document issued since the declaration of the war'. Lloyd George's speech was aimed at national, imperial and international audiences, as well as the TUC. He said nothing to confuse the already chaotic Russian situation, recognizing the growing ideological demands for national self-determination and for greater internationalism, yet he avoided compromising British diplomacy. Brilliantly, Lloyd George conceded nothing to the enemy that might offend his disparate audiences throughout the world.

The careful phrasing of the section on the Middle East illustrates how well Lloyd George walked the political and diplomatic tightrope at the beginning of 1918:

> Outside Europe we believe the same principles should be applied. While we do not challenge the maintenance of the Turkish Empire in the homelands of the Turkish race with its capital at Constantinople – the passage between the Mediterranean and the Black Sea being internationalized and neutralized – Arabia, Armenia, Mesopotamia, Syria, and Palestine are in our judgement entitled to a recognition of their separate national conditions.
>
> What the exact form of that recognition in each particular case should be need not here be discussed, beyond stating that it would be impossible to restore to their former sovereignty the territories to which I have already referred.

Lloyd George had abandoned Russia's past claims to Constantinople and the Turkish Straits, as well as those of France and Italy in Asia Minor. At the same time, by employing the ideology of self-determination, he avoided all restrictions on future British activities in the Asiatic provinces by declaring that non-Turkish elements be accorded 'separate national conditions'.[33] Lloyd George offered both additional justification for fighting the Turks and new propaganda possibilities for the British.

WHITHER RUSSIA?

Historians have reached no consensus about British policy towards Russia either during and after the 1914–18 war. Russia's geographical and demographic immensity and its ethnic diversity have led to the complexities of the tsarist Empire being simplified and misunderstood. Since the mid-nineteenth century Britain had been impressed, if not obsessed, by Russia's territorial expansion into central Asia, its defeats of the Turks, its pan-Slavic identification with southeast European nationalities, and the country's drive to the Pacific. These developments, together with Russia's mineral wealth and industrial potential, led the British to underestimate Russian weaknesses.

Those in London interested in Russia at the beginning of the twentieth century saw the Romanov Empire, even after the defeat of the Russo-Japanese War and the drastic reduction of its navy, as the greatest problem for British imperial security. Despite the Anglo-Russian Convention of 1907, and despite Russia's entry into the war on the side of the Allies in 1914, Russia remained a strategic giant in the eyes of London. Before the war British politicians of the left felt more uncomfortable than those of the right at any association with the tsar. Liberal critics of the Anglo-Russian alliance also exaggerated the autocrat's hold over his empire. Strengthened by prewar Anglo-Russian diplomacy, Russophiles in the Foreign Office cooperated with the tsar mainly because they believed that his huge army from the East would, if adequately supplied by the West, become a steam-roller to crush the German army.

Such ideas persisted from 1914 to 1917. Despite Russia's repeated military failures and its millions of casualties, the British press expected the tsar's armies to do more and more, although in fact Russia proved an increasingly ineffective ally as the war progressed. In the spring of 1917, when Russia's army fell apart and Kerensky failed to lead the provisional government in prosecuting the war successfully, Conservative newspapers blamed him for not being tough enough and accused Jews and 'leftists' of conspiring against the war. The Liberal press attacked the British government for being insufficiently supportive of Kerensky. Partisan divisions widened in 1917, the right fretting over the failure of a Russian military coup in August and the left cheering the Bolshevik seizure of power in November. The British governing class was stunned when the Bolsheviks promised the masses 'peace, bread and land', publicized the secret inter-Allied wartime agreements, signed an armistice with Germany, and called on workers in other countries to compel their countries to end the war. No British official suggested recognition of the Bolsheviks, a few panicked, while most regarded the Bolsheviks as being in the pay of Berlin. London's policymakers wanted to believe that Bolshevism was a transient phenomenon confined to Petrograd.

After consulting with their counterparts in Paris, the Foreign Office decided to avoid a complete break with the Bolsheviks. By signing an armistice with Russia, Germany could in the short term transfer troops from the Russian lines and augment its forces on the western front. There was little the British could do about that. But if Berlin were to sign a separate peace with the Bolsheviks, Germany could begin to exploit Russia's manpower, minerals and cereals, which could counteract the Allied blockade of the kaiser's empire. Britain would keep the door open for the Bolsheviks.[34]

The situation became difficult when the Bolsheviks dismissed the elected members of the Constituent Assembly in mid-January 1918, and in mid-February repudiated almost £600 million in direct war loans that Britain had made to the tsar and the provisional government. Bonar Law, as chancellor of the Exchequer and leader of the House of Commons, reassured Parliament that the Treasury would insure holders of Russian bonds against possible loss up to an 18 per cent premium.[35] Since the prime minister doubted the usefulness of diplomatic initiatives towards the Bolsheviks, he explored a variety of options in and beyond the Middle East for coping with the unpredictable situation in Russia. How would the Turks reassess their participation in the war now that Russia had left it? Would they be more or less likely to make peace?

The first British overture involved Vincent Caillard (1856–1930), a protégé of Ernest Cassel and former president of the Ottoman Public Debt Council who had been associated with Lloyd George at the Ministry of Munitions. Caillard had heard from Basil Zaharoff, a Greek arms merchant living in France, that an agent of Enver Pasha had reported that the Turkish leader was willing to pull out of the war for $10 million. Lloyd George had arranged for $2 million to be set aside from Secret Service funds for this purpose, but not until the end of 1917 did the prime minister hear that Enver was serious. Caillard was told that Britain would make peace with the Turks without the latter having to surrender Constantinople or reinstitute the capitulations, but the freedom of the Straits must be secured, Arabia must be 'independent', Mesopotamia and Palestine should be protectorates analogous to Egypt before the war, and the principle of autonomy for Armenia and Syria should be accepted. Caillard passed these terms on to Zaharoff and deposited $2 million in a Swiss bank in January 1918. The next month Zaharoff met with Enver's agent who informed him that the Turkish officer had changed his mind and would return the money, the agent pocketing $500,000 for his services.[36]

Russia's military collapse even revived Turkish war ambitions to link with other Turkish-speaking peoples in central Asia.[37] In response, Britain sought to strengthen anti-Turkish elements in the East, supporting disparate factions and ethnic groups against the Bolsheviks. British moves into the Caucasus and subsequently into the Trans-Caspian region were as anti-Turkish as they were anti-Bolshevik in inspiration, with encouragement given to the Armenians and Georgians, whose enemies were those of Britain also. Similarly, the War Cabinet authorized Baghdad to send to Baku a military mission consisting of a few officers and a detachment of armoured cars, under General Lionell Dunsterville, to meet a Russian commander who had defied the Bolsheviks. Dunsterville's mission, held up by bad weather, remained south of the Caspian Sea until it was ordered to return to the Caucasus. It reached Baku in August 1918, but soon had to leave the Caspian port when outnumbered by Turks.

During the winter of 1917–18, Lloyd George opposed further military action on the western front and remained determined to defeat the Turks and counter German success in Russia. The death from cholera in November of General Maude raised doubts about what more could be done in Mesopotamia. When Lloyd George urged Allenby to march his troops across Syria to Aleppo, Allenby reported that 90,000 of his 112,000 men were already required to complete the occupation of Palestine that winter and that he would need ten further divisions to march the 250 miles to Aleppo. When Robertson used Allenby's report to buttress his argument that British commitments in secondary theatres be 'cut down' to 'a defensive minimum,' Lloyd George wired Versailles for a second military opinion.[38]

The response came from General Henry Wilson (1864–1922), the first permanent British representative to the Supreme War Council, and later Robertson's successor as commander of the British general staff. With the help of Amery, who had been transferred from the War Cabinet Secretariat to Versailles, Wilson urged 'a decisive offensive against Turkey with a view to the annihilation of the Turkish Armies and the collapse of Turkish resistance'.[39] At the end of January Lloyd George sent General Smuts to the Middle East to meet leading British military and political representatives in order to advise the War Cabinet on 'the best use and coordination of all our resources in that theatre, with a view to the most vigorous prosecution of the war against Turkey'.[40]

The prime minister travelled to Versailles to discuss campaign plans for 1918 with Georges Clemenceau, the French premier and minister of war. Clemenceau emphasized that France had lost more men and property than any country other than Russia. Now Russia was eliminated, the entire war hinged on the western front, and the only other theatre of any importance was the Balkans. Clemenceau opposed stepping up the war against the Turks. Lloyd George retorted that the Allies 'had always over-insured' themselves in the west and pointed out 'the advantages Germany had reaped from her Eastern efforts, and those we might have had and still might get'. Lloyd George had the support of the Italian prime minister, but Clemenceau's opposition led to a compromise. The British could use the forces already at their disposal in the East if it were done without 'diverting forces from the Western Front or in any way relaxing its efforts to maintain the safety of that front which it regards as a vital interest of the whole Alliance'. Robertson, in agreement with Clemenceau, tactlessly reminded Lloyd George of Admiral Fisher's coming under fire for not having spoken out against the Dardanelles.[41]

The prime minister returned to London in early February, having failed to gain Allied support for Allenby's campaign against the Turks, and met the War Cabinet on the eve of Smuts's departure for Egypt and Palestine. Smuts learned that the Admiralty faced vast problems in landing stores on the Syrian coast and that Mesopotamia could transfer few men to Allenby. Only after Allenby completed his occupation of Palestine would he be able to move slowly up the coast of Syria.[42]

Reports reached London that, following Russia's collapse, the Turks had set out to fill the imperial vacuum from the Black Sea to the Caspian Sea and beyond. What should the British do about Russia's old sphere of northern Persia? The War Cabinet asked Balfour to chair a Persia Committee and make recommendations. Whitehall's experts had all kinds of agendas of their own, but the foreign secretary opposed military operations in northern Persia.[43]

Despite Persia's declaration of neutrality in November 1914, the country had nevertheless experienced war. The Cossack Brigade, with Russian officers, had been the only effective military force in the north and managed to hold off the Turks. In the south Germans had harassed the British until 1916, when the South Persian Rifles, with some 11,000 armed men under British commanders, overcame them. From Versailles came a memorandum from Leopold Amery predicting that the Turks were preparing to drive across the Caucasus and Persia into Turkestan and raise 'a holy war against the British oppressor of Islam'. Amery feared German control extending beyond 'the old Berlin–Baghdad idea' and 'the former Ottoman Empire' to the Caucasus, Persia and Turkestan, and recommended that the British encourage Persian ambitions in the Eastern Caucasus against the Turks by promising 'More Persia for the Persians'.[44]

Far-fetched as Amery's Persian anxieties were, Milner wrote coolly to Lloyd George that Persia was only 'an incident' in 'a new campaign, which really extends from the Mediterranean shore of Palestine to the frontiers of India'. Milner doubted that Japan would be able to take over northern Asia, but 'we alone have got to keep Southern Asia'. When Austrian soldiers, formerly imprisoned in Russia, had appeared in northeast Persia, Milner surmised: 'That shows what comes of the collapse of the Power, which used to cover our whole Asian flank.' Recommending that General Smuts be put in charge of the whole Eastern theatre, Milner flattered Lloyd George by writing:

> How right was the instinct, which led you all along to attach so much importance to the Eastern campaign and not listen to our only strategists, who could see nothing but the Western Front. If it were not for the positions we have won in Mesopotamia and Palestine, the outlook

49 The drilling of levies along the road to Hamadan, in the northwestern part of Persia, where some expected the Turks to advance after Russia's collapse in 1917.

would be black indeed. As it is, the position is very serious, but we hold strong cards, if we only play them, have great forces near the points of danger, and prestige and victory at our back.

Milner clearly knew how to engage Lloyd George on the Eastern front.[45]

On 21 March 1918, the meeting of the War Cabinet was primarily concerned with Persia and Russia. It was also the day when Germany launched the first in a series of massive offensives against the western front, offensives which for the moment wholly eclipsed the issue of the Middle East.

CRISES ON THE WESTERN AND HOME FRONTS

In the spring and early summer of 1918, General Ludendorff commanded five great German offensives. The first hit hardest, although French reserves helped to check the advance. The second opened a wide breach in the British army, though Ludendorff lacked sufficient reinforcements to take full advantage. The March and April offensives claimed 300,000 British casualties and eliminated the Fifth Army as a fighting force.[46]

Someone needed to be blamed for this massive reversal. The prime minister defended himself in the House of Commons by denying that he had contributed to the defeat on the western front by ordering troops to the East, as his critics charged. He cited figures purporting to show that

British forces in France had actually been stronger at the beginning of 1918 than they had the year before, and that only four 'White' divisions had been involved in the Middle East. In a letter to *The Times* on 7 May, however, General Frederick Maurice, the director of military operations at the War Office, challenged these figures and accused Lloyd George of lying to Parliament. On 9 May Asquith introduced a motion for a parliamentary enquiry into Maurice's allegations, refusing Lloyd George and Bonar Law's suggestion of an enquiry by two judges. In his defence, Lloyd George stated that the figures he had used had come from Maurice's own department. Although the prime minister prevailed in Parliament, his hold on public opinion appeared to be weakening.[47] In a by-election the official nominee of Lloyd George's coalition was nearly defeated by his Labour challenger.

The mood in London grew angrier as the manpower shortage became more acute. Lloyd George raised the age of compulsory military service to fifty while Fleet Street attacked 'slackers.' Industrial workers and even policemen went on strike over their ranks being depleted by draconian compulsion. Conservative MPs proposed conscription in Ireland and the prime minister agreed, but only after Home Rule had been accepted in Ireland. His attempt to compel the Irish to accept conscription and the Conservative Unionists to accept Home Rule worsened the Irish crisis, and pushed Irish Nationalist MPs into the extremist arms of Sinn Fein. A general strike closed all of Ireland except for the Protestant sections of Belfast and, in retaliation, Lloyd George appointed a British general as high commissioner of Ireland.

German successes in France during the summer, on top of their spring victories on the western front and Russia's collapse, depressed British military experts. General Wilson expected the war to drag on into 1919, while General Smuts thought it would be 1920 before sufficient American troops could take to the field to make a difference. At this point, Milner was even willing to compromise with the Germans. Peace would be restored by the Allies recognizing German victories in eastern Europe in exchange for the cessation of the offensive against the West. The 1918 crises on the western and home fronts led London's policymakers to take further precautions in the Middle East. When the small British military missions to the Caucasus failed in 1918, Lloyd George, Milner and Wilson called a special War Cabinet conference in June. Smuts, Curzon and Balfour, as well as representatives of the War Office and India Office, agreed that 'steps should be taken to interrupt, if possible, the Trans-Caspian railway'.[48] The Trans-Caspian mission was led by General Wilfred Malleson, an intelligence officer of the Indian Army, posted in north-eastern Persia. Malleson and his six officers were instructed to monitor the situation in Trans-Caspia. In the event of Turkish penetration, they were to destroy the Trans-Caspian railway to prevent consignments of cotton getting into enemy hands. When Malleson reached Meshed in August, an

50 Loading mules for the Mesopotamian campaign in 1917, revealing the mounting supply and transport problems arising from successful British military advances in the Middle East.

anti-Bolshevik committee had been organized and Malleson was authorized to deal with it. British reinforcements came from Persia and naval guns were sent to the Caspian, but Malleson could only observe the situation.[49]

Although the small British missions to the Caucasus and Trans-Caspian region were only of local significance, they indicate a general sense of alarm over the East during the summer of 1918. General Wilson declared support for such missions because they related to 'the grave menace to the British Empire created by the collapse of Russia in the Middle East'. The War Office's director of military intelligence reported that the Bolsheviks were ready 'to hand over' central Asia to Germany.[50]

When the Allied leaders met at Versailles in July, they could agree only on the principle that Bolshevism be resisted. Since Lloyd George emphasized the Middle East, and particularly Allenby's campaign, while Clemenceau remained committed to the Balkan offensive, the British and French did as they wanted. Allied military leaders on the western front ignored the politicians at Versailles and ran their own operations. Lloyd George disliked being ignored at Versailles, as Hankey noted in his diary. In mid-July he was 'in his irritated state' over Milner's support of General Ferdinand Foch, and at the beginning of August believed that General Wilson was too much like Robertson: 'It is Irish instead of Scotch, but it is still whisky.'[51]

While the French increasingly took over the Balkans campaign,

51   Aerial photo of the Turkish airfield of Rayak being bombed by the British in September, 1918.
British superiority in the air was significant at the end of the war and beyond it.

Allenby's operations remained virtually his own. British men and material vastly outweighed Turkish resources in Syria, but logistical obstacles still hampered his advance. The Turks had been so eager to take advantage of Russian weakness in and beyond the Caucasus that they did not reinforce their faltering Palestinian and Mesopotamian fronts. Even the arrival of General Liman von Sanders in Syria during 1918 failed to stiffen Turkish resistance. Allenby, after making two abortive attempts to crush the Turks on the east side of the Jordan River, left that area to Lawrence and the Arabs, who blew up the Hejaz railway link with the south. Although Allenby had had to cede a third of his best troops to the western front in the spring of 1918, he added reinforcements from India and kept his men supplied over the summer. Overwhelming British superiority in the air gave Allenby the advantage of excellent reconnaissance.

During the final months of the war, the Allies concentrated on the western front. In mid-July General Foch launched a counter-offensive that spoiled Ludendorff's plans for a great attack in Flanders. In August British tanks attacked at Amiens in mass formation. General Haig, learning from his previous failures and those of Ludendorff, halted his offensive before overextending his line and adopted the tactic of sharp jabs forcing back the Germans. Foch did the same and, by the latter part of September, each side had over ninety divisions involved in battle, with the Allies receiving heavier casualties as they went on the offensive. On 29 September Ludendorff demanded that Berlin sue for an armistice while he could still hold his army together.

ARMISTICES WITH BULGARIA AND TURKEY

After the fall of Bulgaria's pro-German cabinet early in the summer, the French had argued in favour of a major Balkan offensive. General Louis-Félix-François Franchet d'Esperey, commander-in-chief of the Allied forces in Macedonia, began elaborate preparations, but before action could commence, Bulgaria had agreed to an armistice. Taking advantage of the Bulgarian collapse, Franchet d'Esperey proposed an attack on the Turks in Thrace to force them to open the Turkish Straits. But differences between London and Paris blocked progress.

Allenby's offensive into Syria began only after the Bulgarian surrender. The cavalry proceeded up the coastal plain, while part of his infantry defeated the Turks in the hills and to the east. The Turks evacuated Damascus at the end of September. Allenby's forces then moved on to Beirut and up the coast, taking the inland towns of Syria by the end of October. With only 5,000 casualties, Allenby had advanced 350 miles in six weeks and captured over 78,000 prisoners. The Arabs under Lawrence made a limited military contribution, although their association with Allenby and presence in Damascus encouraged Faisal and his Hashemite adherents to claim an Arab victory.

General William Marshall (1865–1939), who had succeeded Maude in Mesopotamia at the end of 1917, continued to consolidate the British position north of Baghdad. Although he had had to turn over several of his divisions to Allenby, Marshall managed to reach Kirkuk by May, his major obstacles being hot weather and an extended supply line. Only after reports reached London of Allenby's success in Syria did the War Cabinet take an interest in 'advancing as far as possible in Mesopotamia'.[52] Marshall encountered little opposition and, early in November, reached Mosul, an area presumed rich in oil.

At the end of September, Lloyd George was taken ill, returning to his duties early in October. By then the War Cabinet and Foreign Office had moved towards an armistice with Turkey, using various strategic initiatives that Lloyd George tried but failed to reverse. He was absent on 1 October, when the War Cabinet discussed the probable impact on Constantinople of Bulgaria's surrender, and instructed General Wilson and Admiral Rosslyn Wemyss (1864–1933), the first sea lord, to draft Turkish armistice terms for the Supreme War Council to consider. Wemyss was also authorized to dispatch two dreadnoughts to the Aegean in case extra force was needed. Wilson and Wemyss prepared a list of twenty-five conditions for the armistice, circulated for Allied discussion at Versailles early in October.

52 Lloyd George, prime minister, and Balfour, foreign secretary, leaving the Crillon Hotel, Paris, during the summer of 1917, on their way to one of many Allied wartime conferences.

Key stipulations were the opening of the Dardenelles, Black Sea and Turkish ports to the Allies; the surrender of Turkish naval arsenals; the demobilization of the Turkish army, with provision for sufficient men to maintain internal order and patrol the frontier; the freeing of Allied prisoners, but with Turkish prisoners still to be held by the Allies; and the Turks to sever all ties with Germany. Allowance was made for further Allied military action after the Turks had signed the armistice: 'The Allies to have the right to occupy any strategic points in the event of a situation arising which threatens the security of the Allies.'[53]

The draft of the Allied armistice was circulated to the War Cabinet on 3 October, the very day Lloyd George returned to Downing Street to chair a cabinet meeting. He raised the possibility of Britain making a separate peace with the Turks rather than negotiating terms with the Allies. The prime minister reminded his cabinet that Britain's secret 1916 agreement with France had 'overlooked the fact that our position in Turkey had been won by very large British forces, whereas our Allies had contributed but little to the result'. Balfour pointed out the flaw in Lloyd George's reasoning by reminding him that 'the original idea' had been that 'any territories that the Allies might acquire should be pooled and should not be regarded as the property of the nation which had won them'. Bonar Law agreed with Balfour, but Lloyd George doubted the Turks would accept any armistice without first knowing about peace terms.[54] The prime minister anticipated French and Italian agreement when he set off for Paris the following day. The armistice was to be negotiated on behalf of the Allies by whichever power was approached by the Turks, but the means of delivering the armistice terms remained open.

The matter of Allenby's occupation of Syria was discussed with the French.[55] After several drafts, a joint Anglo-French declaration was approved by the Foreign Office, the War Cabinet and by France, though not released to the public until after the armistice with Turkey. In the assessment of the Foreign Office, Anglo-French relations appeared to be proceeding smoothly.[56] But at Versailles Lloyd George and Clemenceau conflicted over how to conclude the war with Turkey. Clemenceau wanted to allow Franchet d'Esperey to continue his Balkan operation as far as Constantinople and the Turkish Straits, cutting the Turks off from the Black Sea. Lloyd George wanted the blow to be delivered by Allenby, who would then take command in Macedonia. Lloyd George threatened to turn Syria and Palestine over to the United States, a move calculated to make the French more reasonable. But controversy over the Palestinian and Syrian question was avoided long enough for the Wilson–Wemyss draft to be approved, leaving the armistice to be negotiated by whichever power was approached by the Turks. The conflict over the right to negotiate intensified as the parties awaited President Wilson's response to German peace overtures. Since the commanders-in-chief in both France and the Balkans were Frenchmen, Lloyd George wrote to Clemenceau:

> I do not see how I could possibly justify to the people of the British Empire that at the moment when the final attack upon Turkey was to be delivered, the command of Naval Forces which are overwhelmingly British, in a theatre of war associated with some of the most desperate and heroic fighting by troops from nearly every part of the British Empire, should be handed over to a French admiral as well.[57]

When Clemenceau dug in his heels, Lloyd George did so too.[58]

On 22 October the War Cabinet authorized Admiral Somerset Calthorpe (1864–1937) to begin armistice negotiations with Turkey. When the French protested at being barred from the talks at Mudros, Lloyd George sent Milner to Paris to calm Clemenceau. In the meantime, the prime minister approved Allenby's advance to Aleppo and Marshall's advance to Mosul.[59] At the end of October Lloyd George returned to Versailles to discuss the armistice terms for Austria-Hungary and Germany. To his surprise, the Turks accepted the Allied armistice terms on 30 October. The following evening Hankey noted in his diary the satisfaction of the House of Commons that the armistice had been concluded by a British admiral.[60]

On 1 November *The Times* devoted the first three paragraphs of its daily war column to the Mudros armistice. It described it as 'fitting' that the

Turks had surrendered to a British admiral, and praised the bringing of 'our campaigns in Syria and Mesopotamia to a happy and victorious conclusion'. France and Belgium were the primary operational theatres, but the war could have been shortened if Turkey had been defeated sooner. Britain had been 'entirely right in carrying hostilities to the East'. Its one mistake was that, 'having decided to attack in the East', it failed to do so 'in sufficient strength'.[61]

Chapter 7

Postwar Nationalism: 1918–1920

AFTER THE WAR the British government continued to subordinate the Middle East to imperial interests and to Europe. Allied peace treaties were concluded in 1919 with Germany, Austria-Hungary and Bulgaria, and with the Turks in 1920. During that period, nationalism intensified in the Middle East, as it did worldwide. And in Britain, nationalist hatred stirred up by war propaganda fed Fleet Street's demands for draconian peace terms.

No man could claim greater responsibility for the Near and Middle East than the British prime minister, if only as a result of the fact that Britain had the greatest number of troops, ships and aircraft deployed between Europe and India. At the Paris peace conference, Lloyd George's personal diplomacy followed the precedent of resolving European issues through the rearrangement of non-European territory. But now, in response to post-war British sensibility, he took national self-determination more into account. Nationalism was difficult to apply however in the context of the religious, ethnic and geographical diversity of the Middle East, and the majority of its leaders were dissatisfied with the outcome of the peace conference. When Britain denied Egyptian nationalists a place at the peace conference, fierce demonstrations erupted throughout Egypt. Lloyd George maintained Allied options until harsh terms were imposed on the Turks in the spring of 1920. Apart from backing Greek military action against the Turks and withdrawing British troops from Russia, the prime minister left the Middle East to his colleagues. Milner failed to find a formula acceptable to Egyptian nationalists. Curzon, who succeeded Balfour as foreign secretary in the autumn of 1919, was no more successful with respect to Persia than Lloyd George had been with Turkish militants.

LLOYD GEORGE, WILSON AND CLEMENCEAU

Lloyd George was hailed by the press as 'the man who won the war'. On 11 November 1918, it was he who announced to the House of Commons that the armistice with Germany would begin officially at 11 a.m. – the eleventh hour of the eleventh day of the eleventh month. Parliament immediately adjourned so members could attend a service of thanksgiving at Westminster Abbey.

53   George V welcoming Woodrow Wilson upon his arrival at Charing Cross railway station, Christmas 1918. The US president was warmly received in London on his way to the Paris conference.

In preparation for the post-war general election, Lloyd George, with Bonar Law as leader of the Conservatives, issued a coalition manifesto prioritizing war demobilization and a just peace, but it failed to excite a public grown accustomed to the extremes of war propaganda, and in particular to the xenophobic demands of Northcliffe's *Daily Mail* to rid Britain of Germans, hang the kaiser, and make Germany pay for the war. Having been attacked by Fleet Street for asking Germany to pay for the war only 'up to the limit of her capacity', Lloyd George adopted a more forceful stance at a meeting at Bristol: 'If Germany has a greater capacity, she must pay to the very last penny.' It was this phrase that stuck with the public, along with his promise of a 'nation fit for heroes to live in'.[1]

In the mid-December poll, an electorate that had been increased threefold by the extension in 1918 of the franchise to men over 21 and women over 30, returned the coalition to power with eighty per cent of the seats in the House of Commons. Labour became the official opposition party, while the Sinn Fein candidates who had captured a large majority of Irish constituencies, refused to take their seats at Westminster.

In the two months between the signing of the armistice and the opening of the peace conference in mid-January 1919, Lloyd George received many dominion and Allied leaders at Downing Street, and with some he reached preliminary understandings relating to the Near and Middle East. To Dominion prime ministers in London for the third Imperial War Cabinet in November 1918, Lloyd George confirmed that the lion's share of the Middle East, as well as Germany's colonies in southern Africa and the South Pacific, would become part of the British Empire.

The premiers of France and Italy also visited London in late November. Clemenceau was willing to make concessions in the Middle East in return for British support against Germany at the Paris conference. He formally acknowledged that French claims in Syria did not extend to Palestine, which it was agreed should be part of the British sphere.

The US president paid his first official visit to Britain after Christmas. When President and Mrs Woodrow Wilson's train arrived at Charing Cross from Dover in the afternoon of 26 December, the king and queen were on the platform, with a distinguished company, to greet them. After the obligatory inspection of the guard of honour and associated formalities, the president joined George V in an open carriage for the journey to Buckingham Palace, the route lined with Boxing Day holiday crowds. Wilson's own party had recently lost its majority in both houses of Congress, but the president received a warm reception in London, which placed its hopes upon him and his country.[2]

The following day the president lunched at Downing Street. Wilson had not met Lloyd George, but had established an excellent rapport with Balfour since the latter's mission to Washington in 1917. Such confidence did the foreign secretary have in the prospect of Anglo-American cooperation that he expected the United States to support Britain's demands as long as it worked through the League of Nations, a priority of Wilson's. Neither did he anticipate anything less than full Anglo-American cooperation over the Middle East.

Lloyd George may have anticipated that his energy and determination would compensate for his lack of foreign policy experience, and indeed in his informal meetings with Wilson and Clemenceau, his resourcefulness and persuasive talents usually had immediate effects. The first major blow to his diplomacy came in the autumn of 1919, when Wilson suffered a stroke. The consequent weakening of his presidency coincided with the rise of postwar US nationalism, as an isolationist majority in the Senate refused to ratify the Treaty of Versailles or to join the League of Nations. The same winter, Clemenceau failed to be elected as French president, the electorate believing that the Versailles treaty had made too many concessions to Germany. The fall of Clemenceau – swept away by the tide of postwar nationalism – struck a further blow to Lloyd George's postwar diplomacy.

MAKING PEACE IN PARIS AND SELLING IT TO LONDON

Lloyd George's substantial electoral mandate made him the most powerful politician at the peace conference. In cooperation with other Allied

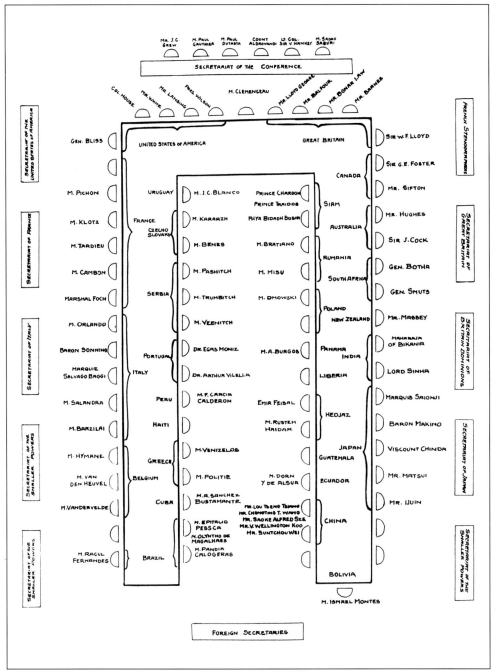

54 The seating chart for delegates at the peace conference in 1919. European and naval matters on the agenda upstaged the Middle East, which Lloyd George primarily handled himself.

leaders, he was expected to settle war differences and establish international order. But how was he to do it when Britain's popular press continued to clamour for revenge on Germany, feared the subversion of Bolshevik agents, and expected new nations to rise from the ashes of defeated empires? The prime minister knew that Britain held most of the military and naval cards in the Middle East. Since his estimation of the number of British troops stationed in the East had been challenged in Parliament in the spring of 1918, the public had identified the prime minister more closely with the war in the Near and Middle East. He therefore had good reason to devise a Turkish settlement acceptable to public opinion, besides ensuring that British casualties from Gallipoli, Salonika, Mesopotamia, Egypt, Palestine, Syria and elsewhere in the region had not been in vain.

By the end of the war, over half a million Imperial troops remained in the Near and Middle East. Table 4 compares the number of troops involved in the region in comparison with those in France.

Table 4
British Empire War Contributions, 1914–18

Theatre	Maximum strength	Total employed	Total casualties
France	2,046,901	5,399,563	2,724,446
Near/Mid. East	1,293,146	2,955,407	303,072
Salonika	285,021	404,207	26,750
Gallipoli	127,737	468,987	119,729
Mesopotamia	447,531	889,702	98,265
Egypt/Palestine	432,857	1,192,511	58,328[3]

The figures for casualties reflect those killed, wounded, diseased, missing or taken prisoner. The losses in the Near and Middle East were much lower than in France. Yet it should be remembered that more than thirty-five per cent of all the British Empire's forces had served in the East.

The level of weaponry and machinery located in the different theatres at the end of the war was also substantial:

Table 5
British Empire Arms & Matériel at end of war, 1918

	France	Egypt/Pal.	Mesopotamia	Salonika
Guns & Howitzers	10,153	445	549	883
Airplanes	1,236	209	45	46
Mechanical Transport	57,051	5,296	6,376	5,080[4]

These figures exclude the ships, port facilities and railway yards that supplied the British armies in the Near and Middle East, and the countless indigenous labourers and animals drafted to build docks, roads, railways, airfields, pipelines and transportation facilities in Egypt and India. Although only a quarter of the hardware required for the western front, the arms and matériel involved in the Near and Middle East made very heavy demands on the British Empire.

Given this enormous investment, the empire expected something in return, and Lloyd George expected to deliver it. Men wiser than he might have known that all belligerents believe their war contributions to have been the greatest. Yet none would have been prepared for the nationalist expectations the war had stirred throughout the world.

The Political Intelligence Department of the Foreign Office had spent months preparing historical information for the British delegation in Paris. Arnold Toynbee, the historian, became so troubled by Lloyd George's handling of the Turkish situation that he spent several months in Greece and Turkey preparing a stinging indictment of Lloyd George's postwar policies. *The Western Question in Greece and Turkey*, first published in the spring of 1922, was an immediate sensation.[5] Mark Sykes, occupying rooms in the basement of the Foreign Office, received disgruntled Armenians, Arabs and Zionists before travelling to Syria to try to accommodate the conflicting parties after the war. The mission so ruined his health that he came down with influenza and died in a Paris hotel early in 1919.[6]

Between January, when the peace conference opened in Paris, and June, when Germany signed the treaty at Versailles, the English-speaking world was kept informed of developments by London's large press corps. The British delegation to Paris was the largest at the peace conference, involving hundreds of military, naval and Whitehall officials, in addition to the representatives from the dominions and India.

Lloyd George's press relations were handled by his close associate, Lord Riddell, a self-made barrister who had amassed a fortune in real estate and publishing. The prime minister was accompanied to Paris by Frances Stevenson, his secretary and mistress, and by Maurice Hankey, indispensable to the organisation of his affairs. The published diaries of Riddell, Stevenson and Hankey provide important clues, beyond the official records, as to how Lloyd George handled eastern matters.[7]

Lloyd George appears to have had a general idea of the settlement he sought in the Middle East. He hated the Turks as much, if not more than Gladstone had loathed them fifty years earlier. While Gladstone wanted to remove the Turks from Europe, including Thrace, Lloyd George's rather more ambitious plan was to oust them from Constantinople, the straits, coastal Anatolia, and the Asiatic provinces. The prime minister's view appears to have been influenced by the Greek premier; to the question, asked by Lloyd George in mid-October 1918: 'Why not leave

55 Lloyd George at the 1919 peace conference in Paris. On his left is Maurice Hankey, secretary to the cabinet, whose published diaries expose the strengths and weaknesses of his chief.

56 Statesmen on a stroll in Paris in 1919. From left to right: Baron Sonnino of Italy, US president Wilson; Georges Clemenceau, the French prime minister, and Balfour, the British foreign secretary.

Constantinople to the Turks?' Venizelos answered that it was because at least one-third of the city's inhabitants were Greek and one-sixth Armenian. As to Italian aspirations in Asia Minor, Venizelos pointed out that there were very few Italians there. When Venizelos reported that Albanians preferred to be part of Greece because their school lessons were conducted in Greek, Lloyd George rejected the principle, which 'would be almost equally valid in order to prove that Wales was really English!'[8]

Like most British policymakers, Lloyd George assumed that the victorious British Empire was stronger at the end of the war than in 1914. Thus he believed that the British were generous in agreeing to a system of mandates whereby the mandatory powers would be trustees accountable to the League of Nations. Three styles of mandates were established: 'A' mandates for the former Ottoman provinces, allowed a good deal of autonomy; 'B' mandates for African lands, more closely supervised by the trustees; and 'C' mandates for Pacific areas, virtually annexed by the trustees.[9]

Lloyd George was away from Paris between mid-February and early March 1919, while President Wilson returned to Washington and Clemenceau recovered from an assassin's bullet. The attempted assassination of Clemenceau brought tighter security once the conference resumed, and a curtailment of large public meetings, which accorded with Lloyd George's preference for intimate sessions with Wilson and Clemenceau alone. The three men discussed Balfour's proposal that the United States assume a mandate over Constantinople and Armenia, and agreed that Britain should acquire mandates over Palestine and Mesopotamia, and France a mandate over Syria.

Clemenceau was content with a French mandate in Syria, although unhappy over Damascus, where Britain continued to back Faisal, son of the Hashemite sharif of Mecca who was conspicuously anti-French. Financially subsidized and militarily protected by British occupation forces under General Allenby, Faisal had little room for manoeuvre, and acknowledged Zionist aspirations in Palestine. Given British and French disagreements over Syria, Wilson suggested the United States send an international commission to ascertain the wishes of the Syrians themselves. But the recommendations of the so-called King-Crane Commission, made in the summer of 1919, were ignored by both Lloyd George and Clemenceau.

Of all the Near and Middle Eastern leaders, Eleutherios Venizelos, the Greek premier who had brought Greece into the war on the side of the Allies, was Lloyd George's favourite. Greek nationalists claimed Thrace, though western Thrace was under Bulgarian control and eastern Thrace under Turkish. Venizelos knew the nationalists also wanted to take over Constantinople, though Lloyd George persuaded him that Britain would insist on some form of international administration over both Constantinople and the straits. Lloyd George did however support

57 Emir Faisal led the Hejaz delegation to the peace conference, with Lawrence advising him. Wartime agreements were scrapped in favour of mandates, the French taking over in Syria.

Venizelos's idea of landing Greeks at Smyrna, a major port on the west coast of the Anatolian peninsula, the population of which was mainly Greek, and persuaded Wilson and Clemenceau to see it as a means of counteracting Italian pretensions in the area. And since the British army was rapidly being demobilized and the situation in Russia remained unpredictable, Lloyd George found it opportune to agree with Venizelos's offer to let the Greeks fight the Turks.[10]

In the spring of 1919 Lloyd George also had to cope with anti-British outbursts in Egypt and India. When the British deported a leading Egyptian nationalist to Malta in March, uprisings broke out not only in Cairo but all along the Nile. Zaghlul Pasha had expected to participate in the peace conference, but was refused. When Zaghlul reached London, Curzon refused to receive him at the Foreign Office. On his return to Egypt, Zaghlul formed a party called the *Wafd* (the delegation), which articulated frustrations against the experience of the British wartime occupation.

Zaghlul Pasha was not alone in being incensed at Britain's parading

Faisal as the spokesman for the Arabs.[11] Within a week of Zaghlul's deportation in early March, foreigners and their institutions were attacked throughout Egypt; Cairo's rail and telegraph communications were cut; mobs hijacked trains in order to murder British passengers. Lloyd George sent General Allenby to Egypt, and when Allenby released Zaghlul, Cairo quietened and order was eventually restored throughout the country.[12]

In a similar way, the Amritsar massacre of April 1919 roused anti-British sentiment in India. The war had driven up the value of the rupee, raised prices and disoriented India's economy. Much of the government of India's revenue had been sequestered to meet war expenses, including those in Persia and Afghanistan. One million Indian soldiers had served in the war, especially in the Mesopotamian campaign, where their casualties were higher than those of 'white' troops. To the ten million war dead and twenty million wounded were added, early in 1919, some fifteen million casualties of an influenza pandemic that also swept the sub-continent.

British anxiety over the Indian situation led to the Rowlatt Acts, repressive measures allowing for trial without jury. Large protest meetings were held in many parts of India, to which British officers responded, in general, with professional restraint. One general, however, ordered his troops to open fire on demonstrators in Amritsar, and 400 were killed. The massacre became a powerful symbol of Indian nationalism.[13]

London's right-wing press blamed the Bolsheviks for the outbursts in Egypt and India, which was easier than acknowledging the legitimacy of Egyptian and Indian war grievances. Senior military officers suggested accelerating British operations in Russia.

The more of the Turkish Empire that the Greeks occupied, Lloyd George argued, the less there would be for the British to do. The Greek landing at Smyrna in mid-May was a success. As the Foreign Office had feared, however, the occupation of Smyrna humiliated Turkish pride and made nationalists more militant. And, as the India Office had warned, British support of Greece in Smyrna also upset India's Muslims, who founded a khilafat movement in reaction to Christian powers taking over the last Islamic imperial capital and the seat of the sultan and caliph.

War Office hopes for an Allied success in Russia were briefly raised by a campaign in May 1919, but its failure in June cooled what little enthusiasm Lloyd George had for Allied intervention against the Bolsheviks; he sought the withdrawal of all British troops after Clemenceau and Wilson had ordered the evacuation of French and US soldiers. To Lloyd George, the way to counteract the popular appeal of Bolshevism was to make peace with Germany, end the war in Russia, and improve working-class conditions.

In August 1919, with Parliament in recess, Lloyd George took a three-week holiday at Deauville, in Normandy, as a guest of Lord Riddell. There, in breaks from rounds of golf, he discussed the problem of the Middle East with his foreign secretary. In the light of American unwill-

58   The British escort women and children after violent demonstrations erupted in Cairo in 1919. The Foreign Office had opposed an Egyptian delegation coming to the Paris conference.

ingness to look after the straits and Armenia, Lloyd George suggested to Balfour that the French might accept a mandate over Armenia as well as over Cilicia. French gains in eastern Anatolia might then be exchanged for a British mandate over Constantinople and western Anatolia. If, however, France insisted on securing all of Anatolia, Britain might acquire Cilicia and Syria. Balfour preferred the wartime solution of Syria for the French, and Palestine and Mesopotamia for the British, but Anatolia remained unsettled.

Balfour retired as foreign secretary after concluding Allied negotiations over the old Austro-Hungarian Empire. He was succeeded by Curzon, whose relationship with Lloyd George was never good. The more Lloyd George acted as his own foreign secretary and the more he ignored the Foreign Office, the more intolerable Curzon found him. Yet Lloyd George knew that Curzon's own ambition would prevent him resigning .

At Deauville, Lloyd George was reassured to hear from Allenby that calm prevailed not only in Egypt but also in occupied Palestine and Syria. The general brought a message from Damascus, where Faisal's precarious rule depended on a sizeable British subsidy and Allenby's military protection. Faisal's note warned that the Hashemites would suffer, as would Britain, if France took over any of Syria, which he termed 'the brain of the Arab Provinces'. Faisal announced his imminent departure from Damascus 'before any decision is taken in London or disaster overtakes us both here and there'. Lloyd George, having agreed that Faisal sought to keep France out of Syria, instructed Allenby to proceed with the removal of British troops from Syria and southeastern Anatolia, their place to be taken by the French. He added that Faisal, if he wished, could remain in Damascus after the British troops left.[14]

59 Former foreign secretary Grey (in glasses) being seen off to the United States in 1919 by Lords Bryce, Reading and Curzon. Grey failed to gain US cooperation in the postwar Middle East.

THE FASCINATION WITH LAWRENCE OF ARABIA

Lloyd George returned to London in September 1919 to find Allenby and Lawrence being lionized for the liberation of the Holy Land from the Turks. London society was captivated by the story of an English crusader, dressed as a bedouin, achieving heroic feats in the desert. A young American journalist, Lowell Thomas, had arrived in London to present a lecture, originally entitled 'With Allenby in Palestine, Including the Capture of Jerusalem and the Liberation of Holy Arabia'. Thomas' delivery was skilful, but the main appeal lay in his vivid photographic slides. While Allenby received the key to the City of London, at a ceremony in the Guildhall, in the presence of Lloyd George, what really captured the imagination were the images of the young T. E. Lawrence. The title of Thomas' lecture was henceforth amended to 'With Allenby in Palestine and Lawrence in Arabia'.[15]

Lawrence himself had neither approved, nor profited from Thomas's lecture. Though known in official circles, he was not a public personality during the war nor even at the peace conference, where he had advised Faisal's delegation. Now, with a fellowship from All Souls, Oxford, Lawrence began work on what would become his most famous work, *The*

60 Lowell Thomas's illustrated lecture created the legendary 'Lawrence of Arabia', and drew sell-out crowds in four different London theatres during 1919–1920.

Seven Pillars of Wisdom. One year later, however, Lawrence would draw upon his new celebrity status to become London's most famous partisan of the Arab 'cause'.

Thomas's travelogue opened in mid-August at the Royal Opera House, Covent Garden. The American had expected to remain in London for a week or two, but his illustrated lecture attracted capacity audiences for four months, moving from Covent Garden to the Philharmonic Hall and then to the Queen's Hall. Among those who attended were members of the royal family and prominent politicians. The lecture also captivated one Elizabeth Monroe, a recent Oxford graduate who later traced the origins of her interest in the Arabs to the lecture, and who went on to be one of Britain's leading journalists on the Middle East.[16]

By and large London audiences were more fascinated by Lawrence himself than interested in the Middle East. And the songs, films and shows about Arab sheikhs that became popular in the 1920s owed little to the writings of such English orientalists as Richard Burton, Gifford Palgrave, Wilfrid Scawen Blunt, or Charles M. Doughty.[17] A series of articles on Lawrence in the *Strand Magazine* featured a prefatory comment by Lloyd George: 'Everything that Mr Lowell Thomas says about Colonel Lawrence is true. In my opinion, Colonel Lawrence is one of the most remarkable and romantic figures of modern times.'[18]

61 Clemenceau arriving at Victoria station, London, in December, 1919. Left to right: Lloyd George, Clemenceau, Paul Cambon, the French ambassador, and Curzon, the foreign secretary.

Ironically, at the very time when London audiences were discovering more about the Arabs, Lloyd George had already ordered Allenby to replace the British troops protecting Faisal's position in Damascus with French forces. Faisal's two visits to Downing Street in late September had been complete failures. The prime minister not only refused to postpone the British withdrawal from Syria, but also reduced Faisal's subsidy from £150,000 to £75,000 per month. In Paris Faisal accomplished even less than he had in London. When he reached Damascus, he found Syrians had lost any enthusiasm for being ruled by the son of the sharif of Mecca: in November 1919, the French high commissioner arrived in Beirut to demonstrate France's determination to rule all of Syria, with or without Faisal.[19]

LLOYD GEORGE'S SETTLEMENT WITH THE TURKS

Without Woodrow Wilson, who had suffered a stroke, and Clemenceau, who had been removed from office, Lloyd George was determined to remain a world statesman. The prime minister had devoted most of 1919 to the peace settlement, and during 1920 and 1921 spent 50 per cent of his time on foreign affairs, 30 per cent on Ireland, and only 20 per cent on domestic matters.[20] His strategy then may have been conditioned by the swingeing attacks on him in the recent book, *The Economic Consequences of the Peace*. Its author, who criticized the harshness of the German peace treaty, was John Maynard Keynes (1883–1946), a Cambridge economist who had served in the Treasury during the war and resigned his advisory post in Paris in June 1919. Macmillan, the book's publisher, had sent advance copies to political and business leaders in Britain and the United States before Christmas. In six months the book sold 160,000 copies.[21] But if Lloyd George's reputation suffered among the literary circles, he remained highly popular among the general public.

Within the Coalition there was disagreement over policy relating to Constantinople. Lloyd George wanted more Greek troops there, while Curzon feared it would foment discontent, as after the Greek occupation of Smyrna. As head of the India Office, Edwin Montagu believed the Turks should retain Constantinople so as not to offend the Muslims. The War Office favoured the Turks in Constantinople as a bulwark against Bolshevism, which Churchill and his senior military advisers continued to see as the main threat to the British in the East. In the end, Lloyd George left the Turks nominally in control of Constantinople while keeping the city under Allied occupation.[22]

In mid-February Lloyd George hosted a conference to draft a peace treaty with the Turks, following the treaties with Germany, Austria-Hungary and Bulgaria. To London came the French and Italian premiers, their foreign ministers and staffs, as well as representatives of the Supreme Council in Versailles, which, founded by Lloyd George during the war, remained essentially his own institution, with his favourite French general, Field Marshal Foch, in charge.

At the conference, Lloyd George attacked Turkish army officers for ignoring the armistice terms and withdrawing, still armed, into the Anatolian hinterland beyond the reach of the Allies. And he was incensed that the recently elected assembly in Constantinople had approved the National Pact of the militants. Threatening that Britain would act alone if the Allies did not agree with him, Lloyd George persuaded France and Italy to approve the announcement of General George Milne (1866–1948) that Constantinople would remain under Allied military occupation. Hankey was given a single night to draft the conclusions that became the basis of the Turkish settlement. Although the new French government was much less cooperative than Clemenceau's had been, the difficulties were overcome: 'The friendly spirit of the conference has been remarkable, in spite of the rivalries and conflicting ambitions of the Powers in Constantinople, Asia Minor, and Syria.'[23]

Early in March, Allenby reported that Arab leaders were becoming restive over the partition of the old Turkish Empire. Meeting in Damascus for their second general congress, a group of Syrians proclaimed their independence and acknowledged Faisal as their Hashemite monarch. At the same time, certain Palestinian leaders petitioned Allenby that Palestine should not be separated from Syria. And some Iraqis chose Faisal's brother, Abdullah, as their Hashemite monarch. But such protests had no effect on Lloyd George who, in mid-April, set out for the peace conference at the Italian resort of San Remo.

In six day-long sessions, the French were highly contentious. They first demanded that Germany pay reparations immediately and then disputed nearly every point of the treaty that had been drafted in London. Lloyd George, encouraged by Coalition victories in two by-elections – the seventh such victory in a row – drove the conference on in high spirits. He pushed through harsher terms than those of the armistice of 1918: the Turkish navy and air force were to be disbanded, and compulsory military service abolished; Turkish forces were to be limited to 50,000, none of which would be allowed in Constantinople. An international commission – dominated by the British – would control the so-called 'neutral Zone of the Straits', which would be permanently occupied by the Allies.

Lloyd George clashed sharply with the French premier on finance. Since France still had a greater financial stake than Britain in the Ottoman Empire, he suspected Paris of attempting to take over Turkish finances. Britain, France and Italy agreed to a tripartite commission to oversee all Turkey's revenue and expenditure, denying the Turks power over their own taxation. The economic and judicial privileges foreigners had enjoyed from the capitulations would remain; Turkey would be responsible for all the costs of the Allied occupation; and French bondholders would be paid by the Ottoman Public Debt.

Having taken the stick to the Turks and French at San Remo, Lloyd George held out carrots to the Greeks. Just as Venizelos had earlier viewed Smyrna as an Allied bridgehead that could be used against the Turks, so he now envisaged Greek rule in Thrace as strengthening the British hold on Constantinople. By facilitating the buildup of large Greek garrisons, Lloyd George encouraged Venizelists to expect that Smyrna and eastern Thrace would eventually be incorporated into a Greater Greece.

At the San Remo conference, Lloyd George also backed Zionism. Palestine, under a British mandate, would become the site of the 'Jewish National Home'. France would have a mandate over Syria and Britain over Mesopotamia. The Arabian peninsula would be left to the Arabs.

It was the Armenians that fared worst. Caught between the Russians and the Turks at the end of the war, as they had been at its beginning, they nevertheless proclaimed their own republic in 1918. Although independence was recognized, the Allies sent no troops to aid the republic, which was supported only by non-governmental relief organizations.

Britain avoided the appearance of partitioning Anatolia by means of what Curzon termed a self-denying ordinance. Under his formula the Allies agreed to mutual support and non-interference in the French south-eastern sphere of Anatolia and the Italian southern sphere. The British had no area of influence in Anatolia, but already dominated Constantinople and the straits; their Greek clients were occupying western Anatolia and eastern Thrace; and Britain controlled all the Asiatic provinces of the old Ottoman Empire except for Syria, along with most of the oil that was expected to be found in northern Mosul, the biggest economic prize of the war in the Middle East.[24]

The question of the demarcation of the Syria-Palestine border was not resolved at San Remo. France wanted no official distinction between Beirut and Damascus, a matter that interested the British since any oil discovered in northern Mesopotamia would require a pipeline to the Mediterranean, either directly through Syria or indirectly through Palestine. In exchange, France won the right to purchase 25 per cent of Mesopotamian crude oil and 25 per cent of any oil produced by the Anglo-Persian Oil Company using the proposed Syrian pipeline.[25]

The formal peace settlement with the Turks, called the Treaty of Sèvres after the Paris suburb in which it was signed, was concluded at the end of April 1920. The same month Turkish nationalists in Ankara, led by Mustafa Kemal, repudiated the Allied settlement and declared themselves the Government of the Grand National Assembly. General Milne, commander of the forces occupying Constantinople and the straits, requested reinforcements in June to deal with Turkish attacks. Lloyd George convened a meeting of seven of his cabinet and, after six hours, concluded that 'to retire from Constantinople before a bandit like Mustafa Kemal would deal a shattering blow to our prestige in the East'.[26] When he asked Greece to send troops to Constantinople, Venizelos complied, provided he be allowed to carry the offensive into eastern Thrace. At a meeting with the French three days later, Lloyd George devised an agreement that allowed Greek troops to replace the French in eastern Thrace and permitted the Greeks to advance from Smyrna into the Anatolian interior. Riddell recorded in his diary how Lloyd George, calling the Turks 'a decadent race' and the Greeks 'a rising people', vilified the army and the Conservatives for opposing his policies.[27]

While the prime minister was still betting on a Greek military victory over Turkish nationalism, the French carefully reoriented their diplomacy away from Greece and towards Turkey. In talks with Mustafa Kemal and Turkish nationalists, France orchestrated the withdrawal of its troops from Cilicia, thereby strengthening its military hold on Syria. When rioters protested against the Syrian mandate, the French army surrounded Damascus. As the French high commissioner was consolidating his rule, Faisal and his partisans escaped. Anti-British outbursts then occurred in Palestine and Mesopotamia.

Protests in Palestine had been modest until April 1920, when violence

62 At San Remo in April 1920, French and Italian representatives met with Lloyd George and Curzon. France obtained a mandate over Syria, as Britain did over Mesopotamia and Palestine.

broke out during the Jewish, Christian and Islamic festivals. In Jerusalem, 5 Jews and 4 Arabs were killed; and 211 Jews and 21 Arabs wounded. Lloyd George approved the immediate introduction of a civilian Palestine administration despite the refusal of the Turks to relinquish their sovereignty. Herbert Samuel, a pro-Zionist Jew and a Liberal who had disassociated himself from Asquith, was nominated Palestine's first high commissioner. Accepting the appointment, he wrote to Lloyd George:

> The fulfilment of the Zionist programme must, from the nature of the case, be gradual, and very considerate for the interests of the Arabs and Christians. Jewry in Palestine would be more likely to practise patience, without losing enthusiasm if the pace were set by an Administrator who was known to be in full sympathy with the ultimate aim.[28]

Curzon, cool towards Zionism, asked Samuel to postpone his acceptance for a year, but the high commissioner refused, and his arrival in Palestine passed without incident. His inaugural address called for the formation of an advisory council composed of Arab, British and Jewish representatives.

The calm in Jerusalem contrasted with widespread turmoil in Mesopotamia during the summer of 1920. Insurrections in Mosul in May had provoked agitation elsewhere. From the War Office, Churchill

63   The announcement of the British mandate in Palestine and reaffirmation of the Balfour Declaration led to disturbances at the Mosque of Omar in Jerusalem, which were quelled by troops.

reported that the fighting was severe, but that the Arabs were being 'bombed and machine-gunned with effect by aeroplanes which cooperated with our troops'. By August Britain declared that 'a state of war exists throughout Mesopotamia'.[29]

MILNER'S MISSION TO EGYPT

Although Lloyd George determined policy in the Middle East, General Allenby was the man on the spot. From military headquarters in Alexandria and his residency in Cairo, Allenby commanded all British forces in the Middle East. In Egypt, he relied on military force and martial law, imposed in the name of Fuad, Egypt's puppet sultan. Allenby had opposed the idea that Milner, the colonial secretary, should come to Egypt in May 1919, but by November announced that Milner would soon arrive in Cairo to explore a new constitutional arrangement, after three decades of British occupation and five years of a British protectorate.

Milner's mission to Egypt marked the end of his imperial career – appropriately, since that is where it had begun. With both Cromer and Kitchener dead, Milner was London's leading expert on Egypt. He hoped to find collaborators willing to negotiate an end to Allenby's military rule. But even before he arrived, Egyptian nationalists announced they would boycott the mission. After three weeks in Cairo, he met a few Egyptians who were willing to see him privately, as he wrote to Lloyd George:

> There are a lot of moderate men about who know that the present
> screaming agitation is folly . . . . But at present they are all terrorised and
> there is precious little backbone in any of them . . . . It is clear that if the
> Moderates are successfully to resist the Extremists, we must have
> something to give the Moderates; they must be able to hold out some
> attractive prospect of self-government.[30]

Milner did not believe that the British could root out nationalism in the
country. In February 1920 he reported to Curzon: 'Further repressive
measures, however necessary, will also supply fresh fuel for agitation and so
we go round in the old vicious circle.'[31] Equally unconcerned with
imperial trappings and Egyptian progress, Milner sought control over
Egypt's foreign affairs simply to protect the vital Suez Canal. This could be
done behind the scenes, using the methods that had worked so well when
Milner had first been in Egypt four decades earlier.

Upon his return to London in March 1920, Milner began to draft his
report. Before it was finished, however, Jerusalem had experienced riots;
Lloyd George had imposed a harsh treaty on the Turks; the Greeks had
joined battle with Turkish nationalists; Faisal had abandoned Syria; and
widespread revolt had broken out in Mesopotamia. All these factors made
Milner adopt a conciliatory position in his talks that summer with Zaghlul,
Egypt's most prominent nationalist. In several meetings, held secretly at the
Colonial Office, Milner agreed to end the British protectorate and reduce
the powers of British civil servants. However, the colonial secretary did not
agree to curtail the police powers of the high commissioner. When
Zaghlul demanded Egypt's complete independence in foreign affairs,
Milner carefully drafted an agreement that allowed diplomatic autonomy
for Egypt and confined the British military presence to the Suez Canal. In
August Milner wrote to Curzon:

> What I want is the acknowledged right, conferred on us by Egypt
> herself in a treaty, to keep a military force on Egyptian soil to guard our
> communications . . . . At the same time the fact that we have such a force
> in Egypt at all, and that Egypt recognizes our right to keep it there for
> our purposes, recognizes, that is, her own permanent place in our
> Imperial system, will lend authority to the 'advice' of our representative
> in Cairo . . . .

The foreign secretary accepted Milner's report, but predicted: 'I can't help
thinking Cabinet will shy rather badly at this.' Zaghlul boasted to London's
press that he had won 'Egypt for the Egyptians', but Lloyd George and his
cabinet were much less willing than Milner to give even the appearance of
surrendering to Egypt's nationalists.[32]

CURZON'S AFGHAN AND PERSIAN IMBROGLIOS

Since Lloyd George paid little attention to Central Asia, either during or after the war, Curzon reigned supreme in devising British policy towards the Persian Gulf, Persia and Afghanistan.

In London, Curzon operated from an imposing town house in Carlton Terrace which afforded one of the city's finest views: St James's Park in the foreground, framed by the Foreign Office, Big Ben, Westminster Abbey and Buckingham Palace. Curzon communicated in an exaggeratedly large hand on engraved writing paper, or through a curiously emphatic style of speech. While a student at Oxford, he had taken elocution lessons and developed a habit of filling his lungs with more air than necessary for normal conversation. The excess air meant that each word received, according to one of his biographers, 'explosive emphasis, and conveyed the impression that his final consonants, and even the commas on which he suspended his periods, were so many external checks or brakes applied to what, but for them, might have been an uncontrollable exhalation'.[33]

In 1917 Curzon had chaired a number of War Cabinet subcommittees, including the Mesopotamia Administration Committee and the Middle East Committee. The meetings were attended by representatives from all the relevant government departments, yet no Whitehall expert could rival Curzon's breadth of knowledge and years of experience. Having made five journeys to Asia during the 1880s and 1890s, prior to becoming viceroy of India, having continued to follow developments there very closely, and having spoken and published extensively on Eastern issues before the war, Curzon quite obviously had an impact upon British policy towards the Middle East.[34]

In March 1918 the War Cabinet subsumed several ad hoc committees within the Eastern Committee. Besides Curzon's Middle East Committee, which met on Saturdays, and Milner's Egyptian Administration Committee, which met irregularly, Balfour chaired an interdepartmental Persia Committee and an interdepartmental Russian Committee. The War Cabinet authorized Curzon to establish the new Eastern Committee according to terms of reference he had drawn up himself. The committee had little effect on military matters, which were determined by the War Cabinet and the general staff. Nor did Curzon have much influence over Palestine, Mesopotamia, Syria or the western part of the Arabian peninsula, all of which were still administered predominantly from the Arab Bureau in Cairo. But he did determine British policy in the area between Persia and India.

After the war, Curzon continued to chair the Eastern Committee on behalf of Balfour, who was at the Paris peace conference. In February 1919, when the emir of Afghanistan was assassinated, several rivals claimed the title. In April, Amanullah Khan proclaimed Afghanistan's complete independence and called upon all Muslims to rise up against British rule.

In a brief contest, labelled the Third Afghan War, Amanullah was subdued. Curzon saw to it that the government of India met the costs of this one-month campaign, estimated at £14,750,000. The war ended with Afghanistan's withdrawal from India, but the Afghan leader retained autonomy within his state. Curzon relinquished control over Afghanistan's foreign relations in 1919, but waited two more years before he officially recognized Afghanistan's independence, by which time the Afghans had already negotiated agreements with the Bolsheviks, Turks and Persians.[35]

Persia, which had remained officially neutral during the war, came under exclusive British control in 1918. The shah was subsidized by Britain, and a pro-British triumvirate – of prime minister, finance minister and minister of justice – was in place in Tehran. Britain maintained several small forces within the country's borders: Indian troops on the coast of the Persian Gulf; the South Persian Rifles, native forces supplied, paid for and trained by Indians; an Anglo-Indian cordon along Persia's border with Afghanistan; another mission in northeastern Persia; a British force in northwestern Persia; and, after the revolutionary upheavals in Russia, the Persian Cossacks who stayed on, paid for by the British. But these forces failed to maintain order in a country that had experienced a decade of political upheaval, military conflict, famine and disease.

During the spring of 1919 Curzon prompted the British ministry at Tehran into a treaty with the shah's three pro-British leaders. Like the fifteen cabinets that had preceded them, the Tehran triumvirate publicly demanded limitations on foreign interference in Persia's territorial and financial independence. Privately, the three collaborators demanded a £200,000 gratuity, and the shah sought assurances that his annual £70,000 subsidy would continue for life. In exchange for British control over external affairs, the Anglo-Persian agreement stipulated that Britain would train the Persian army, reorganize the country's finances, collect customs, undertake railway construction, and improve the country's communication and transportation systems. Curzon arranged a joint British Treasury/government of India loan of £2 million at 7 per cent interest, with Persia's revenues and customs receipts as collateral. The £200,000 gratuity to the Tehran triumvirate was confirmed, though limits were placed on the shah's subsidy. Curzon took pride in the agreement, signed in August 1919, which he believed would make Persia a model for other countries.[36]

Such hopes, however, were soon shattered. Under the Persian constitution of 1905, the treaty had to be ratified by the *majlis*, the parliament that had not met since 1915. Curzon was eager for ratification, but no Tehran ministry was willing to convene the assembly: the nationalists loathed the shah's deal. Nor did military matters proceed as Curzon had wished. In the spring of 1920 Bolshevik forces launched a surprise attack on a British flotilla at Enzeli, a southern port on the Caspian Sea. The British retreated after a Persian Socialist Republic was proclaimed in Gilan, the province where Enzeli was located. Curzon feared that such a reversal would threaten Britain's credibility as defender of Persia's independence, the basis of the Anglo-Persian agreement.

In the autumn of 1920 the War Office sent General Edmund Ironside to northern Persia, where he found that Persian Cossacks were willing to fight against the Bolsheviks. The Cossack division then consisted of two hundred Persian officers, some fifty Russian officers, and several thousand Persian soldiers. Ironside replaced the leading Russian officer with Colonel Reza Khan. Although Reza had little education, he had more than enough experience of Russian commanders. Early in 1921 Ironside informed Reza that Britain would not oppose a coup d'état in Tehran, provided the British-subsidized shah were not deposed.

Tehran's new government formally repudiated the agreement with Britain and signed a treaty with the Bolsheviks. Unlike Curzon's Anglo-Persian agreement, the Russo-Persian treaty gave all Russia's assets, concessions and properties to Persia provided they were not ceded to a third power. The text of the 1920 treaty was widely publicized as a model of anti-imperialism, although one article stipulated that if any third power used Persian territory as a base of operations against Russia, the Russians could send troops into Persia.[37] 'The Russian menace in the East is incomparably greater than anything else that has happened to the British Empire in my time,' Curzon observed when he realized that no British troops would be sent to Persia.[38] The following April Reza clashed with the pro-British premier over whether British advisers should be permitted in the gendarmerie. Reza forced the premier into exile, and named a pro-US Persian as prime minister.

By the end of 1921 Reza's new premier had signed a contract giving Standard Oil exploitation rights to the oil of northern Persia for fifty years. The Anglo-Persian Oil Company (APOC) immediately filed a protest on the grounds that it had purchased this concession for £100,000 in 1916 . The Americans needed British support since APOC had the exclusive right of transporting oil in the Persian Gulf, while the British preferred American oil men over the Bolshevik alternative. APOC and Standard Oil formed a partnership in 1922, while the Persians turned instead to the US-based Sinclair Company, which had rights to market Russian oil. Sinclair, expecting to export the oil of northern Persia through Russian territory, promised to loan the Persian government $10 million.

Anglo-American diplomacy smoothed differences in oil strategy, and not only in Persia. In Mesopotamia, British accommodation of US oil interests prevailed over Curzon's earlier uncompromising imperial stance. Curzon's influence on the postwar politics of Middle Eastern oil was less even than his impact upon events in Afghanistan and Persia.[39]

Chapter 8

Imperial Adjustments: 1920–1922

FROM THE SUMMER of 1920, when Britain declared war on Mesopotamia, to the autumn of 1922, when Britain came close to declaring war against the Turks, the Near and Middle East generated more interest and controversy in London than it had at any point in the century.

Fleet Street comment focused on the costly British presence in Mesopotamia and Palestine, where the new mandates did not yet pay their own way, and the need for economies. Nor were the high costs associated with the occupation of Constantinople and the Turkish Straits met by Turkey. Churchill, at the War Office and subsequently at the Colonial Office, had first to defend the level of expenditure and then find cheaper ways to manage the Arabs. While appointing Faisal king of Iraq, and his brother, Abdullah, the ruler of Transjordan, Churchill created a new Middle East department in London and retained the region's affairs under British control. To ease Arab discontent, he slowed Zionist immigration into the Palestine mandate. To allay Egyptian resentment, General Allenby declared Egypt independent, even though the country's foreign and military affairs, as well as the Suez Canal and Sudan, remained within British jurisdiction. Lowering the British profile in the Middle East was consistent with the naval reductions that Balfour negotiated at the Washington Conference, along with further imperial adjustments being made in India and the dominions.

Lloyd George's alliance with Greece against the Turks failed as the Greeks were driven out of Smyrna and the British threatened at Chanak. And when the prime minister prepared for a further war against Turkey, opposition from the Conservatives, the dominions and the press forced him to resign. He became the scapegoat for the postwar confusion in the Middle East, just as Churchill had earlier carried the blame for Gallipoli.

ECONOMIC AND IRISH PREOCCUPATIONS

What plans Lloyd George had for economic reconstruction after the war assumed the continuation of governmental direction. But the Conservatives, who held the parliamentary majority, demanded and obtained a diminution of state control. As the government ceased to be the largest consumer of goods and services, the postwar economic boom ended. The Conservatives then urged retrenchment, slowing the economy yet further. The City of London, however, adjusted swiftly to postwar realities. Smart capital remained in the still-thriving service sector, while some investors flourished in the growing consumer sector, and many continued to take advantage of attractive opportunities overseas. As a result, Britain's industrial sector became increasingly depressed.[1]

The inflation of the war years continued until 1921: British wholesale prices rose to 225 per cent above their pre-war level. The cost of living increased proportionately, and workers, having grown accustomed to higher wages during wartime, took strike action to maintain their position. Labour in coalmining and railways, appropriated by government in wartime and privatized immediately afterwards, were hit hardest.

The following table indicates the number of workers involved in strikes before and after the war:

1912	1913	1914	1919	1920	1921
1,462,000	664,000	447,000	2,591,000	1,932,000	1,801,000[2]

As Britain's industrial competitiveness declined, so did jobs. Unemployment soared from a level of 5 per cent in 1914 to almost 15 per cent after 1920. The Unemployment Insurance Act of 1920 extended the 1911 provisions to cover more than twelve million workers, at high cost to the Exchequer: whereas £500,000 in benefits had been paid out in 1913–14, £53,000,000 was needed in 1921–2.[3]

After 1918, hardship could no longer be justified by the interests of war or sustained by patriotism, and 'the enemy' was more difficult to identify. Britain was rife with ideological distortions and fears of conspiracy. On the right, many feared that Bolshevik agents had penetrated the trade unions, while the left accused capitalists of pulling the strings of government for profit. In fact, unions leaders probably had no more control over workers than financiers had over politicians. London was trapped in an international economic dislocation beyond its own control. Some suspected an international Jewish conspiracy. In May 1920, for example, *The Times* gave credence to a notorious forgery, *The Protocols of the Elders of Zion*, and a year passed before the newspaper acknowledged that it had been duped.[4]

The real circumstances, combined with unreal suspicions, meant the government was unable to justify a large military presence in the Middle East. With retrenchment at home, how could Britain continue to spend millions on the military occupation of the Middle East? Even if there were oil in the Middle East, who would benefit? The navy needed oil, but was another war sustainable? Such questions were repeatedly raised in Fleet Street during 1920 and increasingly at Westminster. The League to Enforce Public Economy held its first meeting in June of that year. Northcliffe's brother, Lord Rothermere (1868–1940), launched his 'Anti-Waste' campaign in the *Daily Mirror* in October. Fleet Street publicized all manner

64 Faisal, son of Ibn Saud, with British officer and tutor on board ship to London after the war. Since oil had not yet been found in eastern Arabia, the Saudis then seemed unimportant.

of outrageous expenditure in order to make the case for further reductions in government spending. Making severe cuts at the Admiralty, the first lord, Eric Geddes (1875–1937), was applauded for wielding 'the Geddes axe'.

Besides the economic gloom, the Irish problem, or Asquith's 'damnable question', remained.[5] After the war, Ireland encountered mounting tension, and violence spilled over into London, through acts of terrorism. The origins lay in the history of recent decades: the introduction of Home Rule in the late nineteenth century had split the Liberal party; the reintroduction of Irish Home Rule before the 1914–18 war had infuriated the Protestants of northern Ireland, precipitated a constitutional crisis in the House of Lords, and led to a threatened military mutiny in Ulster. The parliamentary statute on Irish conscription of 1917 was never implemented, but it inflamed terrorism and led to the occupation of Ireland under the command of a British high commissioner. The civil war between Republicans and Ulstermen took years to settle, through the eventual separation of the Irish Free State from the six counties of Northern Ireland, which remained united with Great Britain. Even then, it took months to suppress the fighting along the new border.

The continual killing in Ireland frayed British nerves. Conservative newspapers in Fleet Street were hostile to concessions for terrorists, the hardest line being taken by the *Morning Post*. Upon each further outrage, the *Daily Telegraph* and *Evening Standard*, as well as Northcliffe's *Times, Daily Mail* and *Daily Mirror*, fulminated not only at the Irish but also at the governing Coalition. Lloyd George's handling of the Irish question alienated most Conservatives and further reduced their support for the Coalition. Ireland's impact upon British policy towards the Middle East is less obvious, but clearly the press feared that weakness in the Middle East would encourage violence in Ireland. The Middle East and Ireland were moreover often linked by policymakers. At the end of August 1920, for example, when Churchill faced press criticism over the sending of additional British troops to suppress the uprisings in Mesopotamia, the head of the War Office drafted a revealing letter to Lloyd George, though it was never sent:

> There is something very sinister to my mind in this Mesopotamian entanglement, coming as it does when Ireland is so great a menace. It seems to me so gratuitous that after all the struggles of the war, just when we want to get together our slender military resources and re-establish our finances and have a little in hand in case of danger here or there, we should be compelled to go on pouring armies and treasure into these thankless deserts. We have not got a single friend in the press upon the subject, and there is no point of which they make more effective use to injure the Government.[6]

London was spared the economic dislocation of the industrialized north and west, as well as the violence in Ireland. Yet it was perceptibly demoralized. After the war any justification for British involvement in the Middle East appeared to fade. The expanded newspaper readership and huge new electorate knew little about, and cared less for, the Middle East.

FLEET STREET PROTESTS AGAINST THE MILITARY COSTS

Lord Northcliffe died in 1922, his press empire still dominating Fleet Street even though his political influence on Downing Street had waned. The proprietor of *The Times*, the *Daily Mail* and the *Daily Mirror* supported Lloyd George during the war, but when the prime minister marginalized Northcliffe at the peace conference, the two became estranged and embittered. Lord Rothermere too became disaffected, even before succeeding to the newspaper empire, and Lloyd George received diminishing support from the *Daily Express,* published by Lord Beaverbrook (1879–1964), a political ally of Bonar Law. Alone of the press barons to back Lloyd George was Lord Riddell, chairman of the *News of the World* and head of the Newspaper Proprietors' Association. If the proprietors did not exactly

65 The pontoon bridge Anglo-Indians erected in 1917 across the Tigris River at Baghdad. The Turks destroyed much before evacuation, making costly postwar problems for the British

determine opinion, newspaper criticism magnified public impatience with politicians and policymakers after 1918.[7]

Press reaction to the large number of troops dispatched to Mesopotamia in mid-1920 was furious. The government had earlier admitted that the cost of keeping British troops in occupied Ottoman territories was £750,000 a week. Four million soldiers had returned to civilian life since the end of the war, but Fleet Street believed the cost of deploying forces in the Middle East was too high. Churchill had the unenviable task of submitting to the House of Commons the Army Estimates for 1920–21. Privately he remained opposed to Lloyd George's position on intervention against the Bolsheviks and the high level of troop maintenance in the Near and Middle East. In February 1920 Churchill provided the cabinet with the following figures: 14,000 British and 46,000 Indian troops in Mesopotamia; 9,500 British at Constantinople and the Turkish Straits; 9,000 British in Palestine; and 6,000 British in Egypt. He also estimated the cost of involvement in Mesopotamia to be £18 million, and Palestine £9 million per year, a level he believed was beyond justification.[8]

Unsympathetic though he was to expenditure in the Middle East, Churchill nevertheless reacted decisively to the outbreak of violence in Mesopotamia in May 1920. While he dispatched fewer reinforcements than had been requested, he made up the difference through air squadrons until troops could be transferred from Constantinople. Churchill also urged the Royal Air Force to proceed with experimental bombs of 'mustard gas', which he believed 'would inflict punishment upon recalci-

66   British plane at field in Suez starting its first flight to Baghdad in 1918. Air squadrons were to cut postwar costs as Churchill ordered 'police bombing' of rebellious Arabs.

67   Venizelos, the premier of Greece, welcomed after the war by members of the Anglo-Greek community at the Grafton Gallery, London, where he found more loyalty than in Greece itself.

trant natives without inflicting grave injury upon them'.[9] By the end of the summer three-and-a-half months of punitive expeditions had been initiated in Mesopotamia. Some villages were burned, while others were fined. Thousands of rifles and millions of rounds of ammunition were captured. By early October the crisis had passed, but the political and financial repercussions continued in Downing Street and Whitehall.

No sooner had the situation in Mesopotamia eased than another crisis arose in relations between the Greeks and the Turks. It began after Venizelos had recklessly extended his campaign into the Anatolian hinterland towards Ankara, the centre of militant Turkish nationalism. In October the Greek king had died without an heir, prompting the former pro-German king to offer to return. The overly confident Venizelos called an election to block the monarch's return, but lost. He fell from power, while the former king and his queen, a sister of the German kaiser, returned to Athens at Christmas. Lloyd George, however, remained defiant, refusing to change policy towards Greece and insisting that Britain would support it against the Turks.

Early in December the prime minister called a special conference of ministers to discuss military expenditure in the Middle East. According to minutes kept by Hankey, himself as pro-Greek and anti-Turkish as Lloyd George, the discussion noted how 'criticisms of the Government's expenditure' were 'becoming every day more insistent'. It was clear that Parliament would 'demand [that] the permanent military expenditure of the future should be vigorously reduced'. Hankey recorded 'unanimous agreement' neither to negotiate with the Turkish nationalists nor to return Smyrna to Turkey, and it is interesting to note that when Churchill saw the minutes, he took Hankey to task for misrepresenting his views and those of his colleagues.[10]

Churchill pressed Lloyd George to amend his pro-Greek, anti-Turkish policy. Tired of defending the government's policy, he bluntly asked Lloyd George whether 'the line wh you are forcing us to pursue wd commend itself to the present H. of C'.

> I deeply regret & *resent* being forced to ask Parlt. for these appalling sums of money for new Provinces – all the more when the pursuance of the Anti Turk policy complicates and aggravates the situation in every one of them, & renders cheaper solutions impossible.

Churchill's senior military advisers were furious, he explained:

> In the military circles whose op[inio]n it is my duty to understand, there is universal disagreement & protest. These circles exercise much influence in the Conservative party. Altho' while Ireland holds the field all other topics are in suspense, there is a strong & steady undercurrent of disapproval among people who have been & still wish to be yr. most ardent supporters.[11]

Churchill further prepared a cabinet memorandum which urged new terms with Turkish nationalists before their army defeated the Greeks.

In mid-December 1920, Churchill introduced the supplementary Army Estimates, and asked Parliament for an additional £40 million, £9 million of which was for Mesopotamia. A vote against would harm the situation in Mesopotamia, he argued, since British evacuation would only cause more fighting now and higher costs later. The house approved. Churchill then reported to the cabinet finance committee that the forces in Mesopotamia, Egypt and Palestine were still costing £37,000,000 a year.[12]

Lloyd George and Churchill, though differing over policy at the end of 1920, became closer at the start of 1921. Both spent New Year as guests of Philip Sassoon (1888–1939), at his house outside London. Lloyd George invited Churchill to take over from Milner at the Colonial Office, promising him considerable latitude over civil as well as military operations in Palestine and Mesopotamia through a new Middle East Department in the Colonial Office. Churchill accepted.[13]

EMPIRE ON THE CHEAP

As colonial secretary in 1921 and 1922 Churchill cut costs in ways and means that involved both Hashemite Arab leaders and prominent Zionists. He cast Faisal in the role of king in what was now called Iraq, its Arabic name instead of the Biblical Mesopotamia, while Faisal's younger brother, Abdullah, was appointed emir of Transjordan. He agreed to scale down Zionist immigration into Palestine, and slashed British land forces in the Middle East by relying more on Arab soldiers and the Royal Air Force. Initially suspicious, Fleet Street praised him fulsomely once he had achieved his objective.

Churchill's new Middle East Department was led by its permanent undersecretary, James Masterton Smith (1875–1938), whose Whitehall career had begun at the Admiralty in 1901 and who knew his chief well. Assisting Masterton Smith were officials from the India Office, Treasury, Foreign Office and War Office.[14] In an unusual step, Churchill appointed Colonel Lawrence his political adviser, preferring to have this celebrated figure within the government rather than as a critic.[15]

The recommendations of an interdepartmental committee, chaired by Masterton Smith, were that the Middle East Department should focus on Iraq, Palestine and Aden; Curzon had insisted that Turkey, Syria, Persia and Egypt remain under Foreign Office control. Churchill and Curzon later clashed over whether the India Office or Foreign Office was in charge of the Arabian peninsula. The dispute continued an older conflict between the government of India, which for decades had supplied British officers to the Persian Gulf and subsidized the leaders of eastern Arabia, including Ibn Saud, and the Foreign and War offices which, with their personnel based in Egypt and Anglo-Egyptian Sudan, backed the Hashemite Arabs.

68　The Cairo conference in 1921, where Churchill met with forty advisers, including Herbert Samuel (Jerusalem) and Percy Cox (Tehran) on either side of Churchill; in the second row are Arnold Wilson and Gertrude Bell (Baghdad) at the far left, with Lawrence fourth from the right, having accompanied Churchill from London.

Curzon agreed that the Hashemites were useful to Britain provided they did not upset France.

Churchill's staff had made elaborate preparations for the so-called Cairo conference: the leading figures involved in the Middle East converged on the Semiramis Hotel in 'utmost secrecy', according to *The Times*.[16] T. E. Lawrence was reunited with former colleagues at the Arab Bureau: Gertrude Bell and Arnold Wilson came from Iraq, Percy Cox from Persia, and Herbert Samuel from Palestine. The conference took almost fifty sessions over two weeks to work its way through a quagmire of administrative problems in Iraq, Palestine and the Arabian peninsula. The overall goal was to cut costs, with the details worked out by the military as advised by the political experts. British troops would be able to leave as soon as British officers had trained Arab armies, the costs of which were to be paid by the countries themselves. Land and police forces would be supplemented by the Royal Air Force, in accordance with recommendations made by Air Marshall Hugh Trenchard (1873–1956), since air power provided the cheapest means of ensuring British control in the hinterlands

69 Faisal became king of Iraq at Baghdad in August 1921, in accord with the Cairo conference. On Faisal's left is Percy Cox, high commissioner; on his right, General Aylmer Haldane.

70 Churchill, Lawrence and Emir Abdullah in Jerusalem, following the Cairo Conference of 1921. The Hashemite would rule east of the Jordan, as his brother Faisal would in Iraq.

of the Middle East. The Arabs could be appeased by the institution of indirect rule by Britain of Iraq, with Faisal as king, and of Transjordan, with Abdullah as prince. Faisal and Abdullah had become estranged from their father, Husayn, the sharif of Mecca and king of Hejaz. Britain continued to subsidize the leader of western Arabia so long as he was cooperative, and had other collaborators in the eastern parts of the Arabian peninsula, but only later did it increase the provision to Ibn Saud in relation to his greater military prowess. It is important to note that these arrangements were made in Cairo prior to the discovery of oil in the eastern parts of the Arabian peninsula.[17]

During the Cairo meeting Churchill periodically wired London for Lloyd George's approval, now given only after cabinet discussion. The prime minister was swayed by Churchill's prediction that expenditure on Iraq and Palestine would be reduced from £30 million to £8 million by 1922-3.

Following the conference, Churchill spent a week in Palestine, staying at the official residence of the high commissioner in Jerusalem. Samuel arranged for Churchill to meet a delegation of disgruntled Palestinian Arabs, who were duly reminded that Palestine had been liberated by the British, not by the Arabs, and that thousands of British soldiers were buried there. In contrast, Churchill found the Zionists in support of the Balfour Declaration and of the high commissioner, though later they were to be disappointed when Samuel announced that Palestine would be confined to the area west of the River Jordan, the east going to the Arabs. In Jerusalem Churchill met four times with Abdullah, escorted by Lawrence. Britain would support Abdullah both financially and militarily, so long as he avoided troubling the French in Syria, the British in Iraq or the Zionists in Palestine.

Churchill appointed a pro-Zionist, Richard Meinertzhagen (1878–1967), to be military adviser to the Middle East Department. Colonel Meinertzhagen disagreed with many actions taken by the high commissioner in Palestine, particularly after Muslim-Jewish riots broke out in Jaffa early in May 1921, and disagreed with Churchill's support of Samuel's declaration that Jewish immigration must be limited by the 'economic capacity' of Palestine to absorb new immigrants. This historic announcement dismayed London's Zionists, whom Churchill then sought to placate by instructing Samuel to deal more firmly with those Arabs who attacked Jews in Palestine.

In mid-June Churchill ended the secrecy that had surrounded his new Middle East Department and the conference in Cairo. Since Conservative newspapers had expressed the fear that Churchill would extend British responsibilities in the Middle East, the colonial secretary took the opportunity to clear the air in a speech to the House of Commons. He reviewed British policy before and during the war, and reiterated that the British were 'bound to make a sincere, honest, patient, resolute effort to redeem our obligations' in the Middle East. While Ottoman policy had been to rule the Arabs by dividing them, 'setting up administrations of local notables in each particular province or city, and exerting an influence through the jealousies of one tribe against another', Britain was attempting to 'build up around the ancient capital of Baghdad . . . an Arab State which can revive and embody the old culture and glories of the Arab race'. Churchill then turned to the issue of unrest in Palestine, which precluded immediate cutbacks, but said he expected Palestinian Arabs to be satisfied with administrative autonomy in Transjordan. The colonial secretary also justified the restriction on Zionist immigration on the grounds of Palestine's uncertain capacity to absorb them. Acknowledging 'the unknown future' of the Middle East, he concluded by appealing to MPs for their support in 'the difficult and delicate process of reduction and conciliation which lies before us, and on which we are already definitely embarking'.[18]

The speech was well received. Austen Chamberlain wrote to Lloyd George that Churchill had 'changed the whole atmosphere of the House on the Middle East question'. Even Curzon sent him a note of congratulation.[19]

CHURCHILL, THE ARABS AND ZIONISM

Churchill's Middle Eastern success in the spring of 1921 coincided with a period of acute personal tragedy. His mother was recuperating from having had a leg amputated to counteract gangrene, which had set in after she had broken an ankle. At the end of June, however, Lady Randolph Churchill haemorrhaged, lost consciousness and died. Two months later, Marigold, Churchill's three-year-old daughter, fell ill and also died. Churchill coped by continuing to work at full stretch, burdened not only with Near and Middle Eastern problems but also with Irish matters imposed on him by the prime minister. Indeed, during the summer of 1921, the Middle East was overshadowed by events in Ireland.[20] In July Lloyd George finally succeeded in persuading the opposing parties to sign a truce. Despite vociferous Unionist opposition, Eamon De Valera was received at Downing Street, but later rejected the peace accord, just as Churchill failed to make a breakthrough in negotiations between the Zionists and Arabs.

Churchill undoubtedly paid more attention to the Arab than to the Zionist cause, though he did not depart from the Balfour Declaration, reinforced by the terms of the British mandate in Palestine, as agreed at San Remo. Nevertheless, he followed a policy that irritated both the pro-Zionist cause and its opponents in London, the protests of which had, by 1921, degenerated almost into anti-Semitism.

As planned at Cairo, Faisal became king of Iraq, following a British-engineered referendum. British troops were rapidly withdrawn from the country, their place taken by 8,000 British-officered Arab and Kurdish forces, supported by the Royal Air Force. Churchill wanted all British troops out by 1922, but remained concerned that the Turks might return to Iraq. He failed to detach Lloyd George from his pro-Greek position, though other than Hankey and Balfour, the prime minister was alone in his view as Greco-Turkish tensions mounted.

As colonial secretary, Churchill was central to the Imperial Conference held in London during the summer of 1921. Delegates from New Zealand and Canada queried the policy on Zionist immigration to Palestine, which he confirmed would remain open but not 'beyond the numbers which the new wealth of the country, which was created by public works and better agriculture, can sustain'. Churchill repeated that both personally and officially he supported a Jewish 'national home'. Asked if that meant giving the Jews 'control of the government', Churchill replied: 'If, in the course of many years, they become the majority in the country, they naturally would take it over.'[21] Fleet Street too raised questions about the British obligation to Zionists. Could the British afford to maintain the troop levels required to protect the settlement of more Jews in Palestine? Some in London suspected that the Zionist immigrants were really Bolsheviks.

In the latter part of July, and on the eve of the arrival of an Arab delegation to London, Chaim Weizmann, head of the Zionist Executive Committee, met Lloyd George, Churchill and Hankey at Balfour's house in Carlton Terrace. Weizmann believed that restricting Jewish immigration amounted to 'a negation of the Balfour Declaration', which to the Zionist leader had 'meant an ultimate Jewish majority'. Lloyd George and Balfour reassured Weizmann 'that by the Declaration they had always meant an eventual Jewish State'. When Weizmann enquired about representative government in Palestine, Lloyd George told Churchill: 'You mustn't give representative government to Palestine.' Weizmann also impressed upon the three men his concern for the safety of Jews in Palestine in the light of reports that many of the British officials there were hostile to Zionism. He also expressed his willingness to meet the Arabs in London.[22]

The Arab delegation itself attracted public attention. It was received at Lambeth Palace by the Archbishop of Canterbury, who subsequently wrote to Churchill:

> I think I ought to tell you that I have received from a good many quarters requests that I should remonstrate against what is thought to be the undue development of a Zionist policy in Palestine, especially with regard to the purchase of land by or on behalf of Jews and their apparent anticipation that in what are called State lands the development will be entrusted to Jews. Even more important is the possible buying out of reluctant sellers if they are non-Jews with a view to giving the lands to Jews.[23]

Churchill met the seven members of the Arab delegation, led by Musa

Kazim Pasha, in mid-August. Prior to the meeting, Churchill had received a written statement of their five demands: the establishment of a Palestinian government responsible to a parliament elected by Palestinians resident before the war; the reversion of the Balfour Declaration; the banning of further Jewish immigration until a national government had been established; the cancellation of all laws made since the British occupation in 1917; and the joining of Palestine to a confederation of neighbouring Arab states. Churchill suggested that the Arab delegation meet with Weizmann, but they refused to recognize him, much less see him. Churchill again urged the Arabs at least to talk with him. Churchill undertook to arrange for a meeting with the prime minister on condition that the delegation was 'really making an effort to come to a settlement'.[24]

The cabinet discussed the Palestine dilemma. One option was to withdraw the Balfour Declaration and turn the mandate back to the League of Nations, another to hold to the Declaration and arm the Jews with a view to reducing the size of the British garrison. For Lloyd George, Balfour and Churchill, the Balfour Declaration was a matter of honour, and there could be no reneging on it.[25]

Churchill then recalled the Arab delegates to the Colonial Office. He repeated the view that the British government was 'bound to carry out the Declaration', which 'contains safeguards for the Moslems, just as it contains clauses satisfactory for the Jew'. Unable to engage the Arabs, however, Churchill lectured them about gradual Jewish immigration and the necessity of co-operation to develop Palestine, but the meeting ended in failure.[26]

During October, when Lloyd George was still preoccupied with the Irish conference, Churchill feared that the prime minister might carry out his threat to resign rather than impose a military solution on Ireland. He saw clearly that, no matter how much the two of them disagreed on policy, they had to pull together on Ireland as well as on the Near and Middle East in order to survive as leaders of the Liberal Party.

Churchill explored alternatives to the expenditure of £3.5 million annually to maintain British troops in Palestine. He considered setting up a professional gendarmerie such as in South Africa and Canada. If the cabinet allowed him to withdraw all regular British troops, a local force backed by aircraft and armoured cars might be sufficient to police Palestine. Churchill even explored the possibility of transferring the Black and Tans from Ireland to Palestine, Meinertzhagen reporting that 2,000 such mercenaries could be recruited for Palestine at an annual cost of £800,000. The colonial secretary set 1922 as his goal for replacing British troops in Palestine with a professional gendarmerie, backed by the Royal Air Force.[27]

On the fourth anniversary of the Balfour Declaration, in November 1921, the high commissioner in Palestine telegraphed that a disturbance in Jerusalem by 'a small crowd of Arab roughs' had developed into a full-scale attack on the Jewish quarter. Samuel reported that four Jews and one Arab had been killed. Churchill convened a joint Arab-Zionist conference at the Colonial Office, but it accomplished nothing.[28]

In Ireland, meanwhile, negotiations delicately proceeded towards a treaty in December 1921. Lloyd George delegated to a committee, chaired by Churchill, the unenviable task of implementing the treaty, establishing a provisional government in Ireland, and confronting the anxieties of Ulster. The Irish Free State Bill became law in 1922, yet IRA terrorist activity persisted.

With Irish tensions still great, Palestine seemed an unnecessary additional burden. From Jerusalem Samuel complained that the task facing British troops administering the mandate was being made more complex by an additional influx of Jews. Pro-Zionists in London blamed Churchill for not ensuring that the Palestine administration cooperated more fully with Zionism. At the same time, right-wing newspapers in London became increasingly anti-Zionist in tone, the *Morning Post* barely suppressing its anti-Semitism. In February 1922 the *Daily Mail* attacked the Colonial Office for granting an electricity concession to Pinhas Rutenberg, a Russian Jew.[29]

Fighting broke out on the border of Northern Ireland and the Irish Free State in May 1922, when Republican troops occupied certain areas and flouted British authority. With the approval of the cabinet, Churchill ordered that these areas be recaptured in early June. Several Irish were killed or taken prisoner before action was halted. In late June General Wilson was assassinated on the front steps of his house in Eaton Place. Fearing a revival of terrorism in London, Scotland Yard closed the public gallery of the House of Commons and assigned two policemen to each member of the cabinet.

That summer, on the eve of acceptance by the League of Nations of the Palestine constitution and recognition of Zionist aspirations, Parliament debated the Balfour Declaration as the basis for British mandate policy. The House of Lords, despite a strong maiden speech by Balfour, newly created an earl, voted against the Balfour Declaration by 60 to 29. The government's policy was however sustained in the House of Commons by a majority of 292 to 35.[30] Balfour himself presented Britain's case to the League of Nations, which approved the Palestine mandate's incorporation of the British commitment to Zionism.

In Iraq, Churchill's patience was once again tested when Faisal first demanded an Anglo-Iraqi treaty and then declined to sign it unless all references to the mandate were deleted so as to give him complete diplomatic autonomy. The colonial secretary attempted to diffuse the situation by inviting Faisal to London in August, but the king refused to come without prior commitment to the ending of the mandate. Exasperated, Churchill urged an ultimatum: 'we are paying eight millions a year for the privilege of living on an ungrateful volcano out of which we are in no

circumstances to get anything worth having'.[31] But Lloyd George coun-
selled restraint, opposing 'a policy of scuttle'. Britain, he declared, should
be prospecting for oil. 'If we leave, we may find a year or two after we have
that we have handed over to the French and Americans some of the richest
oilfields in the world.'[32]

CURZON AND EGYPT'S INDEPENDENCE

While Lloyd George had placed Churchill in charge of Iraq, Palestine and
some Arabian matters, he had left the remainder of the Middle East to
Curzon. The foreign secretary regarded Churchill as an amateur, and one
in too much of a hurry. Curzon himself continued to view the Middle East
from an Indian perspective. The reforms implemented by Edwin Montagu
through the Government of India Act at the end of 1919 were un-
acceptable to Indian nationalists. Mohandas Gandhi led a non-cooperation
campaign, was arrested early in 1922 and sent to prison. Even more
disturbing to Curzon was that many Muslims on the subcontinent had
embraced the khilafat movement and were protesting against Allied
treatment of the Turks.

During the latter months of 1921, Lloyd George had more pressing
concerns than Egypt. He had begun to negotiate with the Irish and, in
early 1922, to prepare for the major Genoa summit designed to reach a
European settlement with Russia. At Genoa, however, the twenty-fourth
postwar conference Lloyd George had attended, the United States refused
to participate, the French talked only of reparations, and Germany and
Russia showed little interest since they had in advance reached a bilateral
understanding at Rapallo. Balfour, in contrast, achieved success as the
British representative at the Washington conference of 1921–2, where
British naval expenses were significantly reduced by agreeing a ratio of
battleships for Britain, the United States, Japan, France and Italy respectively. While Balfour enjoyed Lloyd George's confidence, Curzon was the
butt of his sometimes cruel humour. In September 1922, during the
Turkish crisis that brought down the coalition, Lloyd George humiliated
the foreign secretary in front of his colleagues by suggesting he never got
anything out of the Foreign Office before 11:30 a.m. The personal and
political antagonism between the two men impaired British effectiveness
within the Middle East; both were to be shaken by events in the region
that forced the Foreign Office and Downing Street to come to grips with
nationalism in Egypt and Turkey.[33]

Lloyd George's government had disassociated itself from Milner's report
early in 1921, while nationalists continued to demand 'Egypt for the
Egyptians' – a phrase which echoed the nationalist demands emanating
from India and Ireland. The cabinet was unwilling to appear to appease
Egyptian nationalism, and it is notable that the more concessions made to

71 Zaghlul Pasha, the Egyptian nationalist, addressing an open-air meeting in Cairo. His attacks on the British led Allenby to deport Zaghlul and five of his supporters to Ceylon in 1921.

Irish nationalists in 1921, the more stubborn Lloyd George and Churchill became towards the Middle East.

While Allenby, as high commissioner, was ready to end the British military protectorate and place Anglo-Egyptian relations on a fresh footing, Curzon delayed the issue. The foreign secretary had difficulty finding Egyptians with whom to negotiate. Instead of meeting Zaghlul, as Milner had done, Curzon opted for the more cooperative Adly Pasha, who visited London in the summer of 1921. But in six meetings no progress was made on the key issues of Egyptian diplomatic representation abroad and British troops in Egypt. The longer the negotiations, the more impatient Allenby became. At the end of 1921 he returned to London declaring that he would require additional troops to check disorder if negotiations were further prolonged. The Egyptian issue came to a head in early 1922, however, when Allenby threatened to resign unless the cabinet took action. Lloyd George dared not remove the soldier hero, risk another explosion in Egypt, or stir up more criticism of his coalition. He therefore invited Allenby back to London, expressed regret over the misunderstandings, and gave him the authority to settle the disturbances in Egypt himself, subject only to Curzon's oversight.

Allenby ignored Egyptian nationalists and reached an accord with the compliant sultan at Abdin Palace. Fuad was made king of Egypt in 1922, and a further coronation under British auspices took place in the postwar Middle East. The Allenby Declaration, issued unilaterally at the end of

February 1922, conceded formal independence to Egypt and ended the British military protectorate. Curzon however ensured that Egypt's 'independence' was more apparent than real by retaining absolute power over four areas: defence, the protection of communications, the control of foreign and minority interests, and the administration of the Sudan. Allenby pledged that Britain would intervene only when its imperial interests, foreign communities, or Egypt's debts were involved. He also accepted that the Egyptian civil service could be filled with Egyptians, although Curzon insisted that no non-Egyptian be appointed without prior approval. Allenby made provision for the establishment of a parliamentary constitutional system in the future. That regime would secure the interests of Egypt's politicians, landowners, foreigners and minorities, but would largely ignore the needs of the impoverished majority.[34]

CHANAK AND LLOYD GEORGE

Just as Curzon was slow to come to terms with nationalism in Egypt, so Lloyd George procrastinated over Turkey. Like the foreign secretary, the prime minister seemed unable to depersonalize Middle East policy. Historians have made much of Lloyd George's personal ties to Venizelos. The men were the same age, and Lloyd George approved of Venizelos more than any other contemporary leader in the Near or Middle East. Nevertheless, he did not agree indiscriminately. Lloyd George remained pro-Greek after Venizelos fell from power at the end of 1920, but although Greek nationalists repeatedly requested that they be allowed to rule Constantinople, Lloyd George never accepted the proposal.

In March 1922 Montagu resigned from the India Office, never having succeeded in opposition to Lloyd George's anti-Turkish stance. Montagu's resignation had no more effect on Lloyd George than the repeated protests of General Wilson, who, as chief of the general staff, had also long insisted that Britain settle with Turkish nationalism. But the prime minister was not alone in his hopes for Greek military success, for his views were reinforced by the apparently omnipresent Hankey and omniscient Balfour. Even Churchill, who had long tried to persuade Lloyd George to come to terms with Turkish nationalists, reverted to a pro-Greek stance over the Chanak 'crisis'.

In August 1922 the Turkish forces, galvanized by Mustafa Kemal (who later took the name of Ataturk, 'father of the Turks') and a militant revival of Turkish nationalism, overwhelmed Greek troops in western Anatolia. In September the Greeks retreated to the city of Smyrna, which the Turks set aflame after more than three years of Greek occupation. Curzon recommended that Greece be encouraged to sign an armistice with Turkey and vacate Asia Minor, though he did not want the British to abandon any point of influence in Europe – the Gallipoli peninsula, the straits,

Constantinople or Thrace. Lloyd George and Churchill agreed, although the prime minister doubted that the Greek army was completely spent. The British navy evacuated tens of thousands of Greeks and Armenians from burning Smyrna, where reports of atrocities stimulated old and new fears.

The War Office was kept informed by reports from General Charles Harington (1872–1940), the commander in chief of British forces in Constantinople. Harrington was also responsible for the security of the British troops in the straits zone at Chanak, a port located on the Asiatic side of the narrows between Smyrna and Constantinople, across from the Gallipoli peninsula. Since the few thousand British forces at Chanak were outnumbered by the Turks, Britain had to decide whether to evacuate its forces or use force against Kemal's army to prevent it entering Constantinople and reasserting Turkish control in Europe.

An atmosphere of war crisis returned to Downing Street. Meetings were held early in the morning until late at night, and throughout two weekends. Whitehall departments sent and received feverish wires, secret messages were busily decoded, and special news releases were prepared for the press. The prime minister delegated Churchill to communicate with dominion leaders and coordinate naval, military and air positions, while Curzon was dispatched to Paris to handle Allied diplomacy.

No longer restricted by war censorship, the press did not jump to automatic patriotic defense. On 18 September the *Daily Mail* attacked the government's press release for being 'deliberately designed to promote a most disastrous and costly war' and demanded: 'STOP THIS NEW WAR!' The next day the same paper sarcastically reported that dominion leaders had refused to send troops 'in order that Mr. Winston Churchill may make a new Gallipoli'. Two days later, the *Daily Mail* demanded that Britain 'GET OUT OF CHANAK' and reported war protest meetings held in London and throughout the country the previous evening. With Parliament in recess, the prime minister had no need or opportunity to inform the House of Commons of the situation. Fleet Street, however, fanned suspicions. Cynics suggested that Lloyd George had deliberately stirred up the threat of war in order to increase his popularity before calling a general election.

So much has been written, and in such detail, about the Chanak crisis and the fall of Lloyd George's coalition that historians have sometimes failed to see the wood for the trees.[35] First and foremost, it is clear that the most influential newspapers in Fleet Street firmly rejected another war against the Turks. The minutes of meetings and diaries kept by participants also make it clear that Lloyd George was revitalized by the Chanak crisis, his hopes stirred not only for a Greek military revival and the return to power of Venizelos, but also for the creation of a larger Balkan union against the Turks. Two trips by Curzon to Paris failed, however, to persuade France to join Britain against Turkey since the French had

72   The Turks recaptured Smyrna in September, 1922, after three years of Greek occupation. The city burned and Greeks fled, but Conservative politicians and newspapers opposed Lloyd George.

already established relations with the Turkish nationalist government at Ankara. The only dominion countries willing to risk more bloodshed at the Dardanelles were New Zealand and Newfoundland. Australia proved very reluctant; Canada was opposed; while in South Africa General Smuts remained firmly silent. Neither were Conservative backbenchers willing to fight in what they regarded as Lloyd George's war. British ships were rushed to the area, aircraft were stopped en route to Iraq, and forces relocated from Malta, Egypt and beyond. But no bandwagon rolled.

The Chanak crisis ended in spite of Downing Street, which had drafted an ultimatum for General Harington to give to Kemal, when the two generals refused to join battle. At the end of September representatives of each agreed to confer at Mudania to discuss the future of Chanak, the straits, and Thrace. The meeting in early October would set the scene for a larger conference at Lausanne in Switzerland, where in 1923 Curzon concluded an enduring treaty between London and Ankara.[36]

The political consequences of the Chanak crisis immediately became clear within Britain when an independent Conservative announced that he would challenge the Coalition candidate at the forthcoming Newport by-election. If the Coalition lost, Lloyd George knew that his government would be finished. Bonar Law, who had stepped down as Conservative leader the previous year, now reasserted his authority and endorsed Curzon's efforts to reach an agreement with France to end hostilities with the Turks. On behalf of the Liberals, Asquith launched an attack on the

Coalition, particularly the 'amateurs in Downing Street'. Churchill planned to take the Coalition's case to the country, but had instead to undergo an emergency appendectomy.[37]

The anti-Coalition candidate won the seat at Newport. On the morning of the result, the Conservatives met at the Carlton Club. Chamberlain spoke in support of the Coalition, but was interrupted by cries of 'Ireland', 'Egypt', 'India' and 'Newport'. Stanley Baldwin (1867–1947), backed by Bonar Law, declared that Lloyd George, having destroyed the Liberal party, should not be allowed to do the same to the Conservatives. The conclusion was clear.[38]

Without Conservative support for the Coalition, Lloyd George had no option but to resign. Hankey rushed to 10 Downing Street, where he saw Chamberlain returning from the cabinet room after informing Lloyd George of the morning's meeting at the Carlton Club. Hankey found Lloyd George in the lavatory. 'Hankey, you have written your last Minutes for me,' he said. 'I have asked the King to come to town, and this afternoon I shall resign and you will have another Prime Minister.'[39]

The leader in *The Edinburgh Review* of January 1923 was headed 'Four Years of Lloyd Georgian Foreign Policy'. Its author was Valentine Chirol, the influential journalist who had first given currency to the term 'Middle East' in 1902. Chirol had left the staff of *The Times* in 1912, but continued to write on India and the Middle East. At the Paris peace conference, he had monitored the French press on behalf of the Foreign Office. More than half of Chirol's new twenty-page article concerned Lloyd George's postwar diplomacy in the Middle East, which he believed had led to

> a resurgent Turkey, flushed with her facile triumph over the unfortunate Greeks, whom we at first encouraged in an adventure far beyond their strength and then abandoned to their fate; anarchy rampant throughout Central Asia; the Middle East from Persia to Egypt seething with new and old discontents amidst the dangerous wreckage of our broken promises and conflicting policies.[40]

Chirol blamed Lloyd George for claiming that his Turkish policy was 'a sort of apostolic succession to Mr Gladstone's', for taking too long to reach a peace settlement with the Turks after the war, for falling under the spell of the Greeks, for ignoring Curzon and the Foreign Office, for offending the world's Muslims, for abandoning Britain's Allies and for breaking wartime commitments. According to Chirol, the only positive British diplomatic achievement between 1919 and 1922 was Balfour's leadership at the Washington Naval Conference. Chirol concluded:

> In the domain of foreign affairs the inheritance which Mr Lloyd George has bequeathed to his successors is more than in any other a *damnosa hereditas*. For if he is to go down to history as the man whose great

qualities did at any rate very much to 'win the war', he will also go down to history as the man whose great defects went far to 'lose the peace'.[41]

Chirol was certainly correct in Lloyd George's overestimation of Greek power and his underestimation of the force of Turkish nationalism. If Britain had concluded a moderate peace sooner with the Turks, the likelihood of a situation such as the Chanak crisis could have been diminished.

But it is nevertheless untrue to suggest that the prime minister was the only person responsible for what had done in the Middle East. Chirol's criticisms of British policy would have been more apt if he had mentioned the other individuals and institutions that had made, conducted and influenced British policy in the Middle East since the beginning of the twentieth century. Chirol might have reconsidered his own imperial strategy, one that had virtually ignored the diverse peoples living in the lands between Europe and India. He might have re-evaluated the preoccupations of the Great Powers that had made the Foreign Office so dismissive of Persia, Turkey and Egypt. At the same time he might have questioned Whitehall for having been so unmindful of the risks and costs involved in extending Europe's war to the Middle East in 1914. He might have noted how the humiliations at the Dardanelles and on Gallipoli in 1915, at Kut in 1916, and in Gaza in 1917, had made London's Eastern strategists more determined to recover the imperial pride lost to the Turks. He might have observed how the British had driven into Central Asia to meet imaginary enemies while attempting to fill the imperial vacuum created by Russia's collapse. Finally, Chirol might have noted how British nationalistic propaganda during the last year of the war had stirred high expectations among the Arabs, Armenians, Greeks, Kurds, Persians, Zionists and others, all of which were shattered by the postwar situation in London.

Conclusion

London's Legacy to the Twentieth Century

LONDON'S IMPACT ON the Middle East was greatest during the first two decades of the twentieth century. After 1922, London was rather more reactive than proactive to Middle Eastern affairs. By the middle decades of the twentieth century, oil in the Middle East had become so important to the British navy and economy that, although the area may still have been less important than Europe, it had become as important if not more so than India. In the final decades of the twentieth century, the Middle East clearly influenced London more than London influenced the Middle East.

As Britain's impact on the Middle East diminished during the 1920s, British involvement in the area increased, mainly because until the 1970s the British obtained most of their oil from the Persian Gulf. Subsequently, oil from the North Sea enabled Britain to become an oil exporter for the first time in its history. British policy in the Middle East after the 1920s had to deal much more with oil and with the various countries and groupings of the Middle East as distinct entities. While the British remained the most powerful foreigners in the Middle East throughout World War II, policymakers had to take much more notice of the Middle East than they had previously in the late nineteenth and early twentieth centuries. The number of British and Allied troops fighting in the Near and Middle East exceeded those in World War I. (During the Cold War, London policymakers increasingly had to consider the aims and interests of Washington.) By the late 1960s, when the last British troops evacuated the area east of Suez, the United States had replaced Britain as the dominant foreign power in the region, allowing for the several Soviet client states in the Arab world. What follows is a brief survey of that twentieth-century shift and some questions about London's legacy in the Middle East for the twentieth century.

From 1922 to 1939 British interests in the Middle East were protected as unobtrusively and as cheaply as possible. Most of the expenses incurred by British armed forces, as well as advisers and equipment in the Middle East, were paid for by Middle Eastern taxpayers. This followed practices adopted by the British in India and Egypt before World War I. Iraq's independence in 1930, like that of Egypt in 1922, favoured the upper classes and minorities who supported government leaders and who identified more with the British than did the masses. British officers and advisers on the spot silenced troublemakers in the countryside by using aircraft for intelligence and for bombing by the police. In urban areas British officials relied on informers and spies to help them locate nationalists, many of whom they imprisoned or exiled with the same determination as the French in North Africa, Syria, and Lebanon.

The Palestine Mandate did not pose very great problems for the British until the late 1930s. The Zionists purchased land, but mostly farmed it themselves, thereby displacing many Palestinian field workers in the 1920s. The arrival of many more Jews who settled in cities during the 1930s sparked an Arab revolt between 1936 and 1939 that took more than 20,000 British soldiers to quell and resulted in 6,500 casualties.[1] Unable to devise a partitioning of Palestine acceptable to the Arabs, Britain at this time favoured the Arabs because of oil and because it was known the Jews could not turn to Hitler. The White Paper of 1939 created a bi-national state, which provided for the equal protection of Arabs and Jews, based on Palestine's population being stabilized at two-thirds Arab and one-third Jewish. Further Jewish immigration was restricted to 75,000 people per year for five years. Outraged by this policy, the Zionists adopted a programme at the Biltmore Hotel in New York City that demanded a Jewish state, and urged Jews to fight the war as if there were no White Paper and the White Paper as if there were no war.[2]

During World War II, the British maintained a massive military presence throughout the Middle East, rid the area of pro-Axis leaders, backed the Free French in Lebanon and Syria, expelled Axis armies from Libya, and encouraged US campaigns in North Africa and US lend-lease subsidies to Ibn Saud. Britain even coordinated the region's economy by means of the Anglo-American Middle East Supply Centre. The rulers and upper classes of the area benefited economically during the war from increased Allied demands for their goods and services. The masses, however, felt the negative impact of the Anglo-American and Free French military occupation of their countries, as wartime inflation made their lives more miserable. Britain kept afloat economically during World War II not only by the US lend-lease agreement, but by borrowing money from Egypt – one of the poorest countries in the world. The Muslim Brotherhood in Egypt, an underground political movement that was hostile to the British, had millions of members that had an impact on mass politics after World War II.[3]

The British withdrawal from the Middle East was determined less by a lack of imperial nerve, than exhaustion after two enormously costly wars. When Churchill was asked to characterize the Exchequer at the end of World War II, he used the word 'bankrupt'. Middle Eastern nationalists, with bitter memories of having been let down by the British after World War I, knew that both the United States and Soviet Union were ideologically opposed to British imperialism in the Middle East. As the British government had gone so heavily into debt during the war and had become so economically dependent upon the United States, special attention had to be paid to the world's only atomic power. Since Washington was at that time quite ignorant of the Middle East, US officials often deferred to Britain's greater experience. British intelligence also played a role in conditioning the official US outlook towards the Middle East.

Israel and oil became the two biggest issues for Britain after World War II, when Zionists paid less attention to Britain after the Israeli state was recognized by the United States in 1948, and with oil companies taking fewer cues from Britain. Apart from some differences over Israel and oil, the United States usually followed the path already well trodden by the British.[4]

The Cold War delayed the British departure from the Middle East. When Soviet forces delayed their departure from northern Iran, Anglo-American fears of the spread of communism were heightened. Britain believed that Soviet communism had to be kept out of the Middle East and the Truman Doctrine strengthened anti-communism in Greece and Turkey even before the Cold War intensified in Europe, and turned into a Hot War in Asia. Cooperation between London and Washington reinstated the shah in Tehran amidst the campaign to nationalize the Anglo-Iranian Oil Company. The shah generously compensated that company, which changed its name to British Petroleum.[5]

In 1956, when the Suez Canal was nationalized, Anthony Eden (1895–1977) as prime minister saw in Nasser another Hitler who at all costs was not to be appeased – as the Nazi leader had been in the 1930s. While seeming to let the United Nations resolve the matter, Britain secretly made plans with France, which repudiated Nasser for supporting Algerian nationalists, and with Israel, which feared an Egyptian invasion. The air and land campaign that Britain, France and Israel waged against Egypt was successful from a military standpoint, but on the eve of a presidential election, the United States became indignant because London had not sought Washington's approval. The US secretary of state, John Foster Dulles (1888–1959) forced the British, French and Israeli troops to evacuate Suez, and this led to Eden's resignation. London and Washington soon resumed cordial relations, however, especially once Nasser's pan-Arab nationalism expanded into Jordan, Syria and Yemen, with the United States adopting an increasingly pro-Saudi stance. Washington backed the Baghdad Pact, which was an Anglo-American variation on the North Atlantic Treaty Organization, but the regional defence organization, the Central Treaty Organization, was shattered in 1958, when the Iraqi revolution demonstrated more hatred for the British and their Hashemite collaborators than love for Soviet socialism.[6]

In 1967 the sudden triumph of Israeli forces over those of Egypt, Jordan and Syria led Washington to start paying more attention to Israeli rather than British intelligence. Israel began to replace Britain as Washington's main external source of intelligence about the Middle East. In the late 1960s, Harold Wilson (1916–1995) as prime minister announced the withdrawal of all British troops east of Suez. To fill the power vacuum in the Persian Gulf, the United States encouraged the shah of Iran to build up his forces and helped establish the Gulf Cooperation Council, which linked Saudi Arabia with the other oil-rich countries of the region. Britain, like other Western countries, competed at such events as the Paris Air Show to sell planes and military hardware to oil-rich Persian and Arab army officers and rulers.

Before Britain obtained North Sea oil in the late 1970s, the country remained largely dependent on Middle Eastern oil. The huge hikes in prices orchestrated during the 1970s by the Organization of Petroleum Exporting Countries (OPEC) meant that the oil-rich states of the Middle East had big shopping lists that various arms dealers and western suppliers competed with each other to fill. The British government supported the United States's protest against the shah's overthrow and the establishment of the Islamic Republic in Iran, the Soviet invasion of Afghanistan, Qaddafi's operations in Libya, the Iraq-Iran war, and Iraq's invasion of Kuwait. By the 1990s it was clear that the Americans had replaced the British as the most powerful and most hated foreigners in the Middle East. At the same time, the City of London put its financial services at the disposal of the oil rich countries of the Persian Gulf in petrodollar marketing and currency speculation.[7]

The unprecedented wealth gained by some from the oil-rich countries of the Middle East, formerly tied to Britain, had an impact on London's hotels, restaurants, hospitals, shops and real estate during the 1970s. An increasing number of merchants in London put signs in their windows welcoming customers in Arabic and Persian script and ever more people from the Middle East worked, studied, lived, and retired in London. British reactions to the many visitors and emigrants from the Middle East required adjustments in the light of the general postwar demographic phenomenon of London becoming racially less homogenous.

Jonathan Raban was so struck by the Arabs he encountered in London during the 1970s that he visited several Arab countries and published his observations. In Dubai, one of the oil-rich Gulf countries of the United Arab Emirates, Raban met the British consul-general, who spoke of there being little goodwill left between the British and the Arabs. Raban asked if the experienced official thought the situation would be improved by more British schools teaching Arabic. The consul-general responded:

It's too late for that. We're much too far behind. Look at all the Arabs who've got degrees – through the medium of English – at British and American universities. How many Englishmen have degrees – through the medium of Arabic – from universities in the Middle East? Name me one. You can't. The Arabs are too far ahead for us to ever catch up. Our only merit is our professional expertise. It's the only thing we've got that the Arabs are remotely interested in. There's hardly a single Englishman alive who can carry on an intelligent conversation in Arabic; but the Arabs you meet here will have digested everything in the *Financial Times* by breakfast time. They're not going to give tuppence for your love of Arabia, or your fourth-year Arabic from the School of Oriental and African Studies; the only thing they want from you is your technical knowledge, your advice on investment or construction. The rest is simply flummery.[8]

Raban then asked the British consul if the Americans were any better than the British in speaking Arabic or understanding the Arabs. 'Worse,' the British official answered with a sigh that gave him some satisfaction: 'Far, far worse.'[9]

The Middle East was a term invented in 1902. Until 1922, London policymaking towards the Middle East involved Britain from naval, capitalist, imperial, European and democratic standpoints. By the 1930s, the British dependence on oil from the region meant that London had to adopt realistic attitudes and actions towards the Middle East, rather than imposing British ethnocentric geopolitical strategy.

Before 1914, London's policymakers saw to it that the British retained supremacy in the area by maintaining their imperial and naval presence as well as the status quo in the Persian Gulf and Suez Canal; by protecting British commercial and financial investments; by dividing the region into diplomatic spheres of interest with France, Russia, Germany, Italy, and Greece; and by extolling their policies to a British public still willing to take up the white man's burden provided it were neither too heavy nor too expensive.

During the 1914–18 war, London's policymakers sent large numbers of British troops to the Near and Middle East, which led to a temporary military occupation of much territory and military control. With the government's imposition of press censorship for the duration of the war, few in London, other than Western military strategists, asked whether this enormous extension of British dominance in the Middle East was either necessary or wise.

After the war, once Fleet Street and Westminster realized the cost of the military occupation of Iraq, Palestine and Turkey, Downing Street and Whitehall had to devise more cost-effective methods of controlling Britain's new Middle Eastern empire. While the British could subsidize and control a ruler and his family, they could neither subsidize nor control an entire nation. The pre-war imperial solutions were no longer effective in a postwar age of nationalism and mass politics.

If criteria other than British interests are used to assess London's invention of the Middle East in the early twentieth century, several questions can be raised. Was London's policymaking more creative or more destructive for the governments and peoples of the Middle East? What precedents did ruling collaborators and members of rich minorities, backed by the British, set for the new nationalist regimes of the Middle East, almost all of which at the end of the twentieth century were dominated in one way or another by military regimes? Has Anglo-American support for the Zionists and for the state of Israel really compensated for what Germany and the Soviet Union inflicted upon Jews? Might the Arab-Israeli conflict have ended sooner if so many had not had a vested interest in the conflict continuing, initially to contain communism but subsequently to find customers for expensive weapons? Has nationalism served the states in the Middle East better than the peoples of these states? Who has benefited the most from the Suez Canal and the oil around the Persian Gulf? Have oil companies and ruling regimes gained at the expense of the majority? Are the English-speaking media any more knowledgeable and tolerant of Arab, Persian and Turkish Muslims at the end of the twentieth century than they were at its beginning? Such questions raise fundamental issues about global power and responsibility in the twentieth century that are relevant to the recent history of the Middle East.

NOTES

Abbreviations

BD 1898–1914   *British Documents on the Origins of the War*, ed. G. Gooch and H. Temperley
BLL   British Library, London
BLO   Bodleian Library, Oxford
CAB   British Cabinet Papers
CCC   Churchill College, Cambridge
CID   Committee of Imperial Defence
FO   Foreign Office, London
HLRO   House of Lords Record Office, London
PRO   Public Record Office, London
WO   War Office, London

Introduction
The World's Greatest Metropolis

1. M. Pearton, *The Knowledgeable State: Diplomacy, War, and Technology since 1830* (London, 1982), p. 107.
2. Ibid., p. 133.
3. The most recent general bibliography is W. Olson, *Britain's Elusive Empire in the Middle East, 1900–1921* (New York, 1982).
4. N. Mathews and M. Wainright, *A Guide to Manuscripts in the British Isles Relating to the Middle East and North Africa*, ed. J. Pearson (Oxford, 1980). Several guides to the archives in the Public Record Office, London, are indispensable for this period: *List of Papers of the Committee of Imperial Defence* (1964); *Classes of Department Papers for 1900–1939* (1966); *List of Cabinet Papers, 1915 and 1916* (1966); *The Records of the Cabinet Office to 1922* (1966); and *The Records of the Foreign Office, 1789–1939* (1969).
5. J. Bullock-Anderson, *A Handlist of Business Archives at Guildhall Library* (London, 1991).
6. C. Hazelhurst and C. Woodland, *A Guide to the Papers of British Cabinet Ministers, 1900–1951* (London, 1974). See also several of the works by A. J. P. Taylor, including *The Trouble-makers: Dissent over Foreign Policy, 1792–1939* (London, 1957); *English History, 1914–1945* (Oxford, 1965); and *Beaverbrook* (London, 1972).
7. The most valuable diary for historians is S. Roskill's monumental study of Maurice Hankey. See his *Hankey: Man of Secrets*, vol. 1, *1877–1918* (London, 1970); vol. 2, *1919–1931* (London, 1972).
8. See *Lloyd George: Twelve Essays*, ed. A. J. P. Taylor (London, 1971); and *Churchill*, ed. R. Blake and R. Louis (London, 1993).
9. The appearance of London's policy-makers and officials in the Middle East is also important for historians and there are rich photographic archives in Britain on the Middle East. See G. Grant, *Middle Eastern Photographic Collections in the United Kingdom* (Durham, 1989).
10. C. P. Snow, *The Corridors of Power* (London, 1963).

1   *British Ascendancy*

1. P. J. Cain and A. G. Hopkins, *British Imperialism*, vol. 1, *Innovation and Expansion, 1688–1914* (London, 1993), pp. 3–52, 397–421.

2. M. Yapp, *The Making of the Modern Near East, 1792–1923* (London, 1987), pp. 47–265.

3. C. Bayly, *Imperial Meridian: The British Empire and the World* (London, 1989), pp. 16–75, 164–216.

4. Cain and Hopkins, *British Imperialism*, vol. 1, pp. 403–8.

5. M. Swartz, *The Politics of British Foreign Policy in the Era of Disraeli and Gladstone* (New York, 1985), pp. 31–122.

6. R. Owen, *The Middle East in the World Economy, 1800–1914* (London, 1981), pp. 216–43.

7. M. Daly, *Empire on the Nile: The Anglo-Egyptian Sudan, 1898–1934* (Cambridge, 1986), pp. 1–39.

8. J. Kelly, *Britain and the Persian Gulf, 1795–1880* (Oxford, 1968), pp. 260–89; B. Busch, *Britain and the Persian Gulf, 1894–1914* (Berkeley, 1967), pp. 1–5, 384–8.

9. See M. Port, *Imperial London: Civil Government Building in London, 1850–1915* (London, 1995).

10. J. Sumida, *In Defence of Naval Supremacy: Finance, Technology, and British Naval Policy, 1889–1914* (Boston, 1989), pp. 3–36.

11. J. Brewer, *The Sinews of Power: War, Money and the English State, 1688–1783* (London, 1989), pp. 70–85; F. Fisher, *London and the English Economy, 1500–1800* (London, 1990), pp. 105–18.

12. R. Sayers, *The Bank of England, 1891–1944*, vol. 1 (Cambridge, 1976), pp. 1–25; D. Kynaston, *The City of London*, vol. 1, *A World of Its Own, 1815–1890* (London, 1994), pp. 9–33.

13. R. Robinson and J. Gallagher, *Africa and the Victorians: The Official Mind of Imperialism* (London, 1967), pp. 1–26, 462–72.

14. D. Watt, *Personalities and Policies: Studies in the Formulation of British Policy in the Twentieth Century* (London, 1965), pp. 1–10.

15. E. Said, *Orientalism* (London, 1979), pp. 31–110; *Culture and Imperialism* (London, 1993), pp. xi–15.

16. D. Read, *The Power of News: The History of Reuters, 1849–1989* (Oxford, 1994), pp. 51, 86–9.

17. Ibid., pp. 19–20, 74.

18. S. Koss, *The Rise and Fall of the Political Press in Britain*, vol. 1, *The Nineteenth Century* (London, 1981), pp. 1–29; vol. 2, *The Twentieth Century*, pp. 1–14; D. Butler, A. Sloman, *British Political Facts, 1900–1975*, 4th edn (London, 1975); A. Morris, *The Scaremongers: The Advocacy of War and Rearmament, 1896–1914* (London, 1984), pp. 1–9.

19. W. Houghton, ed., *The Wellesley Index to Victorian Periodicals* (Toronto, 1966–1979), vol. 1, pp. 7–9, 210–12, 699–700; vol. 2, pp. 551–3, 623–4; M. Steiner, 'British Quality Periodicals on Ireland, India, and Africa, 1880–1930', unpublished M.A. thesis, Arizona State University, 1992. The figures on the Middle East were compiled by W. Hull.

20. J. Altholz, *The Religious Press in Britain, 1760–1900* (New York, 1989), pp. 1–25, 50–67.

21. A. J. P. Taylor, *The Troublemakers: Dissent over Foreign Policy, 1792–1939* (London, 1957); M. Ostrogorski, *Democracy and the Organization of Political Parties*, vol. 1. *England* (New York, 1964), pp. 289–335.

22. Figures compiled from indexes by W. Hull, from UK Parliamentary Debates, House of Commons and House of Lords, 1902–23.

23. Asquith's papers are in the Bodleian Library, Oxford. Asquith's letters as prime minister to the Sovereign, 1908–16, are in the Cabinet Papers, CAB/41/30–6, PRO. See R. Jenkins, *Asquith* (London, 1978).

24. Balfour's papers are in the British Library, London. See also the papers of Balfour's secretary, John Satterfield Sandars, in the Bodleian Library, Oxford. Balfour's letters as prime minister to the Sovereign, 1902–5, are in the Cabinet Papers, CAB/41/27–30. Balfour's letters as

foreign secretary, 1916–19, are in the Foreign Office Private Collection, FO/800/199–217, PRO. See M. Egremont, *A Life of Arthur James Balfour* (London, 1980).

25. Churchill's papers are in Churchill College, Cambridge. The papers of Maurice Hankey are also at Churchill College. See R. Churchill, *Winston S. Churchill*, vol. 1, *Youth, 1874–1900* (London, 1966); vol. 2, *The Young Statesman, 1901–1914* (London, 1967); companion vol. 2 (London, 1969); M. Gilbert, *Winston S. Churchill*, vol. 3, *1914–1916* (1971); companion vol. 3, parts 1 and 2 (1973); vol. 4, *1917–1922* (1975); companion vol. 4, parts 1,2,3 (1977).

26. Curzon's papers are in the India Record Office of the British Library. Curzon's papers as foreign secretary, 1919–24, are in the Foreign Office Private Collection, FO/800/147–58, PRO. See H. Nicolson, *Curzon: The Last Phase* (London, 1934).

27. Grey's papers are at the Public Record Office, London. His papers as foreign secretary, 1905–16, are in the Foreign Office Private Collection, FO/800/43–103, where they have been catalogued by individual countries, including Bulgaria (43), Egypt (46–8), France (49–60), Greece (63), Italy (64–6), Persia (72–5), Serbia and Montenegro (76), Turkey (79–80), USA (81–6). See K. Robbins, *Sir Edward Grey* (London, 1971).

28. Kitchener's papers are at the Public Record Office, London, PRO/30/57/41–91, PRO. See T. Royale, *The Kitchener Enigma* (London, 1985).

29. Lansdowne's papers are in the Public Record Office, London. His papers as foreign secretary, 1900–5, are in the Foreign Office Private Collection, FO/800/114–45, PRO. See T. Legh (Lord Newton), *Lord Lansdowne: A Biography* (London, 1929).

30. Lloyd George's papers as prime minister, 1916–22, are in the House of Lords Record Office, London, with his correspondence in F/2, 3, 8, 10–13, 17, 24–6, 30–1, 38–9, 44–5,

and 49 relevant. The private correspondence must be supplemented by the relevant Cabinet Papers, CAB/27/1–8, 12, 22, 24–39, 50, 91–3, 98, 133–4, 164, 168–70, 189, CAB/28/1–9. See J. Grigg, *The Young Lloyd George* (London, 1973); *Lloyd George: The People's Champion, 1902–1911* (London, 1978); *Lloyd George: From Peace to War, 1912–16* (London, 1985).

31. Milner's papers are in the Bodleian Library, Oxford. Boxes 107–51 relate to the war, 1914–18; boxes 152–77 relate to the postwar, 1918–20. Milner's papers in the Public Record Office, PRO/30/30/2, 7, 10–13, 15, 18–20, 23, are also important. Milner's Mission to Egypt, 1919–20, has papers, FO/848/1–18, PRO. See A. Gollin, *Proconsul in Politics: A Study of Lord Milner in Opposition and Power* (New York, 1964).

32. C. Hitchins, *Blood, Class, and Nostalgia: Anglo-American Ironies* (London, 1990), pp. 110–19.

33. A. Mahan, 'The Persian Gulf and International Relations', *National Review* (London), September 1902, pp. 27–8.

34. Ibid., p. 39.

35. Ibid., pp. 39–45.

36. *The Times*, 14, 17, 20, 25, 27 October; 10, 12, 20, 24 November; 15, 23, 25, 26, 30 December 1902; 14, 17 January; 4, 30 March; 11, 21 April 1903.

37. L. Fritzinger, 'Diplomat without Portfolio: Valentine Chirol of The Times in Berlin, 1892–1896', unpublished Ph.D. thesis, New York University, 1992; papers of V. Chirol, Groups Records Office, New International plc, London.

38. V. Chirol, *The Middle East Question or Some Political Problems of Indian Defence* (London, 1903), p. 176.

39. R. Davison, 'Where is the Middle East?', *Foreign Affairs* (New York), vol. 38, no. 4 (July 1960), pp. 665–75.

40. H. Mackinder, 'The Geographical Point of History', *Geographical Journal* (London), vol. 23 (1904), pp. 431–44.

2   *The Status Quo: 1902–1905*

1. A. Balfour, *Foundations of Belief*, 10th ed. (London, 1912), p. 33.
2. Esher to Balfour, 30 December 1903, Balfour Papers, Add. MS 49718, BLL.
3. As prime minister, Balfour made such distinctions in his extensive royal and political correspondence as well as in cabinet and CID meetings; Balfour Papers, 1903–5, Add. MSS 49683 and 49684, BLL; Minutes and Papers of the Committee for Imperial Defence, 1903–5, Cabinet Papers, CAB/38/1–10, PRO.
4. Supplementary note by the prime minister, 19 December 1904, CAB/38/6/124, PRO.
5. J. Sumida, *In Defence of Naval Supremacy: Finance, Technology, and British Naval Policy, 1889–1914* (Boston, 1989), pp. 18–23.
6. Selbourne to Balfour, 28 October 1903, Selbourne Papers, BLO, as quoted in Sumida, *In Defence of Naval Supremacy*, p. 24.
7. Balfour, 'The British Garrison in Egypt', 21 April 1904, CAB/38/4/32, PRO.
8. Balfour to Edward VII, 2 December 1902, CAB/41/27/36, PRO.
9. Balfour to Edward VII, 23 March 1904, CAB/41/29/14, PRO.
10. Balfour to Edward VII, CAB/41/29/11, PRO.
11. Balfour to Rothschild, 30 January 1914. Balfour Papers, Zionism File, Add. MSS 49745, BLL.
12. The influence of prominent Jewish financiers in the City of London has been grossly exaggerated by decades of anti-Semitic writings. A more balanced, but gossipy treatment is A. Allfrey, *Edward VII and his Jewish Court* (London, 1991).
13. Lansdowne to Balfour, 1 November 1900. Papers of John S. Sanders (private secretary to Balfour 1892–1905), Miscellaneous File, c. 733, Folio 11–12, BLO.
14. Lansdowne's exchanges with Edward VII and Balfour, 22–25 August 1902, Balfour Papers, Add. MS 49727, BLL; Lansdowne to A. Hardinge, 1902–3,

Lansdowne's Foreign Office Papers, Persia, FO/800/137, PRO.

15. Lansdowne's complex roles in the Balkans are covered in *British Documents on the Origins of the War, 1898–1914*, ed. G. Gooch and H. Temperley (hereafter *BD 1898–1914*), vol. 5, *The Near East: The Macedonian Problem and the Annexation of Bosnia, 1903–9* (London, 1928), pp. 49–124.
16. *The Church Times* (London), 2 October 1903.
17. *The British Weekly: A Journal of Social and Christian Progress* (London), 10 September 1903.
18. *The Universe* (London), 19 September 1903.
19. Lansdowne to Balfour, 28 August 1904, Balfour Papers, Add. MS 49728, BLL.
20. Balfour to Lansdowne, 22 February 1904, ibid.
21. Lansdowne's handling of British relations with the United States is covered in B. Perkins, *The Great Rapprochement: England and the United States, 1895–1914* (New York, 1968).
22. Lansdowne's negotiations with Tokyo and Berlin, including the British claims in Kuwait, are covered in *BD 1898–1914*, vol 2., *The Anglo-Japanese Alliance and the Franco-British Entente* (London, 1927), pp. 89–137.
23. Balfour to Lansdowne, a twenty-page letter of dictation dated 12 December 1901, Balfour Papers, Add. MS 49727, BLL.
24. Lansdowne to Balfour, 12 December 1901, ibid.
25. Lansdowne's handling of the Baghdad Railway during 1903 is documented in *BD 1898–1914*, vol. 2, pp. 174–96.
26. R. Owen, *The Middle East in the World Economy* (London, 1981), pp. 191–6.
27. Ibid., p. 199.
28. Ibid., pp. 196–9.
29. V. Chirol, *The Middle East Question* (London, 1903), pp. 214–29. Chirol dedicated his book to Curzon, who invited Chirol to accompany him as the only journalist on the viceroy's tour of the Persian Gulf in 1903.
30. *BD 1898–1914*, vol. 2, pp. 179–93.
31. *UK Parliamentary Debates* (Commons),

4th ser., vol. 120 (1903), 1247–8.

32. *The Times*, 18 April 1903.

33. Balfour's answer to a question put by G. Bowles, *Parliamentary Debates* (Commons), 4th ser., vol. 121 (1903), 122.

34. *The Economist* (London), 25 April 1903.

35. Lansdowne to N. O'Connor, 23 May 1905, Lansdowne Papers, FO/808/143, PRO.

36. Balfour to Edward VII, 1 August 1905, CAB/41/30/30. See also A. Parker's forty-six-page 'Memorandum respecting the Baghdad Railway', 10 March 1906, Turkey File, FO/371/148, PRO.

37. A. Kaminsky, *The Indian Office, 1880–1910* (New York, 1986), pp. 110–11.

38. P. Mason (Woodruff), *A Matter of Honour: An Account of the Indian Army, its Officers and Men* (London, 1974), p. 570.

39. B. Busch, *Britain and the Persian Gulf, 1894–1914*, pp. 187–270. Curzon's papers as viceroy of India are catalogued as vols 195–774 in the India Record Office and Library, BLL.

40. D. McLean, *Britain and her Buffer State: The Collapse of the Persian Empire, 1890–1914* (London, 1979), pp. 29–72.

41. Balfour, 'Defence of India', 30 April, 20 May 1903, Cabinet Papers, CAB/38/2/26, 35, PRO.

42. Viceroy Curzon to Brodrick, Secretary of State for India, 17 December 1903, Curzon Papers, 399, BLL.

43. On Curzon's resignation, contrast Mason, *A Matter of Honour*, pp. 392–402, with D. Dilks, *Curzon in India*, vol. 2, *Frustration* (New York, 1969).

44. Balfour and Lansdowne's handling of Anglo-Russian relations before, during and after the Russo-Japanese War is documented in *BD 1898–1914*, vol. 4, *The Anglo-Russian Rapprochement, 1903–7*, pp. 1–218.

45. Owen, *The Middle East in the World Economy*, pp. 130–5, 216–44.

46. Balfour to Edward VII, 21 July 1903,

Cabinet Papers, CAB/41/28/15, PRO.

47 The extensive exchanges between Lansdowne and Cromer, from 8 October 1902 to 27 March 1904, can be followed in the Lansdowne Papers, FO/800/124, PRO.

48. Lansdowne's diplomacy surrounding the Anglo-French Entente of 1904 is documented in *BD 1898–1914*, vol. 2, pp. 253–407; and in vol. 3, *The Testing of the Entente, 1904–6* (London, 1928), pp. 1–169.

3   *Holding the Ramparts: 1905–1911*

1. G. Dangerfield's *Strange Death of Liberal England* (London, 1935) is a classic in the historical literature on Edwardian decline from Victorian heights.

2. *List of Papers of the Committee of Imperial Defence* (London, 1964), pp. 1–46.

3. K. Robbins, *Sir Edward Grey* (London, 1971), pp. 23–4, 29, 140.

4. Z. Steiner, *The Foreign Office and Foreign Policy, 1898–1914* (Cambridge, 1969), pp. 3, 4, 16.

5. *The Foreign Office List* (London, 1902, 1906, 1910, 1914).

6. For the social gulf between British diplomats and consuls, see D. Platt, *The Cinderella Service: British Consul since 1825* (London, 1971), pp. 1–4.

7. Foreign Office activity is chronicled in *BD 1898–1914*, vol. 4, *The Anglo-Russian Rapprochement* (London, 1929), pp. 183–304, 356–625.

8. N. Keddie and M. Amanat, 'Iran under the Later Qajars, 1848–1922', *The Cambridge History of Iran*, vol. 7, *From Nadir Shah to the Islamic Republic*, ed. P. Avery, G. Hambly and C. Melville (Cambridge, 1991), p. 180.

9. C. Issawi, 'European Economic Penetration, 1872–1921', ibid., pp. 590–607.

10. E. Grey, *Twenty-Five Years, 1892–1916* (London, 1925), vol. 1, p. 148.

11. Keddie and Amanat, 'Iran under the Later Qajars, 1848–1922', *Cambridge History of Iran*, vol. 7, pp. 202–6.

12. *BD 1898–1914*, vol. 4, pp. 374–7.
13. Ibid., pp. 218–304.
14. C. Spring-Rice to Grey, 26 April 1907, Papers of E. Grey, FO/800/70, PRO.
15. Spring-Rice to Grey, 13 September 1907, ibid.
16. More comparative study of Russia's revolution in 1905, Persia's revolution in 1906, and Turkey's revolution in 1908 would help transcend some of the limitations of historical specialization.
17. P. London and A. Hamilton, 'Views on the Anglo-Russian Agreement', *Fortnightly Review* (London), November 1907, vol. 88, pp. 733–4.
18. 'Britain and Russia in the Middle East', *Blackwood's Edinburgh Magazine* (London), January 1908, vol. 183, p. 153.
19. FO/371/324, No. 37605, PRO, as cited in F. Kazemzadeh, *Russia and Britain in Persia, 1864–1914* (New Haven, 1968), pp. 504–6.
20. E. Browne, *The Persian Revolution, 1905–1909* (London, 1910).
21. *Treasury Committee Report on the Organization of Oriental Studies in London,* UK, Parliamentary Papers, Cd 4560 (1909), pp. 1–2.
22. Ibid., pp. 153–6.
23. Ibid., pp. 65–88.
24. Ibid., p. 38.
25. Ibid., pp. 92–8, 101–27.
26. Ibid., pp. 28–31.
27. C. Phillips, *The School of Oriental and African Studies, University of London, 1917–1967* (London, n.d.), pp. 13–14.
28. *The Near East* (London), 9 March 1917, p. 414.
29. B. Lewis, *The Emergence of Modern Turkey* (London, 1961), 2nd ed., p. 217; L. Aroian and R. Mitchell, *The Middle East and North Africa* (New York, 1984), p. 116.
30. *The Christian World* (London), 11 June 1908.
31. *UK Parliamentary Debates* (Commons), 4th ser., vol. 193 (1908), 968–9.
32. Grey to G. Lowther, 31 July 1908, Turkey, FO/371/544, PRO.
33. Minutes on Lowther to Grey, 21 August 1908, FO/371/545, PRO.
34. J. Heller, *British Policy Towards the Ottoman Empire, 1868–1914* (London, 1983), pp. 17–23.
35. Lowther to Grey, 14 December 1908, FO/371/556, PRO.
36. Heller, *British Policy Towards the Ottoman Empire, 1868–1914*, p. 31; E. Kedourie, 'Young Turks, Freemasons, and Jews', *Arabic Political Memoirs* (London, 1974), pp. 243–62.
37. *The Near East*, July–August 1909.
38. Heller, *British Policy Towards the Ottoman Empire,* pp. 32–4. For British diplomacy surrounding the 1908 Revolution, see *BD 1898–1914*, vol. 5, pp. 247–320.
39. H. Feis, *Europe: The World's Banker, 1870–1914* (London, 1930, 1961), p. 5.
40. Ibid., p. 10.
41. P. J. Cain and A. G. Hopkins, *British Imperialism*, vol. 1, *Innovation and Expansion, 1688–1914* (London, 1993), pp. 407–8.
42. *The Near East*, March 1908.
43. Ibid., April 1908.
44. Copies of *The Near East* are rare, but available at Colindale, BLL.
45. *The Near East*, May 1908.
46. *The Near East*, June 1908.
47. F. de Rancourt, *History of the Ottoman Bank* (privately printed in Istanbul on the 125th anniversary of the bank, 1988); rare copy available in Guildhall Library, London, pp. 1–16; R. Owen, *The Middle East in the World Economy* (London, 1981), pp. 191–200.
48. Cain and Hopkins, *British Imperialism*, vol. 1, pp. 406–7.
49. Rancourt, *History of the Ottoman Bank*, p. 17.
50. Cromer to Strachey, 3 April 1906, quoted in P. Mellini, *Sir Eldon Gorst, The Overshadowed Proconsul* (Stanford, 1977), pp. 103, 267.
51. Exchanges between Grey and Cromer, 25 November 1905–9 May 1906, Grey Papers, FO/800/46, PRO.
52. *The Times*, 28, 29 June 1906; *The Egyptian Gazette* (Alexandria), 29 June 1906.
53. Cromer, *Modern Egypt* (London, 1908), vol. 2, p. 161.

54. Mellini, *Gorst*, p. 176; M. Daly, *Empire on the Nile: The Anglo-Egyptian Sudan, 1898–1934* (Cambridge, 1986), pp. 125–6.
55. Owen, *The Middle East in the World Economy*, pp. 216–43.
56. *The Egyptian Gazette*, 12 February 1908; al-Rafi, as quoted in J. Ahmed, *The Intellectual Origins of Egyptian Nationalism* (London, 1960), p. 79.
57. Gorst to Grey, 1 February–18 December 1908, Grey Papers, FO/800/47, PRO.
58. W. Churchill, 25 October 1909, no. 1143, CAB/37/101, PRO.
59. See Mellini, *Gorst*, pp. 185ff.
60. The last section was the caption to the drawing of T. Roosevelt on the cover of *The Illustrated London News* (London), 4 June 1910.
61. *UK Parliamentary Debates* (Commons), 5th ser., vol. 17 (1910), 1123–54.
62. Cromer, *Ancient and Modern Imperialism* (London, 1910), pp. 117–18.
63. Grey Papers, 1911, FO/800/47, PRO.

4   *Anticipating War: 1911–1914*

1. A. Morris, *The Scaremongers: The Advocacy of War and Rearmament, 1896–1914* (London, 1984), pp. 286–306.
2. J. Altholz, *The Religious Press in Britain, 1760–1900* (New York, 1989), pp. 63–4.
3. J. Grigg, *The Young Lloyd George* (London, 1973), pp. 58–85.
4. J. Grigg, 'Churchill and Lloyd George', *Churchill*, ed. R. Blake and W. Louis (Oxford, 1994), pp. 97–103.
5. A massive volume is devoted to the Moroccan Crisis of 1911, *BD 1898–1914*, vol. 7, *The Agadir Crisis* (London, 1932), pp. vii–846. That Agadir was the decisive turning-point towards war is argued by G. Barraclough, *From Agadir to Armageddon: Anatomy of a Crisis* (New York, 1982), pp. 177–81.
6. Lloyd George's speech at the Mansion House, as quoted in *BD 1898–1914*,
   vol. 7, p. 391; see the analysis of Barraclough, *From Agadir to Armageddon*, pp. 131–3.
7. Minutes of 114th meeting, 23 August 1911, Committee of Imperial Defence Papers, CAB/38/19/49, PRO; D. Read, *The Power of News: The History of Reuters* (London, 1992), pp. 88–9.
8. S. Roskill, *Hankey: Man of Secrets, 1877–1918*, vol. 1 (London, 1970), pp. 101–2, 107–8.
9. J. Sumida, *In Defence of Naval Supremacy: Finance, Technology, and British Naval Policy 1889–1914* (Boston, 1989), pp. 189–96.
10. *BD 1898–1914*, vol. 9, *The Balkan Wars*, part I, *The Prelude: The Tripoli War* (London, 1933), pp. 259–448; U. Trumpener, *Germany and the Ottoman Empire* (Princeton, 1968), pp. 21–61.
11. *BD 1898–1914*, vol. 9, pp. 513–773.
12. *BD 1898–1914*, vol. 11, *The Balkan Wars*, part II, *The League and Turkey* (London, 1934), pp. 1–1004.
13. Grey's diplomacy can be followed in his papers on Turkey, 1911–14, FO/800/80, and on Russia, 1911–14, FO/800/74, PRO.
14. Grey's note, 12 June 1913, in *BD 1898–1914*, vol. 10, part 1, *The Near and Middle East on the Eve of War* (London, 1936), p. 901.
15. T. Royale, *The Kitchener Enigma* (London, 1985), p. 4.
16. Kitchener to Tyrrell, 30 March 1912, Grey Papers, Egypt, FO/800/48, PRO.
17. Grey to Kitchener, 8 May 1912, Grey Papers, FO/800/48, PRO.
18. Kitchener's participation in the Malta meeting of the CID. Kitchener Papers, PRO/137/57/41; CID Minutes and Papers, May–July 1912, CAB/38/20–1, PRO.
19. Grey to Kitchener, 3 November 1912, Grey Papers, FO/800/48, PRO.
20. For the negotiations on the Baghdad Railway from 1910 to 1914, see *BD 1898–1914*, vol. 10, part 1, pp. 549–723; vol. 10, part 2, *The Last Years of Peace* (London, 1938), pp. 1–420.
21. Ibid.
22. Grey to L. Mallet, 23 December 1913,

Grey Papers, FO/800/80, PRO.

23. *BD 1898–1914*, vol. 10, part 1, pp. 724–900.

24. Grey to Townley, 14 October 1912, Grey Papers, FO/800/70, PRO.

25. P. Morrell, 'Our Persian Policy', *Nineteenth Century*, January 1912, vol. 71, pp. 40–7.

26. R. Machray, 'The Fate of Persia', *Fortnightly Review*, February 1912, vol. 97, pp. 291–302.

27. L. Fraser, 'The Problem of Persia', *Edinburgh Review*, October 1912, vol. 216, pp. 489–512.

28. R. Ferrier, *The History of the British Petroleum Company*, vol. 1, *The Developing Years, 1901–1932* (Cambridge, 1982), pp. 15–157.

29. Churchill to Fisher, 11 June 1912, quoted in R. Churchill, *The Young Statesman*, vol. 2, *1901–1914* (London, 1964), pp. 608–9.

30. Ferrier, *British Petroleum*, vol. 1, pp. 165–82.

31. *UK Parliamentary Debates* (Commons), vol. 55 (1913), 1465.

32. *The Times*, 18 July 1913.

33. Ferrier, *British Petroleum*, vol. 1, p. 190.

34. Ibid., p. 198.

35. Ibid., p. 199.

36. *The Times*, 20 June 1914.

37. Churchill's 'piracy' was defended by the Foreign Office on the grounds that the two ships, 'not having hoisted the Turkish flag were in no sense public vessels of the Turkish state'. A. Ryan, Foreign Office Papers, FO/800/240, PRO.

38. Asquith's diary, 17 August 1914, as quoted in H. Asquith, *Memories and Reflections, 1852–1927* (Boston, 1928), vol. 2, pp. 32–3.

39. M. Gilbert, *Winston S. Churchill*, vol. 3, *The Challenge of War, 1914–1916* (Boston, 1971), pp. 274–82.

40. Asquith, *Memories and Reflections*, vol. 2, p. 36.

41. Anglo-Ottoman diplomacy can be followed in the dispatches in FO/371/2139–43, PRO.

42. Crewe, quoted in F. Moberley, *The Campaign in Mesopotamia, 1914–1918* (London, 1923), vol. 1, p. 80.

43. Grey to Cheetham, 31 October 1914. Grey's deference to Kitchener on Arab questions is evident in his minute on this telegram: 'Does Lord Kitchener agree? If so, I will approve', FO/800/48, PRO.

44. Trumpener, *Germany and the Ottoman Empire*, pp. 50–6.

45. P. Cox to Hardinge, 23 November 1914, copied for the Foreign Office, Turkey File, FO/371/2143, PRO.

46. J. Marlowe, *Anglo-Egyptian Relations, 1800–1956*, 2nd ed. (London, 1965), pp. 69–73.

47. Copy of Colonial Secretary's Order in Council, 6 November 1914, in FO/371/2143, PRO.

48. *The Times*, 30 October–6 November 1914.

49. Lord Mayor's Day (1914) Remembrance Book, City of London Record Office, London.

50. *The Times*, 10 November 1914.

51. Parliamentary Papers 1914–16, Col. 7628, vol. 84, pp. 179–273. The precedent for this White Paper was Cd 7467, 'Correspondence between the Foreign Office and European capitals from 20 July to 4 August 1914'.

52. *UK Parliamentary Debates* (Lords), 5th ser., vol. 17, 3–4.

53. Ibid., 7–11. Bryce's deep involvement with the Armenian tragedy may be followed in his papers, MSS Bryce, 195–210, BLO.

54. The most recent account of the war and its aftermath in the Middle East is D. Fromkin, *A Peace to End All Peace: Creating the Modern Middle East, 1914–1922* (New York, 1989).

5   *The Empire Adrift: 1914–1916*

1. R. Adelson, 'The Formation of British Policy Toward the Middle East, 1914–1918', unpublished Ph.D. diss. (St Louis, 1972), pp. 1–24, 480–90.

2. J. Mackintosh, 'The Role of the Committee of Imperial Defence before 1914', *English Historical Review*, vol. 77 (Oxford, 1962), pp. 490–503.

3. *List of Cabinet Papers, 1915 to 1916* and *The Records of the Cabinet Office to*

1922; Minutes and Papers, War Council, Dardanelles Committee and War Committee, 1914–16, Cabinet Papers, CAB/22 (82 folders); photocopies in chronological order with G series, CAB/42 (26 volumes), PRO.

4. J. Fisher, *Memoirs*, vol. 1 (New York, 1921), p. 72.

5. P. Rowland, *David Lloyd George: A Biography* (New York, 1975), pp. 289–90.

6. Asquith's diary, 27 February 1915, as quoted in H. Asquith, *Memories and Reflections 1852–1927* (Boston, 1928), vol. 2, p. 76.

7. Fisher, *Memoirs*, vol. 1, pp. 63–5.

8. The wartime debate between Easterner and Westerner strategists has persisted in memoirs and partisan histories, most of which confuse strategy with tactics. The most convincing case remains that made in C. Cruttwell's *History of the Great War* (Oxford, 1940).

9. Hankey to Balfour, 28 December 1914, 5 January 1915; Balfour to Hankey, 2 January 1915; Add. MS 49703, Balfour Papers, BLL

10. Minutes of War Council, 25 November 1914; 7, 8, 13, 28 January 1915; 9, 16, 19, 24, 26 February 1915; CAB 42/1, PRO.

11. Minutes of War Council, 10, 19 March, 6 April; 14 May 1915; CAB/42/2, PRO.

12. M. Gilbert, *Winston S. Churchill*, vol. 3, *1914–1916* (London, 1971), pp. 417–41.

13. C. Hazelhurst, *Politicians at War, July 1914 to May 1915* (London, 1971), pp. 223–82.

14. Kitchener, 'The Dardanelles', 28 May 1915, CAB/37/128; Minutes of Dardanelles Committee, 7, 12, 17, 25 June; 5, 24 July; 19, 20, 27 August 1915; Hankey's 'Memorandum on the Situation', 30 August 1915, CAB/42/3, PRO.

15. At the Cabinet meeting on 4 October 1915 it was decided to rename the Dardanelles Committee the War Committee, although Hankey's CID Secretariat continued to use the Dardanelles Committee until 1

November 1915.

16. Minutes of Dardanelles Committee, 23, 24, 29, 30 September 1915, CAB/42/3; 4, 6, 11, 14 October 1915, CAB/42/4, PRO.

17. Churchill's memo, 20 October 1915, CAB/42/4. He leaped on the first reports of the Armenian massacres as a justification for using gas; Gilbert, *Churchill, 1914–1916,* vol. 3, pp. 555–6.

18. War Committee Conclusions, 3 November 1915; Minutes and Papers, November to December 1915, CAB/42/5, 6; Cabinet Papers, November to December 1915, CAB/37/137, 138, 139, PRO.

19. Hardinge to Nicolson, 23 September 1915, Nicolson Papers, FO/800/379, PRO.

20. Reports and Papers of Interdepartmental Committee on Mesopotamia, 16 October 1915, CAB/42/4, PRO.

21. Minutes of Dardanelles Committee, 14 and 21 October 1915, CAB/42/4, PRO.

22. Before his death in 1992, E. Kedourie, editor of *Middle Eastern Studies*, published more extensively than anyone on British policy towards the Middle East in the twentieth century, including *England and the Middle East: The Destruction of the Ottoman Empire, 1914–1921* (London, 1956); *The Chatham House Version and Other Middle Eastern Studies* (London, 1970); *Arabic Political Memoirs and Other Studies* (London, 1974); and *In the Anglo-Arab Labyrinth: The McMahon-Husayn Correspondence and its Interpreters, 1914–1939* (Cambridge, 1976).

23. M. de Bunsen's 'Committee on Asiatic Turkey', papers and reports, CAB/27/1, PRO.

24. R. Adelson, *Mark Sykes: Portrait of an Amateur* (London, 1975), pp. 34–8, 43–5, 100–2, 106–23.

25. Ibid., pp. 180–95.

26. The McMahon-Husayn Correspondence, as published by G. Antonius in *The Arab Awakening* (1938), as Parliamentary Papers, Cmd. 5479, 5957, and 5979 (1938–9), and in

E. Woodward et al., eds, *Documents on British Foreign Policy*, series 1, vol. 4 (1952), vol. 13 (1963).

27. Minutes and papers for Nicolson's Committee, November–December 1915, Nicolson Papers, FO/882/2, PRO.

28. Sykes-Picot memorandum, 'Arab Question', 5 January 1916, CAB/42/11, PRO.

29. Nicolson's committee met for the last time on 21 January 1916, FO/371/2767, PRO.

30. Nicolson, 'Arab Proposals', 21 January 1916, CAB/42/11, PRO.

31. Sykes to Foreign Office, 15 March, FO/371/276; Sykes to Nicolson, 18 March 1916, FO/800/381, PRO.

32. Cambon to Grey, 9 May; Grey to Cambon, 15 May; Grey to Cambon, 16 May; Grey to Berckendorff, 23 May, CAB/37/147; Berckendorff to Grey, 1 September 1916, CAB/24/9, PRO.

33. Grey to Rodd, 6, 21 September, CAB/37/155; 4, 18 October, CAB/37/157; Grey to Bertie, 9 November, CAB/37/1593; Grey to Buchanan, 21 November 1916, CAB/37/160, PRO

34. 'Attitude of Great Britain and France to the Sherif's proclamation of the title 'Malik el Bildad el Arbia'', undated, FO/882/5, PRO.

35. W. Robertson, 'Note Prepared by the C.I.G.S. for the War Committee on the Assistance that Diplomacy Might Render to Naval and Military Operations', 12 February 1916, CAB/42/9, PRO.

36. Grey, 'The Position of Great Britain with Regard to her Allies', 18 February, CAB/24/9; Minutes of War Committee, 7 June 1916, CAB/42/15, PRO.

37. Minutes and Papers of the War Committee, June–August 1916, CAB/42/12–17; Minutes of the War Committee, 25 September 1916, CAB/42/20, PRO.

38. W. Robertson, 'The Occupation of El Arish', 19 November, to which was appended T.E. Lawrence's report of 17 November, Minutes of War Committee, 20 November 1916, CAB/42/24, PRO. See also B. Westrate, *The Arab Bureau: British Policy in the Middle East, 1916–20.* (University Park, Pa., 1992).

39. *UK Parliamentary Debates* (Lords), 5th ser., vol. 19 (1915), 994–8.

40. *The Economist*, 16 October 1915, vol. 81, pp. 590–1.

41. *UK Parliamentary Debates* (Commons), 5th ser., vol. 82 (1916), 2976–7.

42. Minutes of War Cabinet, 20, 25 September 1916, CAB/42/20, PRO.

43. Report of the Dardanelles Commission, Parliamentary Papers, Cd 8490, pp. 419–86; papers, CAB/17, PRO; J. Masefield, *Gallipoli* (London, 1916).

44. Report of the Mesopotamian Commission, Cd 8610, pp. 773–965, papers, CAB/19, PRO.

45. *The Times*, 8 December 1916.

6 War Imperatives: 1916–1918

1. D. Watt, *Succeeding John Bull: America in Britain's Place, 1900–1975* (Cambridge, 1984), pp. 24–39

2. K. Burk, *Britain, America and the Sinews of War, 1914–1918* (London, 1985), pp. 13–27.

3. Ibid., pp. 137–8.

4. Ibid., pp. 263–8.

5. Unless the historian distinguishes among Easterner strategists in all their Arabist, Balkanist, Dominionist, Imperialist, Internationalist and Zionist variations, Middle Eastern policy-making is simplistically linked to the Near Eastern and Russian theatres, both of which turned out to be far more significant to the war's outcome than all the British campaigns in the Middle East.

6. D. Woodward, *Lloyd George and the Generals* (Newark, 1983), pp. 334–6.

7. Historians still disagree about the numbers of British troops and other personnel involved in the different war theatres. According to statistics drawn up for the autumn of 1918, the western theatre employed 5.4 million British, with 2.7 million British

228 NOTES TO PP.141–56

casualties, as opposed to 2.9 million British employed in the Near and Middle East, with only 300,000 British casualties. Gray and Argyle's *Statistics of the Military Effort of the British Empire during the Great War, 1914–1920* (London, 1922), pp. 451–2, 502, 595.

8. M. Sykes, Eastern Report, 21 February 1917, CAB/24/143, PRO; E. Browne to C. Scott, 16 April 1917, Scott Papers, Add. MS 50909, BLL.

9. See J. Turner, *Lloyd George's Secretariat* (Cambridge, 1980).

10. Proceedings of the War Cabinet, 9 December 1916, CAB/23/1, PRO. When Lloyd George became prime minister, Hankey ceased recording the views of individual members of the War Cabinet, although those of non-members were still recorded; Hankey's diary, 11–14 December 1916, S. Roskill, *Hankey: Man of Secrets, 1877–1918,* vol. 1 (London, 1970), pp. 339–42.

11. Proceedings of the War Cabinet, 28 February 1917, CAB/23/1, PRO.

12. Milner to Lloyd George, 17 March 1917, Lloyd George Papers, F/38/2/3, HLRO.

13. Proceedings of the War Cabinet, 2 April 1917, CAB/23/2, PRO.

14. Minutes of Committee on Territorial Desiderata in the Terms of Peace, 17–23 April; Report of the committee, 25 April 1917, CAB/21/77, PRO.

15. Robertson, 'Military Effect of Russia Seceeding from the Entente', 9 May; Jellicoe, 'Naval Effect of Russia Seceding from the Entente', 10 May 1917, CAB/24/12, PRO.

16. Curzon, 'Policy in View of Russian Developments', 12 May, CAB/24/12; Proceedings of the War Cabinet, 14 May 1917, CAB/23/2, PRO.

17. Stevenson's diary, 19 and 26 May 1917, quoted in *Lloyd George: A Diary by Frances Stevenson*, ed. A. J. P. Taylor (New York, 1971), pp. 158–9.

18. Hankey's diary, 30 May 1917, quoted in Roskill, *Hankey*, vol. 1, p. 393.

19. The terms of reference for the War Policy Committee were specified by the War Cabinet, 8 June 1917,
CAB/23/3; Minutes of the War Policy Committee, 11–25 June 1917, CAB/27/6, PRO.

20. Minutes of the War Policy Committee, 18 July 1917, CAB/27/6, PRO.

21. Robertson, 'Palestine', 19 July 1917, CAB/27/7, PRO.

22. Hankey penned a compromise between Lloyd George and Robertson for the War Cabinet in 'Report of Cabinet Committee on War Policy', 10 August, CAB/27/6; Proceedings of the War Cabinet, 28 July, 10 August, 3 September 1917, CAB/23/3, 4; Robertson's communications with Allenby, 13 June–31 December 1917, WO/106/718; Arab Bureau Papers on Arab Legion, FO/882/2, PRO.

23. Hankey's diary, 13 September 1917, quoted in Roskill, *Hankey*, vol. 1, p. 435.

24. C. Cruttwell, *History of the Great War* (Oxford, 1940), pp. 610–16.

25. L. Stein's *Balfour Declaration* (New York, 1961) has stood up well since the opening of British archives at the Public Record Office in the late 1960s, which were used by I. Friedman, *Question of Palestine, 1914–1918* (London, 1973) and *Germany, Turkey, and Zionism: 1897–1918* (Oxford, 1977).

26. Rothschild to Balfour, 18 July 1917, CAB/24/24; R. Adelson, *Mark Sykes: Portrait of an Amateur* (London, 1975), pp. 235, 241–5.

27. Proceedings of the War Cabinet, 3 September 1917, CAB/23/4, PRO.

28. Proceedings of the War Cabinet, 4 October 1917, CAB/23/4, PRO.

29. Proceedings and Conclusions of the War Cabinet, 31 October 1917, CAB/23/4. See also Montagu's 'Zionism', 9 October, CAB/24/28; Hankey's 'Zionist Movement', 17 October, CAB/24/4, and Curzon's 'Future of Palestine', 26 October 1917, CAB/24/30, PRO.

30. *The Times*, 9 November 1917.

31. Ibid., 15 December 1917.

32. Proceedings of the War Cabinet, 19 December 1917, CAB/23/4; 1, 3, 4 January 1918, CAB/23/5, PRO.

33. *The Times*, 7 January 1918.

34. Proceedings and Papers of the War Cabinet, December 1917, CAB/23/4, PRO.

35. Proceedings and Papers of the War Cabinet, 21–22 January 1918, CAB/23/5, PRO.

36. This diplomacy may be followed in the Lloyd George Papers, F/6/1, HLRO; V. Rothwell, *British War Aims and Peace Diplomacy, 1914–1918* (Oxford, 1971), pp. 175–8.

37. See Balfour's Foreign Office Papers, FO/800/206, 214, PRO; Rothwell, *British War Aims and Peace Diplomacy*, pp. 173–5.

38. Lloyd George to Robertson, 14 December 1917, William Robertson Papers, I/19/13, Liddell Hart Archives, King's College, London; Robertson, 'Future Operations in Palestine', 26 December 1917, CAB/24/37; Proceedings of War Cabinet, 31 December 1917, CAB/23/4; Hankey to Wilson, 31 December 1917, CAB/25/43, PRO.

39. Wilson, Supreme War Council, to War Cabinet, 'The Turkish and South Russian Situation', 4 January 1918, CAB/25/44, PRO.

40. Proceedings of the War Cabinet, 28 January 1918, CAB/23/5, PRO.

41. Procès verbal of the meeting of the Supreme War Council, 31 January, 1 February 1918, CAB/25/120, PRO; Roskill, *Hankey*, vol. 1, pp. 489–92.

42. Report on Smuts's Mission, 1 March 1918, CAB/24/42, PRO.

43. Proceedings of the War Cabinet, 26 February 1918, CAB/23/5, PRO.

44. L. Amery, 'Germany and the Middle East', 12 March 1918, CAB/25/120, PRO; 'Policy in Persia and Trans-Caucasia', included in a letter to Lloyd George, 15 March 1918, Lloyd George Papers, F/2/1/16, HLRO.

45. Milner to Lloyd George, 20 March 1918, Lloyd George Papers, F/38/3/20, HLRO.

46. Cruttwell, *History of the Great War*, pp. 505–42.

47. Roskill, *Hankey*, vol. 1, pp. 539–52.

48. Conclusions of Conference on Middle Eastern Affairs, 17 June 1918, CAB/24/55, PRO.

49. See C. Ellis, *The British 'Intervention' in Transcaspia, 1918–1919* (Berkeley, 1963).

50. H. Wilson, 'British Military Policy, 1918–1919', 25 July 1918, CAB/27/8; G. Macdonogh to Tyrrell, 13 July 1918, WO/106/60, PRO.

51. Roskill, *Hankey*, vol. 1, pp. 575, 586.

52. Proceedings of the War Cabinet, 2 October 1918, CAB/23/8, PRO.

53. Conditions of the Allied Armistice with Turkey, drafted by Wilson and Wemyss and concluded by Calthorpe, October 1918, WO/106/1571, PRO.

54. Proceedings of the War Cabinet, 3 October 1918, CAB/23/8, PRO.

55. Memorandum on Cecil's Conference at the Foreign Office with the French, 30 September 1918, FO/371/3383, PRO.

56. Cecil, 'Future Government of the Middle East', opposed by Curzon, also opposed by the War Cabinet, 14 October 1918, CAB/23/8, PRO.

57. Lloyd George to Clemenceau, 15 October 1918, CAB/24/67, PRO.

58. Proceedings of the War Cabinet, 11–22 October 1918, CAB/23/8, PRO.

59. Proceedings of the War Cabinet, 22 October 1918, CAB/23/8, PRO.

60. Hankey's diary, 31 October 1918, quoted in Roskill, *Hankey*, vol. 1, p. 625.

61. *The Times*, 1 November 1918.

7   *Postwar Nationalism: 1918–1922*

1. *The Times* (London), 25, 30 November, 12 December 1918.

2. *The Illustrated London News* (London), January 1919.

3. *Statistics of the Military Effort of the British Empire during the Great War, 1914–1920,* ed. Gray and Argyle (London, 1922), p. 739.

4. Ibid., pp. 451–2, 502, 595.

5. A. Toynbee, *The Western Question in Greece and Turkey: A Study in the Contact of Civilisations* (London, 1922). The first edition was published in March 1922; the second in November

1922.

6. R. Adelson, *Mark Sykes: Portrait of an Amateur* (London, 1975), pp. 279–95.

7. S. Roskill, *Hankey: Man of Secrets,* vol. 2, *1919–1931* (London, 1972), pp. 43–98; G. Riddell, *Lord Riddell's Intimate Diary of the Peace Conference and After, 1918–1923* (London, 1933), pp. 9–102; F. Stevenson, *Lloyd George: A Diary by Frances Stevenson,* ed. A. J. P. Taylor (New York, 1971), pp. 169–88.

8. Lloyd George's interview with Venizelos, 15 October 1918, London, F/92/10/1, Lloyd George Papers, HLRO.

9 H. Temperley, ed., *A History of the Peace Conference at Paris,* vol. 6 (London, 1924), pp. 502–5.

10. Temperley, *Peace Conference,* vol. 6, pp. 1–22, 41–104; B. Busch, *Mudros to Lausanne: Britain's Frontier in West Asia, 1918–1923* (Albany, 1976), pp. 81–192.

11 The outbreak of venereal disease in Egypt is covered in 'The Report of the Cairo Purification Committee, 1916', chaired by the Bishop of Jerusalem. Director of Military Operations and Intelligence Papers, War Office, WO/106/1544, PRO; see also A. Marsot, *Egypt's Liberal Experiment, 1922–36* (Berkeley, 1977), pp. 43–72.

12. Temperley, *Peace Conference,* vol. 6, pp. 193–200; J. Darwin, *Britain, Egypt, and the Middle East: Imperial Policy in the Aftermath of War 1918–1922* (New York, 1981), pp. 47–79.

13. S. Wolpers, *A New History of India,* 4th ed. (New York, 1993), pp. 286–300.

14. Roskill, *Hankey,* vol. 2, *1919–1931,* pp. 115–19.

15 J. Wilson, *Lawrence of Arabia: The Authorized Biography* (London, 1990), pp. 623–5.

16. See E. Monroe, *Britain's Moment in the Middle East, 1914–1971* (Baltimore, 1981).

17. K. Tidrick, *Heart-Beguiling Araby* (Cambridge, 1981), pp. 57–163, 183–6.

18. *Strand Magazine* (London), vol. 59 (January 1920).

19. D. Fromkin, *A Peace to End All Peace: Creating the Modern Middle East, 1914–1922* (New York, 1989), pp. 409–10.

20. P. Rowland, *David Lloyd George: A Biography* (New York, 1975), p. 523.

21. D. Moggridge, *Maynard Keynes: An Economist's Biography* (London, 1992) p. 335.

22. Conclusions of the Cabinet, 6 January 1920, CAB/23/20, PRO.

23. Roskill, *Hankey,* vol. 2, *1919–1931,* pp. 147–8; Temperley, *Peace Conference,* vol. 6, p. 28.

24. On oil, the Cadmen-Bertholet Agreement was confirmed by Lloyd George and Millerand on 25 April 1920, Cmd 675, misc. no. 11, *Parliamentary Papers* (1920).

25. Roskill, *Hankey,* vol. 2, pp. 159–63.

26. Conclusions of the Cabinet, 17 June 1920, CAB/23/22.

27. Riddell, *Diary 1918–1923,* p. 208.

28. Papers of Herbert Samuel, File A/65, HLRO, as quoted in A. Klieman, *Foundations of British Policy in the Arab World: The Cairo Conference of 1921* (Baltimore, 1970), pp. 62–3.

29. Cabinet meeting, 7 July 1920, CAB/23/22 PRO; M. Gilbert, *Winston S. Churchill,* Vol. 4, *The Stricken World, 1916–1920* (Boston, 1975), pp. 490–95.

30. Milner to Lloyd George, 28 December 1919, Lloyd George Papers, F/39/1/52, HLRO, as quoted in Darwin, *Britain, Egypt, and the Middle East,* p. 91.

31. Milner's sketch of a report, dated 12 February 1920, Milner Papers, BLO, as quoted ibid., p. 96.

32. Curzon to Milner, 17 August 1920, Milner Papers, 163, BLO, as quoted ibid., p. 109.

33. H. Nicolson, *Curzon: The Last Phase, 1919–1925* (London, 1934), pp. 45–6.

34. Minutes and papers of the Mesopotamia Administration and Middle East Committees, 1917, are in CAB/24; those of Milner's Egyptian Administration Committee and Curzon's Eastern Committee are in CAB/27, PRO.

35. Fromkin, *A Peace to End All Peace,* pp. 421–3.

36. W. Olson, *Anglo-Iranian Relations During World War I* (London, 1984), pp. 224–45.
37. R. Ullman, *Anglo-Soviet Relations, 1917–1921* vol. 3, *The Anglo-Soviet Accord* (Princeton, 1973), pp. 374–88.
38. Conclusions of the Cabinet, 17 November 1920, CAB/23/23.
39. Ferrier, *History of the British Petroleum Company*, vol. 1, *The Developing Years, 1901–1932* (Cambridge, 1982), pp. 570–80.

8   *Imperial Adjustments: 1920–1922*

1. P. J. Cain and A. G. Hopkins, *British Imperialism*, vol. 2, *Crisis and Deconstruction 1914–1990* (London, 1993), pp. 11–20.
2. P. Rowland, *David Lloyd George: A Biography* (New York, 1975), p. 505.
3. W. Arnstein, *Britain Yesterday and Today* (Lexington, Mass., 1992), pp. 273–5
4 N. Rose, 'Churchill and Zionism', *Churchill*, ed. R. Blake, W. R. Louis (Oxford, 1993), p. 155.
5. G. Dangerfield, *The Damnable Question: A Study in Anglo-Irish Relations* (London, 1979), pp. 305–52; R. Foster, *Modern Ireland, 1600–1972* (London, 1988), pp. 494–515.
6. Churchill to Lloyd George, 31 August 1920, CCC, as quoted in Gilbert, *Churchill*, vol. 4, *1916–1922*, pp. 495–6.
7. The press cuttings on the postwar Middle East in the library of the Royal Institute of International Affairs, Chatham House, provide a large sample of Fleet Street reactions to the British military in Mesopotamia and Palestine.
8. Churchill's memo, 7 February 1920, CCC, as quoted ibid., p. 478.
9. Churchill to Trenchard, 29 August 1920, CCC, as quoted ibid., p. 494.
10. Conference of Ministers, 1–2 December 1920, CAB/23/23, PRO; Gilbert, *Churchill*, vol. 4, *1916–1922*, pp. 503–4.
11. Churchill to Lloyd George, Churchill Papers, 2/111, CCC, as quoted ibid.,

p. 499.
12. Ibid., p. 507.
13. Ibid., pp. 507–10.
14. Ibid., pp. 507–43.
15. J. Wilson, *The Authorized Biography: Lawrence of Arabia* (London, 1990), pp. 643–72.
16. *The Times*, 26 March 1921.
17. A. Klieman, *Foundations of British Policy in the Arab World: The Cairo Conference of 1921* (Baltimore, 1970), pp. 105–38.
18. *UK Parliamentary Debates* (Commons), 5th ser., vol. 142 (1921), cols 265–72.
19. Gilbert, *Churchill*, vol. 4, *1916–1922*, pp. 598–9.
20. In an analysis of over 3,000 articles on Ireland, India and Africa, published from 1915 to 1929 in *Blackwood's Edinburgh Magazine*, the *Contemporary Review*, the *Edinburgh Review*, the *Fortnightly Review*, the *Nineteenth Century*, the *Quarterly Review*, and the *Westminster Review*, 31 per cent were about Ireland, 33 per cent on India, and 36 per cent on Africa. M. Steiner, 'British Quality Periodicals in Ireland, India, and Africa: 1881–1930', unpublished M.A. thesis (Arizona State University, 1992), p. 91.
21. Gilbert, *Churchill*, vol. 4, *1916–1922*, pp. 616–17.
22. Meeting at Balfour's house, 22 July 1921, Weizmann Papers (Israel), as quoted in Gilbert, *Churchill*, vol. 4, *1916–1922*, p. 621.
23. Archbishop of Canterbury to Churchill, 10 August 1921, Colonial Office Papers, 733/14, as quoted in Gilbert, *Churchill*, *1916–1922*, companion vol. 4, part 3 (Boston, 1978), p. 1585.
24. Gilbert, *Churchill*, vol. 4, *1916–1922*, pp. 625–7.
25. Cabinet meeting, 17 August 1921, CAB/23/26, PRO.
26. Gilbert, *Churchill*, vol. 4, *1916–1922*, pp. 628–31.
27. Ibid., pp. 634–5.
28. Ibid., pp. 637–41.
29. Ibid., pp. 642–62.
30. *UK Parliamentary Debates* (Commons), 5th ser., vol., 156 (1922), cols 341–4; (Lords), 5th ser., vol. 50 (1922), cols

1033–4.

31 Churchill to Lloyd George, 1 September 1921, Lloyd George Papers, HLRO, as quoted in Gilbert, *Winston S. Churchill,* vol. 4, *1916–1922,* p. 817.

32. Lloyd George to Churchill, 5 September 1921, CCC, as quoted ibid., p. 818.

33. Rowland, *David Lloyd George,* pp. 578–84.

34. J. Darwin, *Britain, Egypt, and the Middle East: Imperial Policy in the Aftermath of War, 1918–1922* (New York, 1981), pp. 115–37.

35. The most recent narrative is D. Walden, *The Chanak Affair* (London, 1969).

36. A. J. P. Taylor, *English History 1914–1945* (Oxford 1965), pp. 190–3.

37. Gilbert, *Winston S. Churchill,* vol. 4, *1916–1922,* pp. 865–7.

38. D. Fromkin, *A Peace to End All Peace: Creating the Modern Middle East, 1914–1922* (New York, 1989), pp. 530–57.

39. S. Roskill, *Hankey: Man of Secrets,* vol. 2, *1919–1931* (London, 1972), p. 296.

40. V. Chirol, 'Four Years of Lloyd Georgian Foreign Policy,' *The Edinburgh Review,* 237 (January–April, 1923), pp. 1–20.

41. Ibid. For Lloyd George's diplomacy, see G. Craig, 'The British Foreign Office from Grey to Austen Chamberlain, The Diplomats 1919–1939', ed., G. Craig and F. Gilbert (Princeton, 1981), pp. 15–35.

Conclusion   *London's Legacy*

1. D. Hirst, *The Gun and the Olive Branch: The Roots of Violence in the Middle East* (London, 1977), pp

75–107.

2. C. Sykes, *Cross Roads to Israel: Palestine from Balfour to Bevin* (London, 1965), pp. 205–12.

3. See W. R. Louis, *Imperialism at Bay: The United States and the Decolonization of the British Empire* (London, 1977), and see V. Ponko, *Britain in the Middle East, 1921–1956: An Annotated Bibliography* (New York, 1990).

4. Ibid. See W. R. Louis, *The British Empire and the Middle East, 1945–1951: Arab Nationalism, The United States and Postwar Imperialism* (Oxford, 1984); *The End of the Palestine Mandate,* ed. W. R. Louis and R. Stookey (Austin, 1986); *The Special Relationship: Anglo-American Relations since 1945,* ed. H. Bull and W. R. Louis (Oxford, 1986).

5. B. Kuniholm, *The Origins of the Cold War in the Near East: Great Power Conflict and Diplomacy in Iran, Turkey, and Greece* (Princeton, 1994), pp. 378–82. See *Mussadiq, Iranian Nationalism and Oil,* ed. J. Bill and W. R. Louis (London, 1988); J. Bamberg, *The History of the British Petroleum Company,* vol. 2, *The Anglo-Iranian Years, 1928–1954* (Cambridge, 1994).

6. See *Suez 1956: The Crisis and its Consequences,* ed. W. R. Louis and R. Owen (Oxford, 1989); *The Iraqi Revolution of 1958: The Old Social Classes Revisited,* ed. R. Fernea and W. R. Louis (New York, 1991).

7. R. Owen, *State, Power, and Politics in the Making of the Modern Middle East* (London, 1992), pp. 3–133; E. Monroe, *Britain's Moment in the Middle East, 1914–1971* (Baltimore, 1981), pp. 178–206.

8. J. Raban, *Arabia: A Journey Through the Labyrinth* (New York, 1979), p. 187.

9. Ibid.

EUROPE

Odessa

Crimean Peninsular

BLACK SEA

Caucas

Sarajevo

Sofia

Edirne

Istanbul
Bosporus

Batum

Erzerum

Gallipoli Pen

Salonika

Ankara

Dodecanese Is

Izmir

Antalya

∧ ∧ ∧ ∧ ∧
∧ Taurus Mts

Aleppo

Mosu

Athens

Euphrates Riv

Hama

Homs

Tunis

Malta

Crete

Rhodes

Cyprus

Tripoli

Beirut

Damascus

MEDITERRANEAN SEA

Jerusalem

Jordana
River

Port Said

Dead Sea

Tripoli

Alexandria

Cairo

Suez Canal

Aqaba

Sinai
Pen

AFRICA

Nile River

RED SEA

Me

N

Khartoum

White Nile

Blue Nile

EARLY TWENTIETH - CENTURY
MIDDLE EAST

0   100   200   300 mls